BARDIC ETHOS AND THE AMERICAN EPIC POEM

Jeffrey Walker

BARDIC ETHOS AND
THE AMERICAN EPIC POEM

Whitman, Pound, Crane, Williams, Olson

Louisiana State University Press
Baton Rouge and London

99 98 97 96 95 94 93 92 91 90   5 4 3 2 1

Designer: Laura Roubique Gleason
Typeface: Garamond #3
Typesetter: G & S Typesetters, Inc.
Printer: Thomson-Shore, Inc.
Binder: John H. Dekker & Sons, Inc.

Library of Congress Cataloging-in-Publication Data
Walker, Jeffrey, 1949–
    Bardic ethos and the American epic poem: Whitman, Pound, Crane,
Williams, Olson / Jeffrey Walker.
        p.   cm.
    Bibliography: p.
    Includes index.
    ISBN 0-8071-1478-2 (alk. paper)
    1. Epic poetry, American—History and criticism.   2. American
poetry—20th century—History and criticism.   3. Whitman, Walt,
1819–1892.   Leaves of grass.   4. Bards and bardism in literature.
I. Title.
PS309.E64W35   1989
811'.03—dc19   88-37650
                                                        CIP

73365

for
Y. & E.

襟懐

kinkai
the heart; thought; magnanimity

I demand races of orbic bards,
with unconditional uncompromising sway.
Come forth, sweet democratic despots of the west!
   —Walt Whitman, *Democratic Vistas*

Contents

Preface

This book is about a line of perplexing, obsessive, and often brilliant poems, poems we tend to call "important failures." Or, at times, we call them *"splendid* failures." That oxymoronic status is, to say the least, puzzling. Even as they frustrate and disturb us, these odd, sprawling poems win for themselves devoted readers, generate almost endless commentary, and inspire new ventures in the enterprise they represent (quixotic as that enterprise may be). The poems of which I speak, or at least the poems on which I concentrate, are the *Cantos, The Bridge, Paterson,* and *The Maximus Poems*—and behind them, standing as the definitive prototype, the 1855 *Leaves of Grass.* Individually, and no matter the judgment we put upon them, these problem poems are major representatives of what we habitually, uneasily call "American modern epic verse," and together they constitute a live tradition, one that I suspect is yet to be played out. I do, however, think the direction of that tradition is predictable, and of interest to anyone concerned with the ways of our literary culture or with the legacies of American modernism.

The claim from which I start is that the fundamental enterprise in which the modern poems participate is Whitmanesque. And because it is Whitmanesque, it is necessarily suasory as well. Pound, Crane, Williams, and Olson all want to constitute themselves, like Whitman, as an American epic bard—as a "call in the midst of the crowd . . . orotund sweeping and final." They would become, moreover, a polemical call: they would speak with a voice equipped to foster revolutionary change in their reader's consciousness, to induce a "new paideuma," to put "ideas into action," and ultimately to alter and direct the national will. What is implied in this desire, or complex of desires, is a discourse whose ultimate goal is victory in the forum of public (ethical, political, economic) values, and thus a poetry involved profoundly in the condition of persuasion. The question to be asked, however, is Which kind of persuasion? In what way does the poetry persuade, or want to persuade? The problem that the writers of modern epic have faced, and will continue to face, is a problem of rhetoric—of finding the means of persuasion adequate to their grand, and sometimes grandiose, suasory desires.

I propose, then, a rhetorical criticism: a close, critical examination of the poets' suasory desires, as well as the means of persuasion they found available. *Availability* is crucial. The would-be modern epic bard has worked, and has largely been obliged to work, with a set of inherited conventions and assumed beliefs—the already given topoi from which his suasory constructs rise and in which, perhaps, those constructs are logically implicit from the start. These topoi derive, through Whitman and with curious transformations, from two eighteenth-century mythologies: a Jeffersonian historico-political vision, as revised according to vitalistic premises; and a bellettristic theory of bardic utterance, as filtered through an Emersonian and subsequently modernist orphism. From the intersection of these mythologies, the discourse of the modern epic bard arises. We get, as the Ezratic phrases have it, a "poem including history" that is also "the voice of a nation through the mouth of one man," and the result is a striking rhetoric of (what is meant to be) sublime authority. But striking as it is, that rhetoric is also troublesome. In fact, it accounts completely for the puzzling outcomes and the success-in-failure of the American modern epic poem, or what I will call the "*bardic* poem." The poet's available, conventional means at once create, inhibit, and promote his suasory purposes.

In the first four chapters of this book, my focus is primarily on the motives and the conventions that the moderns have inherited from Whitman and revised. The object is, in general, to define what sort of rhetoric the modern would-be epic bard has been committed to in principle—and thus I am looking more for a generic construct than for individual differences (but without wanting to ignore or minimize those differences). The next four chapters demonstrate, extend, and qualify the theoretical argument through close rhetorical analysis of the *Cantos, The Bridge, Paterson,* and *The Maximus Poems.* In these chapters, the individual differences between poets become a central concern, as we see the poets working out (or not working out) the possibilities available to them.

Here I must note a peculiarity of structure: in my argument, I approach *The Maximus Poems* as a third-wave effort, with Pound, Crane, and Williams representing the second wave after Whitman himself. Olson works consciously from a tradition embodied for him in his modernist precursors, thereby carrying that tradition to a summation, a kind of terminus (though not, perhaps, the only possible terminus). For this reason, and for reasons of economy as well, I do not discuss Charles Olson and *Maximus* until Chapter Eight.

The selection of poems herein is meant to be representative and not encyclopedic; but there may be a stronger argument as well for this particular selection. What sets these poems apart from other poems that are sometimes also called "American modern epic"—the so-called personal epic or long poem—is their intention to be more than extended lyric sequences representing a private consciousness experiencing the texture of contemporary life. Their rhetoric sets them apart from poems such as Robert Lowell's *Notebooks,* John Berryman's *Dream Songs,* Allen Ginsberg's *Howl,* or even Louis Zukofsky's *"A"* (if what Barry Ahearn says about that book is right, and I suspect it is). Of course, those poems have their Whitmanesque inspirations also, and they frequently work within similar stylistic and other formal conventions.

I have generally preferred the term *bardic poem,* or variants thereon, to mark the distinction I am making here—to separate the rhetoric with which I am concerned from the cousin, second-cousin, and perhaps more closely related rhetorics of other poems sometimes labeled "American modern epic," and also to separate it from the basically hopeless question whether my exemplar poems are "epic" in some timeless, generic sense. The term is, in effect, a memorandum of the differences I wish to emphasize. Those differences have more to do with Whitmanism than with anything else. I am not, for example, intending a close identification (such as Donald Wesling makes) between "the bardic" and orality, nor do I mean to focus (as C. Carroll Hollis does, with Whitman) on "oratorical" style, or some specific method of delivery. Voice is, in fact, a major concern in my analysis, but my interest lies less with the possible orality or "oratoricality" of the bardic voice, and more with its broad rhetorical function as an instrument of ethical authority.

In sum, then, I am not concerned with "rhetorical poetry" per se or with poetry in a "rhetorical style"—as if there were unrhetorical poetries or styles. All discourse is rhetorical, and there are many kinds of rhetoric;

rhetoric is more than style, while style is a part of rhetoric. I work from an assumption that rhetoric is, in the classical and basically Aristotelian sense, the art of "observing the available means of persuasion" in any given discourse. Persuasion, in a literary context, means the use of logological, structural, stylistic, and other means to create an intended effect in the mind of a reader (or listener). What the would-be modern epic bard ultimately intends, or desires, is moral education and transformation, leading to cultural revolution: the bardic poet is considerably beyond the urge to generate merely aesthetic effects. What concerns me, therefore, is a particular rhetorical tradition that is central and crucial to the history of modernism, a tradition that calls for a rhetorical critique.

If rhetoric is the art of observing the available means of persuasion, it is also the art of the preferable—of finding (and recognizing) good reasons, of deciding what we want and what we want to do. A rhetorical criticism, of necessity, is both these things. Most of this book is taken up with "observation" or with analysis; but in my final chapter, the art of the preferable will also have its say. My general warrant I take from Whitman himself, who said to Horace Traubel in 1888, "I do not love a literary man as a literary man. . . . [I]t [literature] is a means to an end, that is all there is to it: I never attribute any other significance to it." [1] Possibly, the ever-posturing Whitman was in this case just posturing; but I will take him, for present purposes, at his word. Whitman's is a rhetorician's attitude. A work of literature, and in particular the bardic poem that Whitman invented and gave to the moderns, is a suasory construct—a means to an end, or ends. That is all there is to it. From the perspective of this stance, I seek to weigh the means and the ends, and measure the means against the ends. And most essentially, since Whitman would have us look at literature so pragmatically and without a veneration-in-advance, I have not committed this book to the rhetoric of encomiastic celebration, apologia, or reverent exegesis, though there are grounds for praise along the way.

1. Horace Traubel, *With Walt Whitman in Camden* (New York, 1961), I, 58.

Acknowledgments

For the help and advice they gave me while I was writing this book (and before that), I owe much gratitude to Leonard Nathan, James E. B. Breslin, V. P. Bynack, Seymour Chatman, and Thomas O. Sloane.

I personally wish to thank the University of California Press for its enlightened policy regarding scholarly fair use of *The Maximus Poems,* as well as other materials.

The permission of New Directions Publishing Corporation to reprint or quote short excerpts from the following works is gratefully acknowledged:

1948, 1956, 1959, 1962, 1963, 1966, 1968 by Ezra Pound, © 1972 by the Estate of Ezra Pound. Reprinted by permission of New Directions Publishing Corporation and Faber & Faber Ltd.

Ezra Pound, "A Pact," *Personae.* Copyright 1926 by Ezra Pound. Reprinted by permission of New Directions Publishing Corporation and Faber & Faber Ltd.

Ezra Pound, *Selected Prose.* Copyright © 1973 by the Estate of Ezra Pound. Reprinted by permission of New Directions Publishing Corporation and Faber & Faber Ltd.

Ezra Pound, *Literary Essays.* Copyright 1935 by Ezra Pound. Reprinted by permission of New Directions Publishing Corporation and Faber & Faber Ltd.

Ezra Pound, *Guide to Kulchur.* Copyright © 1970 by Ezra Pound. All rights reserved. Reprinted by permission of New Directions Publishing Corporation and Faber & Faber Ltd.

Ezra Pound, *The Spirit of Romance.* Copyright © 1968 by Ezra Pound. All rights reserved. Reprinted by permission of New Directions Publishing Corporation and Faber & Faber Ltd.

Charles Olson, *Selected Writings.* Copyright © 1966 by Charles Olson.

Permission to quote short excerpts from the following is also gratefully acknowledged:

John Milton, *Paradise Lost,* in *The Complete Poetry of John Milton,* ed. John T. Shawcross. Doubleday & Company, 1971.

P. D. Ouspensky, *Tertium Organum,* tr. Nicholas Bessaraboff and Claude Bragdon, © 1970 Alfred A. Knopf, Inc.

Ezra Pound, *ABC of Reading.* Yale University Press, 1934.

Noel Stock, *The Life of Ezra Pound,* © 1982 by Noel Stock. Published by North Point Press and reprinted by permission. All rights reserved.

William Carlos Williams, "The Later Pound" and "A Study of Ezra Pound's Present Position," reprinted from *The Massachusetts Review,* © 1973 The Massachusetts Review, Inc.

Parts of Chapter IV appeared previously in "Classical Rhetoric and/or the Modern Lyric: A Contra-Fiat," and are reprinted (in revised form) by permission of McFarland & Company, Inc., Publishers, Jefferson, N.C., from Vol. IV, no. 3 (Spring, 1987), of *American Poetry:* A Tri Quarterly, © 1987 Lee Bartlett and Peter White. Parts of Chapter V appeared, in an earlier version, in "Aristotelian Poetics: Reading Ezra Pound with Michael Riffaterre," *Style,* Vol. XVIII, no. 1 (Winter, 1984).

BARDIC ETHOS AND THE AMERICAN EPIC POEM

I. Prospects

A second time? why? man of ill star,
Facing the sunless dead and this joyless region?
　　　—Ezra Pound, Canto I

An epic, Ezra Pound repeatedly said, is a poem including history. Certainly, that definition applies to the *Cantos,* as well as those modern poems we customarily take as major exemplars of the so-called American epic—namely, *Paterson, The Bridge,* and *The Maximus Poems.* They are all "poems including history." And yet the Ezratic definition, for all its fame, tells us almost nothing. It does not tell us, for example, about how an epic "includes" history, or even to what end. Nor does it tell us whether history is what an epic, or an American modern epic, is centrally about, even if the presence of a history is somehow necessary to the rhetoric of the poem (as indeed it is). It is not clear, either, that Pound, Crane, Williams, and Olson had really worked these questions out on paper or in mind, in any concentrated way, before they tried to work them out in actual epic poetry. But these were and are the crucial questions, for the would-be American epic bard has been engaged, in the twentieth century, in a grand, quixotic, *suasory* enterprise in which the public ends are troublesome and the poetic means are problematic. They are, as well, the questions this book explores.

The central question is not whether it is possible to "write an epic" in the twentieth century; the question, rather, is what the possibilities are for the kind of literary rhetoric the poets have chosen to adopt. The poets, of course, thought they were writing epic in some sense, and said so. But whether they did write *epic,* in the grand generic sense, or failed or succeeded in writing it, is a question that would only draw us into a trap. We would be trying to elaborate a platonic definition of the epic *sub specie aeternitatis,* and then match our poems to the definition. We would only find out whether we have a match or not. Whether the poems *should* match the definition, or the definition the poems, becomes either a matter of mere taste or an exercise in celebrating some preferred authority.

The truth is that the American modern epic has little to do with the traditions and conventions of the classical epic, however much the poets might have gestured ostentatiously toward Homer, or the Homeric (or even pre-Homeric) world, or some other poet and world where *epos* seems to flourish as a form of culture-shaping public discourse. Much more central to the suasory motives of the poets, and to the rhetorical means by which they sought to achieve their ends, was and is the basically (but not entirely) homegrown, homemade tradition of Walt Whitman, and of what might be called—partly for convenience, and partly to remind ourselves of its differences from classical or other models—the *bardic* poem of the Whitmanesque "sacerdotal literatus." For the ambition of the poets was not simply to write an epic. Their ambition was to be Walt Whitman or, rather, the American bard that Whitman had tried to be, and to accomplish the "great psalm of the republic" that was to be the bardic poet's ultimate achievement. And therein lies the tale.

The American modern epic poem begins, early in the twentieth century, from a surge of Whitmanesque and bardic yearnings, ambitions, identifications. We see this, clearly and dramatically, in Ezra Pound's now-famous "What I Feel About Walt Whitman," written in 1909, when Pound was just beginning to find his way in literary London. The piece deserves to be quoted at some length:

> From this side of the Atlantic I am for the first time able to read Whitman, and . . . I see him America's poet . . . the only one of the conventionally recognized "American poets" who is worth reading. . . . *I honour him for he prophesied me* [emphasis added] while I can only recognise him as a forebear of whom I ought to be proud. . . . In America there is much for the healing of the nations, but woe to him of the cultured palate who attempts the dose. . . . The expression of certain things related to cosmic consciousness seems tainted with this [Whitman's] maramis. . . . I am (in common with every educated man) an heir of the ages and I demand my birthright. . . . The vital part of my message, taken from the sap and fibre of America, is the same as his. Mentally I am a Walt Whitman who has learned to wear a collar and a dress shirt. . . . And, to be frank, Whitman is to my fatherland . . . what Dante is to Italy and I at my best can only be a strife for a renaissance in America of all the lost or temporarily mislaid beauty, truth, valour, glory of Greece, Italy, England and all the rest of it. . . . It seems to me I should like to drive Whitman into the old world. I sledge, he drill—and to

scourge America with all the old beauty. (For Beauty *is* an accusation) and with a thousand thongs from Homer to Yeats, from Theocritus to Marcel Schwob . . . I am fain set my own hand to the labour.[1]

There is an almost messianic fervor in this copious confession—which did not appear in public until 1955—as Pound declares himself *prophesied* by Whitman, and proposes Whitman as the instrument for a "strife" that already sounds like the *Cantos,* and that is to produce an American renaissance. (If a renaissance of, or scourging by, old European beauties does not sound exactly like the Whitmanesque "message," it does share, as we will see and as Pound suggests, certain vital similarities: both poets are "heirs of the ages," each according to his lights, and both are, as Pound believes, poets of "cosmic consciousness.") But Pound is also anxious to emphasize his distance from the previous American bard. Pound is Whitman in a collar, and as his essay elsewhere says, Whitman is "a beginning and not a classically finished work." Pound puts on the bardic mantle with misgivings.

These ideas become official four years later in the 1913 poem "A Pact," in which Pound goes through the ostentatious, belated gestures of making peace with a spiritual father: "It was you that broke the new wood, / Now is a time for carving." In fact, these identifications with Whitman and a Whitmanesque message, combined with simultaneous, uneasy distancing gestures, are a constant and already well documented feature in Pound's career. The feature appears most distinctly, perhaps, in *ABC of Reading* (1934) and "National Culture" (1938), as well as "Carta da Visita" (1942), the *Pisan Cantos* (1948), and the textbook-anthology *Confucius to Cummings* (1964), in which Whitman is very substantially represented. Whitmanism appears to have been an enduring part of Pound's self-conception, though it is a Whitmanism to which important qualifications are attached. Whitman represents a fundamental message, and a literary rhetoric to be significantly revised, recarved, or reinvented for the modern age. Whitman indicates the means of a strife for renaissance.[2]

1. Ezra Pound, "What I Feel About Walt Whitman," in *Selected Prose 1909–1965,* ed. William Cookson (New York, 1973), 145–46.

2. Ezra Pound, "A Pact," in *Selected Poems of Ezra Pound* (New York, 1957), 27; Pound, *ABC of Reading* (New Haven, 1934), 162, 181; Pound, "National Culture: A Manifesto" and "Carta da Visita," in *Selected Prose,* 161–66, 306–35; Pound, *Confucius to Cummings* (New York, 1964). See also Roy Harvey Pearce, *The Continuity of American*

Agreements with this view are easy to find in the writings of Crane and Williams. Crane's "Modern Poetry" (1930) holds that "the most typical and valid expression of the American *psychosis* [is] still found in Whitman . . . but his bequest is still to be realized in all its implications." In addition, Crane's overt though sometimes defensive Whitmanism, both in *The Bridge* and in his letters, is fairly well known. Williams, as early as "America, Whitman, and the Art of Poetry" (1917), states that "Whitman created the art in America," but also that "the only way to be like Whitman is to write *unlike* Whitman. Do I expect to be a companion to Whitman by mimicking his manners?" Similarly, in "Against the Weather" (1939), he writes that "from Whitman, we draw out—what we have to do today . . . to study what we have put down, as he seems not to have done, and to take out what is useful and reject what is misleading." Like Pound, Crane and Williams found in Whitman not only a project for the American poet to pursue but also a specific manner from which they wished to distance themselves or that they regarded as merely a rough beginning.[3]

The actual project was defined for them, in Whitman's *Democratic Vistas*: "Our fundamental want today in the United States, with closest, amplest reference to present conditions, and to the future, is of a class, and the clear idea of a class, of native authors, literatuses, far different, far higher in grade, than any yet known, sacerdotal, modern, fit to cope with our occasions, lands, permeating the whole mass of American mentality, taste, belief, breathing into it a new breath of life, giving it decision, affecting politics far more than the popular superficial suffrage . . . accomplishing . . . a religious and moral character beneath the political and productive and intellectual bases of the States." Whitman indicates a double project: the creation of a "class" of sacerdotal literati and, through this class, the cultivation of a national moral consciousness to enliven politics, economics, and intellectual life in general. The ultimate issue of this project—its definitive accomplishment—is to

---

Poetry (Princeton, 1977), 88; and James E. Miller, *The American Quest for a Supreme Fiction: Whitman's Legacy in the Personal Epic* (Chicago, 1979), 74.

3. Hart Crane, "Modern Poetry," in *The Complete Poems and Selected Letters and Prose of Hart Crane*, ed. Brom Weber (New York, 1966), 263; William Carlos Williams, "America, Whitman, and the Art of Poetry," *Poetry Journal* (November, 1917), 27, 31; Williams, "Against the Weather: A Study of the Artist," in *Selected Essays* (New York, 1969), 219.

be what Whitman's 1855 Preface calls a "great psalm of the republic," or what *Democratic Vistas* calls the sort of "epical presentation" found in Isaiah, Homer, and Lucretius. This epical presentation, however, is distinctly *not* epic poetry in the classical, generic sense. As the 1855 Preface contends, the American bard's great psalm shall not be "direct or descriptive or epic," apparently precluding Homeric narrative, Hesiodic description, and Lucretian discursus. According to *Democratic Vistas*, the sacerdotal literature to be produced in America must be "far different, far higher in grade, than any yet known." The massive psalm or epical presentation or bardic poem that Whitman foresees is, in general and wonderfully vague terms, to be "great literature" that "penetrates all, shapes aggregates and individuals, and after subtle ways, with irresistable power, constructs, sustains, demolishes at will." The bardic poet, somehow, is to appropriate to himself the role of a Shelleyan legislator of the world (though ultimately, as Whitman maintained, he would not go unacknowledged) and to seek an extraordinary power over the public consciousness. This influence in effect abridges the moral authority of actual, politically constituted legislatures and, rather ironically for Whitman's celebrations of democracy, the electoral workings of the democratic process itself (the "popular superficial suffrage"). And he is to fulfill this role, somehow, by means of his great psalm.[4]

Pound, Crane, and Williams agreed substantially with Whitman's understanding of the bardic poet's public role: the poet, in Pound's formulation, provides the "data for ethics" and maintains the "clarity of thought" without which a smoothly functioning state or a highly developed civilization cannot exist or endure. Artists, according to Pound, "are the antennae of the race," and the literatus, as he argues in *ABC of Reading* and elsewhere, is to provide not a "mental bed" but knowledge leading to "increase of capacities." Insofar as this knowledge is essential to construct and preserve (or demolish) the institutions of a national culture, Pound, like Whitman, believes it to be preeminently supplied by epic bards. He maintains in "How to Read" (1928), for example, that "a civilization was founded on Homer, civilization not a mere bloated empire." Like Whitman's projected great psalm, moreover, Pound's imagined epic aims less at specific moral instruction and more at the cultivation of a generalized moral character. As Pound says, the real epic poet is not to serve the state by "coercing or persuading, or bullying or

4. Walt Whitman, *Complete Poetry and Collected Prose* (New York, 1982), 932–33, 8.

suppressing people into the acceptance of any one set or any six sets of opinions," nor is he, like Milton and Virgil, to "muck about with a moral." He is, rather, to be (like Dante, supposedly) "concerned with a *senso morale,* which is a totally different matter." *Senso morale* is ethical will, or what Pound calls in his later essays "guided will" or *"directio voluntatis"*—or, to use a simpler if non-Ezratic term, ethos. Ethos is the general sensibility, the deep-down character-core that underlies and determines the specific moral choices any individual will make, and that underlies also the communal institutions a society of individuals will devise. If Whitman is the American Dante, as Pound's 1909 essay proclaims, and if Pound is a modern Whitman-in-a-collar, then his strife for an American renaissance will also, and of necessity, be concerned with cultivating a new "religious and moral character beneath the political and productive and intellectual bases of the States."[5]

Crane and Williams had somewhat less to say on the matter than did Pound, but their positions were relatively similar. Crane thought that poetry should not "limit its goal" to "exact factual data" or "moral classifications," but he did believe that poetry could transmit a sort of "absolute experience" that gains "our unquestioning assent" to an apprehension of life, one that would become "an active principle in the reader's consciousness henceforward." This implies an ethical training of some kind. Likewise, Crane was interested in discovering a "new hierarchy of faith" and in developing a literary art that stopped short of propaganda but went beyond "pure aesthetique" to matters of social concern—the sort of art he found in *Winesburg, Ohio* or *Spoon River Anthology,* which he actually called a "chapter in the Bible" of American consciousness. Crane's bardic literatus was to shape the national ethos by means of what amounted to secular scripture.[6]

Williams, who could at times vacillate into formalistic declarations that a "religious or social tinge" mars the aesthetic quality of a poem, could also be much more aggressive than either Pound or Crane in formulating the sacerdotal mission of the poet. His strongest statement came in the essay "The Basis of Faith in Art" (1937), which argued (like Shelley in a hostile mood) that "poetry is a rival government always in opposition to its cruder replicas" and that "the poet has to serve and the

---

5. Pound, *ABC of Reading,* 75; Pound, *Literary Essays of Ezra Pound,* ed. T. S. Eliot (New York, 1968), 21, 217.

6. Crane, *Complete Poems and Selected Letters and Prose,* 205–206, 217–23.

reader has to—be met and won—without compromise." The poet contributes his vision, moreover, so that "society may be built more praiseworthily" or that society may be anything but a chaos of clashing self-interests. Williams repeated this opinion in "Against the Weather" and in a 1950 defense of Pound's *Cantos,* which, as the argument implied, was an essential poem for the health of America's national culture: "The poem should be read. It isn't even necessary to understand every nuance; no one can do that. Read! Read the best and the thing will come out in a cleaner, more timely, more economically adjusted business world and in better statesmen." In Williams' essay, "the best" means the best *modern* literature—"Pound rather than Marlowe or Donne" and "even Dada rather than Racine." Williams' general position aligned with the project for a bardic literature outlined in *Democratic Vistas*: the poet must inculcate the values or the moral stance that eventuates in actual policies, and to the extent that he fulfills this role, his authority is indeed more profound than that of the "popular superficial suffrage."[7]

These Whitmanesque, sacerdotal aspirations were by no means confined to Pound, Crane, and Williams. They were part of a resurgent and highly fashionable Whitmanism that moved the American avant-garde (or, at least, the younger intellectuals) just after the turn of the century—a Whitmanism that, ironically, was largely derived from European sources. As Pound observed in *Patria Mia* (1913), Whitman became acceptable in America "when he was properly introduced by William Michael Rossetti, and not before then." Although Pound was clearly scornful of American turn-of-the-century culture, his statement could easily have been turned upon him. The Pound of 1909 who suddenly found he could read Whitman for the first time was, after all, living in the intellectual milieu of Edwardian London. As Samuel Hynes has shown, the dominant early modernist ideas of that place and time were strongly influenced by the neotranscendental and social-revolutionary visions of the self-appointed sages Edward Carpenter and R. M. Bucke, both of whom were direct disciples of Whitman himself. Pound's 1909 linking of himself to Whitman's "cosmic consciousness" reveals, in particular, the influence of Bucke, or of Bucke's *Cosmic Consciousness* (1901). Bucke claimed that Whitman's "gospel" had brought him to a sudden,

7. William Carlos Williams, "The Basis of Faith in Art," and "The Poem as a Field of Action," in *Selected Essays,* 180–83, 288; Williams, "The Later Pound," *Massachusetts Review,* XIV : 1 (Winter, 1973), 129.

revelatory experience of the higher awareness while he was riding home
in a hansom cab from a poetry reading. Bucke's Whitmanian gospel, as
James E. Miller has pointed out, was also a crucial factor in Crane's
conception of his bardic destiny: Crane found the kernel of Bucke's ideas
quoted at length (ten pages) in P. D. Ouspensky's *Tertium Organum*
(1920), and shortly afterward experienced what he believed to be the
"higher consciousness" while under ether in a dentist's chair. In 1923,
Crane told Waldo Frank that he had found a vision "that not only
America needs, but the whole world." There was much in America, and
in the possibilities of a Whitmanesque American bard, for the healing of
the nations. Between the Pound of 1909 and the Crane of 1923, then,
British Whitmanism seems to have persisted as an instrumental force in
the revival of the bardic project in America.[8]

France was likewise instrumental. As Betsy Erkkila has shown—and
as Pound's *ABC of Reading* implicitly recognizes, by tracing the development of English poetry through Whitman to Gautier, Corbière, Rimbaud, and Laforgue—Whitman's "indirect" poetry, with its strong af-
finities to Sainte-Beuve's poetics of suggestiveness, found a home among
the early Symbolists, who could see in *Leaves of Grass* a practical demonstration of their own literary theories. Further, turn-of-the-century social radicals in France looked upon Whitman as a prophet of socialism
and political activism or, more generally, of twentieth-century modernism, with all the liberation and renewal that the brand-new century was
supposed to bring. The result was a rage for Whitman among the more
radical French literati of the prewar years, an enthusiasm validated for
their American counterparts through the prestige of French writing and
thought, and through direct appeal as well. Here, for example, is the
then-eminent critic Romain Rolland in a lead-off editorial for the inau-
gural edition of the *Seven Arts* magazine in November, 1916: "My faith is
great in the high destinies of America. . . . On our old continent,
civilization is menaced. It becomes America's solemn duty to uphold the
wavering torch. . . . You must make of your culture a symphony that
shall in a true way express your brotherhood. . . . You must make real
the dream of an integrated and entire humanity. . . . Behind you, alone,

8. Pound, *Selected Prose*, 112, 145; Samuel Hynes, *The Edwardian Turn of Mind*
(Princeton, 1968), 9, 14, 135–56; P. D. Ouspensky, *Tertium Organum*, trans. Nicholas
Bessaraboff and Claude Bragdon (1920; rev. ed. 1922; rpr. New York, 1970), 286; J. E.
Miller, *The American Quest for a Supreme Fiction*, 167–68.

the elemental Voice of a great pioneer, in whose message you may well find an almost legendary omen of your task to come,—your Homer: Walt Whitman." Who could resist this sort of exhortation?[9]

Like Pound, Crane, and Williams, a number of significant American critics agreed with Rolland—but, again, with reservations. Van Wyck Brooks, in *America's Coming-of-Age* (1915), found in Whitman the beginnings of an American "middle tradition" combining the pragmatic, catchpenny opportunism of "low-brow" commercialism and the vaporous, ineffectual idealism of "high-brow" aspiration. He believed that this fusion of real and ideal provided (or could provide) the national consciousness with a "focal centre" that was "the first requisite of a great people." In *Letters and Leadership* (1918), Brooks went further to propose, with perorative flourish, a Whitmanesque sacerdotal class to serve as the catalyst for national transformation and national greatness:

> [N]o true social revolution will ever be possible in America till a race of artists, profound and sincere, has brought us face to face with our own experience and set working in that experience the leaven of highest culture. . . . Is it imaginable that we shall fail to rise to the gravity of our situation and recreate, out of the sublime heritage of human ideals, a new synthesis adaptable to the unique conditions of our life? When that occurs, we will cease to be a blind, selfish, disorderly people. We shall become a luminous people, dwelling in the light and sharing our light.

Brooks's projected social revolution paralleled Pound's notion of artistic strife for a renaissance, and it pointed clearly to the polemical motivations of the Whitmanesque enterprise—a motive central to the rather considerable rhetorical problem the poets faced. American society, with its gap between ideals and reality, was "blind, selfish, disorderly." Unlike Homer (or at least an imagined Homer), who could be the spokesman *for* the values of an existing aristocracy, the American bard would not be the exemplary spokesman of American public culture, its unequivocal celebrator. The moderns' American bard was imagined from the start as an opponent to the public culture that surrounded him, a Jeremiah combating the perversions of the actual world and seeking not so much to guide the national mind but, more radically, to transform it.

9. Betsy Erkkila, *Walt Whitman Among the French* (Princeton, 1980), 50, 171–74, 176; Pound, *ABC of Reading,* 162; Romain Rolland, editorial, *Seven Arts* (November, 1916), 47–51.

In fact, the bard might out-Jeremiah Jeremiah, since what he proposed was frequently to be a revision of fundamental values, a "new synthesis," rather than a return to values of traditional authority. As Williams put it, the poet was not only an unacknowledged legislator but also something of a king in exile—or a king who had never yet come into his own—speaking, "against the weather" indeed, *in opposition to* his cruder replicas. How this would be done was far from clear. To stand on a soapbox and hurl invective was not enough, since cultural revolution (and not self-righteous indignation) was the goal. Whitman, though on the right track, was still inadequate. As Brooks declared, his "social ideal" was merely a "collection of raw materials" needing to be rescued from its own self-indulgent, self-absorbed disorder "by adding intellect to emotion." So again, the modern bard was to be Whitman in a collar. He was to carve the new wood, which could not be left as is. But how this carving and this collaring were to be done, and how the carved and collared Whitman would contribute to a cultural revolution, were questions that remained unanswered. Detailed considerations of the necessary rhetoric were not available, from Brooks or from anyone else.[10]

Still, the sacerdotal call continued to be called. Lewis Mumford, in *The Golden Day* (1926), borrowing a line of argument from D. H. Lawrence's *Studies in Classic American Literature* (1923), agreed with Brooks and extended his argument. Mumford's American was an "outcast European," stripped of his old culture and wandering in a new world "without a Moses" to guide him. The writers of the "Golden Day" (Whitman, Emerson, Thoreau, Melville, and Hawthorne) had essentially brought him to a "verge" by accomplishing the final dissolution of European sensibility, but had stopped there. Moreover, the society for and to which they had spoken had irretrievably disappeared in the "brown decades" after the Civil War. A "modern Moses," it seemed, was urgently needed. F. O. Matthiessen, acknowledging his debt to *The Golden Day* and *America's Coming-of-Age,* took the argument still further in his epochal *American Renaissance* (1941). There, he sought to assess the abilities of his (and Mumford's) five major authors to reconcile crass reality and a redemptive *senso morale* in a culture-crystallizing vision "commensurate with America's political opportunity." Matthiessen's study was a persuasive culmination of concerns that had begun, more

10. Van Wyck Brooks, *Three Essays on America* [*America's Coming-of-Age, Letters and Leadership, The Literary Life in America*] (New York, 1934), 63, 77–89, 126, 189–90.

obscurely, with writers such as Romain Rolland and R. M. Bucke; it became a formative influence in Charles Olson's somewhat late resuscitation of the bardic enterprise.[11]

Examples of the early twentieth century's resurgent Whitmanism could be extensively cataloged; but Brooks, Mumford, and Matthiessen will stand for present purposes as major markers, indicating a continuity. There was, in short, an available and continuing audience—a critical one, if not a popular one—for twentieth-century bardic poetry. There were as well a number of poets more than willing to try the epic task. Expectations and aspirations were fairly congruent. Both audience and poets saw in Whitman, or in what they understood as Whitman's cultural context, the rudiments of a sacerdotal tradition that would serve to cultivate a national ethos, but that would first have to be reworked for the modern age. Further, like Pound and Brooks, they tended to regard the sacerdotal enterprise as a polemical *strife* with a national culture that was, in its present state, chaotic and blind. What rhetoric transforms the benighted and corrupt? To whom does the bardic poet speak, and how? The poet's problem was to find some way to be a Whitman equal to the twentieth-century job.

The widespread early modernist desire for a "great psalm of the republic"—as well as some sense of the problem—is epitomized in James Oppenheim's editorial for the *Seven Arts* in April, 1917:

> America, the old America, exists no longer. We have gone through a hiatus, a terrible pause of disillusion and aimlessness. . . . We are merely part of the civilization of Europe, and the role of Messiah-nation is ours no longer. We stand at the faint beginnings, the trembling dawn, of our second great epoch. There is no doubt of that. And throughout our country there is a great desire, an overwhelming need. . . . What poet and prophet shall clarify for us and project a vision which shall lead us on to a new nationality? . . . [T]he time has come. A new poet must appear among us.[12]

Oppenheim, it seems probable, was advertising himself: his own poetry, also published in the *Seven Arts,* identifies him as one of Whitman's imitative disciples. Oppenheim, like Pound, was both sounding and

11. Lewis Mumford, *The Golden Day: A Study in American Experience and Culture* (New York, 1926), 44, 89, 90, 92, 278; F. O. Matthiessen, *American Renaissance* (Oxford, 1941), xv. See also Mumford, *The Brown Decades: A Study of the Arts in America* (New York, 1931).

12. James Oppenheim, editorial, *Seven Arts* (April, 1917), 629–30.

responding to the general call. What Oppenheim failed to understand, however, was that the notion of America's destiny as a messiah nation was still a central feature of the Whitmanesque enterprise and was still essential to its rhetoric. America was, somehow, to be the redemptive culmination of the long historical dialectic of human aspiration. Indeed, Oppenheim's gesture toward a "second great epoch" implies a renewed (if troubled, and indeed rather self-contradictory) faith in what Rolland had called the "high destinies of America." So, likewise, did Pound's early belief in the imminence of an American twentieth-century renaissance. However, this nation had indeed passed through Oppenheim's "hiatus," and the modern grounds of an epic poetry fit for promoting a modern renaissance were not entirely clear. As we will see, the moderns responded to their changed, post-hiatus conditions by reconstituting the Whitmanesque vision of apocalyptic history in ways that substantially transformed the nature of the bardic project and affected the grounds of its rhetoric. In fact, the changes the moderns wrought exacerbated the problems inherent in the rhetoric that Whitman had bequeathed to them. Our immediate concerns, however, are with what the modern bard would have to modify as he sought to enter and transform the selfish, blind, disorderly national mind, to make it realize its destinies and rediscover "all the lost or temporarily mislaid beauty, truth, valour, glory of Greece, Italy, England and all the rest of it." Thus we come straight to the paterfamilias of American bardism, and to the rhetoric of his most distinctive poem, the 1855 *Leaves of Grass*.

II.   The Rhetoric of 1855

Worse and worse .... Can't you stand it?
  —Whitman, "A Boston Ballad"

In 1888, Whitman told Horace Traubel that "Passage to India"—that paean to Manifest Destiny—was his "most essential poem." The vision of futurity that appears there was a commonplace in Jeffersonian and Jacksonian political rhetoric, and indeed it had a central place in Whitman's work. Moreover, it was a commonplace deeply rooted in the American psyche, from the Puritan belief in national election onward. America was to be the fulfillment of a process simultaneously historical and supernatural, a fulfillment visible in the renewal of God's covenant with Israel, a New Jerusalem, a redeeming and redeemed *Theopolis Americana*. By Whitman's time, this providential history had modulated into the real Whig "secret history," or such versions of it as appeared in Noah Webster's Introduction to his 1828 dictionary or Emerson's *English Traits* (1856). American destiny was redefined as an Anglo-Saxon golden age, a renaissance of archaic (but also Teutonic-Christian) commonsense virtue that had flourished in England, from the collapse of corrupted Rome to what Emerson called the "debacle" of the Norman Conquest. The prospective *Theopolis Americana* became an agrarian, continental civilization/empire founded on the democratic, egalitarian virtues of the neo-Saxon rural yeoman. It thus finished the westward course of empire, linking East and West, and at last fulfilled humanity's noblest aspirations. America would bring the process of the centuries to closure. Thomas Jefferson had symbolically fused these mythic, providential histories, in his 1776 proposal for the shield of the nation: on one face, the children of Israel in the wilderness, and on the other, the Saxon chieftains Hengist and Horsa. The specific terms of American apocalyptic history could be transformed, but its essential, paradigmatic shape remained stable. The *true* America was a society of persons with a special destiny, a communal destiny, in which to participate—insofar, at least, as they belonged to an elect of saints, or were guided by the ethical sense of an uncorrupted Saxon yeomanry, or at least were Whigs in some original and Jeffersonian sense.[1]

For Whitman, however, as for Emerson and Webster, and others, a better phrase than Manifest Destiny is "untransacted destiny," with the stress on *untransacted*. The phrase appears in an 1846 report to the U.S. Senate by William Gilpin, the principal heir of Thomas Hart Benton's Jeffersonian-Jacksonian social philosophy: "[T]he untransacted destiny of the American people is to subdue the continent . . . to establish a new order in human affairs . . . to stir up the sleep of a hundred centuries— to teach old nations a new civilization—to confirm the destiny of the human race . . . to absolve the curse that weighs down humanity, and to shed blessings around the world!"[2] For the most part, Gilpin's is standard period rhetoric, a conventionally "sublime" and fervent accumulation leading to the inspirational climax, in the manner of a platform orator. Indeed, aside from the telltale *un-* that flags his glorious and still-deferred American imperium, Gilpin seems intent on ostentatiously (perhaps too ostentatiously) declaring confidence—as does Whitman, much of the time. In truth, the *un-* looms large. Whitman's optimistic, even jingoistic enthusiasms are framed by a distinctly pessimistic, polemical mood.

Whitman's mood appears explicitly from at least as early as the 1850s, in such pieces as the satirical, pre-bardic "Dough-Face Song" (1850), the lurid pamphlet *The Eighteenth Presidency!* (1856), and the open letter to Emerson in 1856—not to mention the original *Leaves of Grass*. As his critics and biographers have more than once observed, Whitman the poet starts in disillusion, and not only with politics but with American public culture as a whole. Later, we see the bard's dark mood nowhere

---

1. Traubel, *With Walt Whitman in Camden,* I, 156; Perry Miller, *Errand Into the Wilderness* (Cambridge, Mass., 1956); Sacvan Bercovitch, *The Puritan Origins of the American Self* (New Haven, 1975); Henry Nash Smith, *Virgin Land* (Cambridge, Mass., 1950); Alan Trachtenberg, *Brooklyn Bridge: Fact and Symbol* (New York, 1965); Vincent P. Bynack, "Noah Webster and the Idea of a National Culture: The Pathologies of Epistemology," *Journal of the History of Ideas,* XLV : 1 (January-March, 1984), 99–114; Ralph Waldo Emerson, *English Traits* (1856; rpr. New York, 1903); Merrill D. Peterson, *The Jefferson Image in the American Mind* (Oxford, 1960), 415.

2. William Gilpin, *Mission of the North American People, Geological, Social, and Political* (Philadelphia, 1873), 124. See also Smith, *Virgin Land,* 37.

more emphatically than in *Democratic Vistas*. He reiterates the central themes of his career and agitates for the sacerdotal literature that has not yet appeared (except, of course, in himself): "I say we had best look our times and lands searchingly in the face, like a physician diagnosing some deep disease. . . . The spectacle is appalling. We live in an atmosphere of hypocrisy throughout. . . . The best class we show, is but a mob of fashionably dress'd speculators and vulgarians. . . . Are there, indeed, *men* worthy the name? . . . Is there a great moral and religious civilization—the only justification of a great material one? . . . [A] sort of dry and flat Sahara appears, these cities, crowded with petty grotesques, malformations, phantoms, playing meaningless antics." Whitman's indictment of American actuality, early and late in his career, is sweeping: the business classes are depraved, the government is corrupt, the judiciary tainted, and the arts "infidelistic." The national ethos manifests itself in virtually no public institution that escapes contagion. If the future vistas are sublime, the present vistas are appallingly, distressingly ugly. And worse, the present makes the future dubious. For if it is true, as the argument of *Democratic Vistas* holds, that the United States is "either to surmount the gorgeous history of feudalism, or else prove the most tremendous failure of time," then the national ethos that is everywhere evident, the real-but-false America lost in its spiritual wasteland, seems to shift the probabilities toward failure. The existing national character, uncultivated by the great literature of Whitman's uncreated sacerdotal class, is unequal to the American apocalypse imagined in the rhetoric of destiny.[3]

What is needed, then, and as Whitman says to Emerson in his 1856 letter, is a man who will "face round at the rest," illustrate in himself the true identity of "these States," speak (if need be) "with terrible negative voice," and refuse "all terms to be bought off from his own eye-sight, or from the soul that he is."[4] Whitman's bard, moreover, must be or poetically represent such a man and must also help create such men. He must either cultivate in his fallen audience the ethical awareness of the true American, or he must demonstrate to them the true American's ethical authority and legitimate claims to leadership, so that the national destiny may be fulfilled. Indeed, the sacerdotal literatus Whitman calls for must do both these things. He is set for confrontation with official

3. Whitman, *Complete Poetry and Collected Prose*, 937–39, 930.
4. Whitman to Emerson, August, 1856, *ibid.*, 1331–32.

public culture, and he must find a rhetoric that will serve his suasory intents. This necessity drives the bard to literary theory.

Whitman declares in *Democratic Vistas* that the proper "process of reading" is not to be "a half-sleep" but "in highest sense, an exercise, a gymnast's struggle" in which the reader must "construct indeed the poem, argument, history, metaphysical essay—the text furnishing the hints, the clue, the start or framework." The idea that such a *proper* reading-process, and a literature appealing to it, will serve to cultivate an ideally American ethos is rooted in the Scottish commonsense philosophy underlying much of American transcendentalism and all of the Emersonian poetic. If we can assume what Emerson calls a nature "saturated with deity and with law," we can further assume what he considers an "aboriginal" human nature likewise saturated and thus endowed with a univocal, intuitive Reason or Taste. Moral truth is universal and self-evident—just as colors and shapes are instinctively self-evident to the well-formed eye, and tastes to the unjaded tongue—as long as the divinely given inner nature is uncorrupt. As Emerson argues in "The Poet," then, an orphic discourse of symbolistic indirection, intimating the ineffable realities of universal Spirit beyond and/or beneath the formulas and stale conventions of quotidian discourse, will coax the mind from its spiritual inanition and call its deeper and diviner faculties into play. The "gymnast's struggle" of tropistic interpretation in such a discourse is, as the Emersonian line of thought invites us to believe, a spiritual and moral calisthenic that liberates, regenerates, and educates the aboriginal self. And the "aboriginal Self" is just what the myth of untransacted destiny proposes as the spirit of the true America: the long-suppressed (under "feudalism") and likewise presently dormant (or dulled and smothered) "deific" sensibility that is common to all, but needs to be awakened, exercised, and cultured by the sacerdotal literatus to a state of fine acuity.[5]

5. *Ibid.*, 992–93; Ralph Waldo Emerson, "Montaigne, or the Skeptic" and "The Poet" in *Essays and Lectures* (New York, 1983), 708, 461–62ff. (The terms "aboriginal Self" and "Reason" appear in "Self-Reliance" and *Nature*.) See also Charles Feidelson, Jr., *Symbolism and American Literature* (Chicago, 1953), esp. Chap. 2. For an overview of the Scottish commonsense tradition in ethics and belles-lettres, see William Charvat, *The Origins of American Critical Thought, 1810–1835* (Philadelphia, 1936), esp. 36–37. For a persuasive discussion of the comparatively slight influence exerted on Emerson and his peers by German romanticism, see René Wellek, "Emerson and German Philosophy" and "The Minor Transcendentalists and German Philosophy," in *Confrontations: Studies in*

The truth, however, is that despite his urge to be the orphic Poet described by Emerson, Whitman as a polemical sacerdote has much more in mind than simply exercising his reader's mental muscles. The reader's struggle, in Whitman's account, is to produce some fairly definite realizations, or what Whitman calls the "argument, history, metaphysical essay" for which the bardic discourse will provide the artfully scattered "hints" (some of which are, in fact, outright declarations). For a reader with an appropriate degree of aboriginal and deific intelligence, after all, the perhaps ineffable truths and American vistas reflected and betokened in the poet's utterance *ought* to become self-evident, even if they are so sublime as to resist an adequate verbal formulation or description. The poet's fragmentary indirectness, then, is both an indication of the impossibility of adequate articulation and an exegetical prompt that will put the reader on the path to self-reliant, independent understanding of what all participants in American destiny must understand. The reader, in sum, is to become a genial exegete, deriving from the interaction of his own imagination with the text a meaning only latent in the poet's utterance. That meaning is nevertheless certain, reasonably determinate, and finally inevitable—given the shared spiritual ground of author and audience and the assumption (one that Whitman made) of a univocal human intuition, or common sense.

But why would a reader do that? A fundamental problem for the sacerdotal enterprise in general, and in particular for the Emersonian, orphic Poet, is the educability of the fallen popular mass that needs to be redeemed or moved forward by enlightened leaders whose moral authority must be recognized. The problem is evident in Whitman's pessimisms and in Emerson's perception (in a journal entry for March, 1845) of "the real love and strength of the American people." The "active, enterprising, intelligent, well-meaning, and wealthy part of the people" have been overwhelmed and paralyzed by "hordes of ignorant and deceivable natives and . . . armies of foreign voters," who are in turn hypnotized by unscrupulous, demagogic "editors and orators." The problem is more evident still in *Walden*. Thoreau, in the "Baker Farm"

---

the Intellectual and Literary Relations Between Germany, England, and the United States During the Nineteenth Century (Princeton, 1965). For an impression of Emerson's distance from Coleridge and Wordsworth (and his relative closeness to Carlyle), see the first chapter of *English Traits*, as well as the later chapter "Literature."

chapter, discovers the "boggy Irishman" John Field quite satisfied with his apparently degraded version of the bucolic life. The highest imaginable good, for Field, is his ability to get "tea, coffee, and meat every day," despite Thoreau's attempts to talk to him "as if he were a philosopher, or desired to be one." Field just isn't interested. Worse yet are the Abnaki Indians of *The Maine Woods*. Despite their lifelong contact with uncivilized Nature, they seem as indifferent as is Field to higher values. They see the woods as little more than a source of moose meat. In consequence, they are susceptible to all the white man's corruptions, as well as their own. If the actual America finds that its population increasingly includes hordes of immigrants, "foreign voters," and ignorant natives with sensibilities as blunt, un-aboriginal, and unresponsive as those of John Field or Thoreau's ignoble savages, the *popular* national ethos may well be past redemption, at least from a transcendentalist point of view.[6]

The transcendentalist response to this perception is to narrow the focus of the sacerdotal enterprise. The sacerdotal literatus, as the representative of a higher self maintained or proposed against the actual downward drift of national culture, turns aside to cultivate the sensibilities of the worthy part of the public world from which he necessarily stands aloof. As Thoreau says, near the end of *Walden,* "The words which express our faith and piety are not definite; yet they are significant and fragrant like frankincense *to superior natures.*" Likewise, Emerson in *English Traits*: "It is the condition of religion to require religion for its expositor. Prophet and apostle can only be rightly understood by prophet and apostle." Here, a literatus talks to an inner circle, perhaps only a literary priesthood. E. T. Channing, the Boylston professor of rhetoric at Harvard from 1819 (Emerson's senior year) to 1851, provides the justification for this strategy:

> Of one thing we may be very sure, that a writer of character little troubles himself to learn whether he shall have an audience. . . . Possibly the interpretation may come. . . . But who shall be the interpreters? He [the literatus] has thus far educated none to his purpose. Yet some may be growing up round him,—his unknown disciples,—impatient like himself of drowsy acquiescence. . . . [T]he utterer of cloudy oracles has at last touched ears

6. Emerson, *Journal,* March, 1845, quoted in Stephen Whicher (ed.), *Selections from Ralph Waldo Emerson* (Boston, 1960), 278; H. D. Thoreau, *Walden and Civil Disobedience* (1854, 1849, respectively; rpr. New York, 1966), 137.

that can hear. . . . This may look a little exclusive and selfish. The few favored ones are shutting in the truth from the common eye and touch, and making it the property of the master's inner school. No, indeed. They are preparing to teach it. They will by-and-by proclaim it from the house-top.

This is, in effect, an evangelical and charismatic theory of literature and of national culture—or counterculture—within an assumed hierarchy of enlightenment best epitomized by the relationship between Christ, the apostles, and the Christian multitude, with a vast and unconverted pagany beyond. Or, in other words, there are a sacerdotal class, an elite of enlightened sensibility, and a revelation gradually disseminated to individuals who come, by varying degrees, into the communion of the true America.[7]

Whitman's goal, however, is a larger audience than Emerson's prophet and apostle, Thoreau's superior natures, or Channing's secretive unknown disciples. His ultimate ambition is to end the long preparatory phase that Channing speaks of, and proclaim the revelation from the housetop, sounding his barbaric yawp to the world beyond genteel literary circles. Whitman's bard is to address, or try to address, the regenerate and the unregenerate alike. What he faces (as *The Eighteenth Presidency!* and the letter to Emerson put it) is a nation of "thirty millions of live and electric men" who are, despite their potent energies, a lot of "large boys" with "no determined tastes" and no sense "of the grandeur of themselves, and of their destiny." They are thus at the mercies of a depraved and infidelistic public culture. How shall they and that culture be redeemed?[8]

Whitman's fundamental problem, for which the Emersonian poetic really offers no solution, is to find some ground upon which polemical bard and fallen (or simply unawakened) audience can meet. The poet needs to mount a discourse with sufficient authority to overrule the conventional attitudes and expectations of the public culture, which presumably holds the unregenerate reader in thrall, and to persuade that reader to a vision of his better self or, more ambitiously, to waken him to a sensibility commensurate with America's apocalyptic destiny. (Or, less

7. Thoreau, *Walden and Civil Disobedience*, 215 (emphasis added); Emerson, *English Traits*, 255; E. T. Channing, *Lectures Read to the Seniors in Harvard College* (1856; facsimile, Carbondale, 1968), 158–59.

8. Whitman, *The Eighteenth Presidency!* and Whitman to Emerson, August, 1856, in *Complete Poetry and Collected Prose*, 1325, 1332.

ambitiously, to recognize the moral leadership of such a sensibility.) But where will the bardic poet get such overpowering authority? It cannot come from insistence alone; it must be granted by an audience to which the sacerdotal literatus stands initially in opposition, as did Paul before the Corinthians. Whitman's position is not that of the ancient epic poet, who at least in theory could constitute himself as the mouthpiece of the culture to which and for which he spoke. Nor, for that matter, is Whitman's position exactly that of Northrop Frye's "contrast epic" poet, who could excoriate (or view with ironic contempt) the sins of his society from an ethical perspective already recognized by that society as authoritative.[9] The ethical perspectives to and for which Whitman's bard proposes to speak are in large measure antagonistic; the ethical center he proclaims is not, in fact, the center for the culture that surrounds him. Whitman's bard goes forth in peril of being understood, and responded to, in terms of the very infidelistic attitudes his enterprise is meant to overturn or modify. He projects himself into a situation that is not, indeed, impossible, but neither is it favorable.

In the 1855 *Leaves of Grass,* we find Whitman preoccupied with establishing the needed authority to speak, in the face of a nation of genteel infidels, corrupt vulgarians, and overgrown boys, as one who is "the arbiter of the diverse" and "the key." This text is especially useful as an example of essential American bardic rhetoric because it is prototypical Whitman and is Whitman's longest sustained performance in the bardic mode: twelve untitled, unnumbered sections that ask, in their original form (a form the author would soon dismember and disperse, however), to be read as a single poem. And considered as such, the 1855 poem gives a fuller, if sometimes redundant, impression of the rhetorical intents and strategies of Whitman's American bard than does any other single piece in the Whitman canon. "Song of Myself," often considered his contribution to American epic, is in 1855 an element (though certainly the major one) within a larger purpose that continues to develop through the subsequent eleven sections. "Song of Myself," in essence, is that part of the work—*half* of it—in which Whitman focuses the authority-building aspect of his rhetoric, though there is really no part of the text, including the Preface, where this activity is far from center stage. Let us look at the grounds upon which Whitman's 1855 version of the sacer-

9. See Northrop Frye, *Anatomy of Criticism* (Princeton, 1957), 317.

dotal, polemical bard acquires authority within his poem. We will look at what the bard then does, or can do, and with whom, given the ground on which he stands.[10]

Whitman opens with his famous announcement, almost a fiat, of consubstantiality between himself and his audience. "What I assume you shall assume, / For every atom belonging to me as a good belongs to you" (27). He moves straightway to the standard Romantic antithesis between civilization and nature, retreating from the "fragrance" of "houses and rooms" and turning toward the odorless "distillation" of the atmosphere:

> It is for my mouth forever . . . I am in love with it,
> I will go to the bank by the wood and become undisguised and naked.
> I am mad for it to be in contact with me.   (27)

This is the ground, then, upon which Whitman first engages his audience—a sort of Wordsworthianism in the nude. Insofar as this opening move succeeds, the decorums of official culture ("houses and rooms") are at a remove while poet and audience converge toward a source of higher value, namely Nature. And as they converge Whitman promises his readers that they will soon "possess the origin of all poems" (an odd inducement, it seems, for an unregenerate reader), and then proclaims: "You shall not look through my eyes either, nor take things from me, / You shall listen to all sides and filter them from yourself" (28). This is also odd—the opening command was to assume what Whitman assumes. Whitman's reader is asked to become, or be, a self-reliant understander in a state of aboriginal nature, even as the poet presents some incompatible-looking statements to be sorted out. At this point, Whitman really lacks the authority to elicit such an attitude toward his text, or a willing participation in the sorting out, unless the reader already has a sensibility so transcendental that the poet's declarations can pass for truisms—or unless the commanding self-assurance of Whitman's tone is in itself a sufficient bluff. But whether Whitman is successful or not, his initial intent is clearly to distance his audience from the authority of existing culture ("poems" or "houses and rooms"), on the strength of an appeal to the higher truths of nature and, more crucial, to the direct and

10. Walt Whitman, 1855 Preface, in *Complete Poetry and Collected Prose*, 8–9. All page numbers accompanying citations of the 1855 *Leaves of Grass* are from *Complete Poetry and Collected Prose*, which offers the best and most widely available edition of this poem.

true perceptions of a free romantic self, which will not "look through the eyes of the dead" or "feed on the spectres in books" (28). The speaking poet begins his poem with a Wordsworthian sort of appeal that is, somewhat paradoxically (given what Whitman is asking for), already a literary convention by 1855.

The reader who responds, at least partially, to the conventions invoked is rapidly drawn with the speaker into solitude, or a place removed from "trippers and askers" and "linguists and contenders," against whom the poet "sweated through fog" in his former days (29). Then Whitman can invoke his soul and invite it to speak:

I believe in you my soul .... the other I am must not abase itself to you,
And you must not be abased to the other.

Loafe with me on the grass .... loose the stop from your throat,
Not words, not music or rhyme I want .... not custom or lecture, not even the
    best,
Only the lull I like, the hum of your valved voice.   (30)

What immediately follows is the celebrated pseudo-erotic passage, presented as a reminiscence, in which the union of the speaker (or "the other" that he is, a social identity) with his soul results in the sudden attainment of "the peace and joy and knowledge that pass all the art and argument of the earth." The speaker resists a stable identification: perhaps the soul that has just been invited to "loose the stop" from its throat (though, possibly, that line itself is spoken by the soul), or "the other," namely, Walt Whitman, son of Manhattan, or the Poet who has been speaking from the opening lines. The Poet, the Soul, and the "actual" Walt Whitman, in fact, are present and speaking (from this point, at least) throughout the poem; since they are consubstantial, they are fused. In the dramatic action of the poem, the Poet emerges from the transfiguring union of a limited personal identity with its Self, its immortal Soul.

The convention invoked is, again, distinctly Romantic, or transcendentalist. Whitman clearly speaks as Emerson's Poet, withdrawn into pristine solitude, permitting the currents of Spirit to well up through him—"Through me the afflatus surging and surging" (50)—so that he may, as Emerson puts it, ejaculate thought as Logos, or Word.[11] "Song of Myself," and all subsequent sections of *Leaves of Grass* by implication,

11. Emerson, "The Poet," in *Essays and Lectures,* 466.

must be read in terms of this convention. Indeed, Whitman would later have to insist that we must construe *"Leaves of Grass* entire . . . as a radical utterance out of the abysms of Soul, the Emotions and the Physique."[12] If the reader comes to *Leaves of Grass* with different assumptions regarding the nature of poetic utterance, the text is likely to make little sense—or to make a sense different from what Whitman intends. The preferred audience of *Leaves of Grass,* if not the audience Whitman originally hoped to reach, thus emerges rather quickly as persons of a sufficiently Romantic or transcendentalist stripe to accept the convention that poetic utterance is an orphic revelation from "the abysms of Soul" as a working assumption in the interpretive act. Or, more strongly, the audience implied by *Leaves of Grass* is one that can accept or does accept the convention as an outright truth. Whitman's poet, then, commits himself, and despite his populist ambitions, to speak primarily to Thoreau's superior natures, or to those who fancy themselves as such. Certainly, this audience might include what Whitman thought of as people with infidelistic tendencies—sensualists, aesthetes, readers of gothic novels, devotees of Poe—in need of a moral calisthenic. But the western agrarian yeomen, Whitman's "thirty millions of live and electric men," appear to be effectively left out, however much the poet may discuss them. And paradoxically, what leaves out those thirty millions is the poet's choice of an audience-specific convention that asks to be seen as natural and therefore universal—a false but reasonable enough assumption, given the transcendentalists' up-to-date beliefs in 1855.

Given his point of departure, with all its attendant expectations, and given the audience he does engage, Whitman then reveals the nature of the Self who speaks, amplifying his claim to authority as he goes. Iteratively, through hints and indirections, as well as through outright statement, the voice that emerges from Walter Whitman declares itself a manifestation of the universal soul in which all single identities participate. It is "an acme of things accomplished" and "an encloser of things to be" (79), present and taking part in virtually all events at all places and times in the cosmic unfolding—from the primordial "lethargic mist" (80) and the "orchards of God" (63), through all the scenes and events that Whitman partially catalogs, to the present moment of utterance. By making his transfigured self the voice of transcendental spirit, and to the extent that his reader accepts this representation, Whitman gives

12. Walt Whitman, 1876 Preface, in *Complete Poetry and Collected Prose,* 1011.

himself a warrant to persuasively claim that he utters "the thoughts of all men in all ages and lands" (43) and that he is the channel of "many long dumb voices" (50). Through him, the spoken and the unspoken (and the unspeakable) of all history speak. With his voice thus established, Whitman can move to strong reconfirmation of the essential unity between himself and his reader: "It is you talking just as much as myself .... I act as the tongue of you, / It was tied in your mouth .... in mine it begins to be loosened" (84). This declaration explains why Whitman's reader is to assume what he assumes, and reaffirms (if somewhat imperiously) the obligation or necessity to do so. The reader is presented with what claims to be the voice of his own soul, his deeply embedded and divinely implanted conscience. Insofar as he grants this premise, he must acknowledge that the poet's claims on his belief are more powerful than are those of superficial society. By keeping the status of his voice frequently before the reader's mind, Whitman gives himself the means to widen and maintain the split between his audience and the infidelistic values of public life.

The second major feature of this voice, and its second major source of appeal, is its being the voice of destiny. This is, after all, the voice of an *evolving* identity, one that still looks forward to its ultimate realization. As Whitman says or, rather, as the voice for which he is the channel says:

One world is aware, and by far the largest to me, and that is myself,
And whether I come to my own today or in ten thousand or ten million years,
I can cheerfully take it now, or with equal cheerfulness I can wait.   (46)

Moreover, Whitman speaks with the "long dumb voices" of "interminable generations of slaves" and other innumerable "deformed," despised, and oppressed persons for whom the "password primeval" is "democracy" (50). So his and the reader's yet uncompleted Self may be understood as the motivating end of universal human aspiration, and the end that a democratic society such as the United States must seek. When this Self at last comes into its own, "the curse that weighs down humanity," as William Gilpin said, will be absolved. This event, as Whitman suggests, may be fast approaching. After reviewing its sufferings and humiliations, "my own crucifixion and bloody crowning" (71), the voice discovers itself trooping forth "replenished with supreme power, one of an average unending procession" across the North American continent and beyond: "Our swift ordinances are on their way over the whole earth,

/ The blossoms we wear in our hats are the growth of two thousand years"
(71). The untransacted destiny may be transactable. The path of human
evolution (and of the long dialectic of human history, as a part of that
evolution) lies through the American republic. Thus, toward the close of
"Song of Myself," Whitman can take his reader upon a knoll, hook him
round the waist, and point to "landscapes of continents, and a plain
public road" where "wonderful cities and free nations" may be "fetched"
through enterprise and self-reliance—a splendid prospect, and one now
"within reach" (82). Whitman thus uses his authority as a spokesman for
(or, rather, as the voice of) the universal aspirations of the human spirit,
in order to valorize the myth of American destiny as the fulfillment of
those aspirations. And on the strength of these two basic appeals, spiritual and patriotic, he arrives at a position where he can announce whatever specific values (in addition to "democracy") may be commensurate
with and necessary for the great national achievement that must occur if
America would escape ignominy as "the most tremendous failure of
time."

An extensive account of the specific values Whitman uses his authority to propose is beside my central purpose. Indeed, within the
terms of the Emersonian poetic to which he largely appeals, specific
propositions ought to be unnecessary. Theoretically, it ought to be
enough to sensitize the reader to the promptings of his inward soul,
which on its own would apprise him of the moral truth. But as a bard (or
in his mimesis of one), Whitman would be not only a "terrible negative
voice" but also "judgment" (9), a "call in the midst of the crowd . . .
orotund, sweeping and final" (75). This function is partly fulfilled in
"Song of Myself," but chiefly taken up in the eleven sections of the
second half of the 1855 *Leaves of Grass*. The main end is that Whitman
can widen and deepen the split between his audience and the depraved
values of a public life they presumably live. He can also consolidate his
position as the authoritative voice of the one true American ethos. As he
announces toward the close of "Song of Myself," having "stood up" and
begun to "explain" himself (79), "Long enough have you dreamed contemptible dreams, / Now I wash the gum from your eyes" (83).

Washing away the gum begins, in "Song of Myself," with an aside to
the unredeemed, the "down-hearted doubters, dull and excluded," for
whom he has a sort of consolation: "Be at peace bloody flukes of doubters
and sullen mopers, / I take my place among you as much as among any"

(78). Whitman enforces a considerably distanced attitude toward the "atheistical," despairing mopers—who would be addressed as a "bloody fluke"?—even as he invokes a compassionate patience toward them. The audience stands with Whitman and regards the miserable state of the unredeemed, allotting itself, in proportion as it joins with him, a measure of implied redemption. As the text unfolds, the category of the unredeemed, at once pitiable and despicable, is extended and amplified with its own collection of types. "I Sing the Body Electric," in its 1855 version, concludes with an unequivocal denunciation of the slave trader: "Who degrades or defiles the living human body is cursed" (124). "Faces" makes what now may seem a rather harsh distinction between acceptable American types (the bearded he-men and statuesque "perfect mothers" so characteristic of Whitman's vision) and their unacceptably degraded urban-commercial counterparts. As the bard says, with terrible negative voice,

This face is an epilepsy advertising and doing business .... its wordless tongue
    gives out the unearthly cry,
Its veins down the neck distend .... its eyes roll till they show nothing but
    their whites,
Its teeth grit .. the palms of the hands are cut by the turned-in nails,
The man falls struggling and foaming to the ground while he speculates well.
                                                                    (126)

"An epilepsy advertising and doing business" is, clearly, Whitman's metaphor for an avaricious commercial civilization in general, what *Democratic Vistas* would later call "these cities, crowded with petty grotesques . . . playing meaningless antics." This "epilepsy" and his ilk are not allowed even the backhanded compassion Whitman has for the "bloody flukes." As he says, "Do you suppose I could be content with all if I thought them their own finale?" (125). Concluding his catalog of wretches, he surveys the lot with a disgusted, half-sarcastic amazement: "Those are really men! .... the bosses and tufts of the great round globe" (126). Finally, he dismisses them as splaying and twisting "fishes or rats" eventually to be "unmuzzled" by the inevitable advance of "The Lord" (126–27). The audience, again, is asked to stand at a considerable moral distance from these specimens of blinded sensibility—figures of the business ethos that absorbs so much of the national energy—and to look on in judgment.

Whitman's negativism reaches its peak in "A Boston Ballad." This ninth segment of the original *Leaves of Grass* was probably written in 1854 as a response to the disturbances in Boston brought on by the trial of a fugitive slave.[13] It appears in 1855, however, without title and without any explicit references that would clearly attach and limit it to that one event. Its effect is generalized, and the intention is bluntly obvious. Assembling a crowd of respectable Yankees and "Yankee phantoms" at a procession of "Federal foot and dragoons" headed by the president's marshal, Whitman disperses the seemingly outraged ghosts —"old maniacs," shades of the Revolutionary army, who do not "belong here anyhow"—and then proposes to the "gentlemen of Boston" the "one thing that belongs here": King George's skeleton, glued together, with a crown clapped on its skull (135–37). In the conventional world of well-dressed citizens, those who are the grandsons of the banished ghosts, the principles of the Revolution have been betrayed. And, by implication, so have the values the nation must embody to fulfill its apocalyptic destiny. The 1855 *Leaves of Grass* presents the audience with as negative an opinion of the prevailing national culture as does the later *Democratic Vistas*. It also validates the judgment on the appeal to a potentially more powerful mode of authority than Whitman could ever muster in his oratorical prose (where he must really speak from an authority no more than equal to that of his hearers), or in the ordinary, "public voice" of Walter Whitman, private citizen. The audience, so far as it grants to Whitman his claimed authority and subscribes to the vision of national destiny promoted in *Leaves of Grass,* has virtually no place to stand within the conventional attitudes of genteel social life, which now as a whole is under the sign of infidelism. If Whitman's engaged, actual audience does consist of genteel Romantics or transcendentally inclined "ladies and gentlemen" who would otherwise talk "in subdued tones" of "astral and bric-a-brac" or "Longfellow and art,"[14] they are asked to migrate out of that condition and into a better one, or at least to recognize where the true path lies.

The true path—the positive side of Whitman's antithesis between the morally superior but unachieved national ethos for which he speaks,

13. Stephen D. Malin, "'A Boston Ballad' and the Boston Riot," *Walt Whitman Review,* IX (September, 1963), 51–57.

14. Whitman, "Emerson's Books (the Shadows of Them)," in *Complete Poetry and Collected Prose,* 1052–53.

and the unacceptable society that exists—lies through everything the text affirms: democracy, an agrarian yeomanry (the "live and electric" population of workingmen), sexual frankness, beards ("Washes and razors for foofoos .... for me freckles and a bristling beard" [48]), and so forth. Most important, the audience is to recognize the moral authority of individuals over the workings of government and politics: "The President is up there in the White House for you .... It is not you who are here for him" (93). The audience is also to understand that "all doctrines, all politics and civilization exurge" from itself (93). This "truth," announced in "A Song for Occupations," serves as the basis in "To Think of Time" for an appeal to take action, so that whatever is in the audience may be "exurged" and given articulation in a realized identity:

It is not to diffuse you that you were born of your mother and father—it is to
    identify you,
It is not that you should be undecided, but that you should be decided;
Something long preparing and formless is arrived and formed in you,
You are thenceforth secure, whatever comes or goes.   (104)

The audience, to the degree that it really is genteel or cultured, is invited out of its subdued world of polite hyperaesthesia and into the rough-and-tumble of direct experience: they are to act upon the world that is, at present, dominated by the corrupted and maimed sensibility *Leaves of Grass* rejects. But Whitman also gives assurances against the regenerate reader's fears and timidity—he is secure, as long as he pursues his true identity, whatever happens.

The righteous and secure path, moreover, can be unequivocally recognizable; and that also is a source of security. In "Faces," Whitman elaborates the notion of "true" action as a manifestation of the will of God ("The Lord advances and yet advances" [127]), placing "superb" faces in direct antithesis to the epileptic speculator and the muzzled rat-faces:

This face is a lifeboat;
This is the face commanding and bearded .... it asks no odds of the rest;
This face is flavored fruit ready for eating;
This face of a healthy honest boy is the programme of all good.

These faces bear testimony slumbering or awake,
They show their descent from the Master himself.   (127)

For a self not blinded to its intuitive, divinely given moral sense, virtue should be as self-evidently perceivable as are colors. The true American need have no doubts and can instantly recognize his tribe. Whitman goes on to admire "a fullgrown lily's face," her "limber-hip'd" lover, and—in contrast to "the rich ladies in full dress at the soiree"—a white-haired Quaker on her farmhouse porch ("Behold a woman!") who is "the justified mother of men" (128). In effect, the governing will of a correct national ethos is located in a rural yeomanry and, at the same time, in a virtual elect of perfect and "commanding" types in whom divinity is unmistakably manifest. To Whitman's credit, he does not exclusively identify the leading edge of God's will with what Emerson calls the "fair Saxon man," though, indeed, many of Whitman's chief examples seem to fit the type.[15] But his attempt to elicit affirmation of what amounts to a natural aristocracy of healthy-looking and therefore "justified" persons, in whom the higher laws reveal themselves, has troubling implications for the also affirmed but vaguely defined term *democracy*. When the Master's face is plainly visible in certain persons, after all, some sort of moral hierarchy and a restriction of political authority seem to follow as natural consequences.

The curiousness implied in Whitmanesque democracy completes itself in "Song of the Answerer" as Whitman "answers for" the poet:

Him all wait for .... him all yield up to .... his word is decisive and final,
Him they accept .... in him lave .... in him perceive themselves as amid light,
Him they immerse, and he immerses them.   (129)

This is a clear version of Emerson's epoch-defining genius, as described in "The American Scholar," "Self-Reliance," and "Fate."[16] The speaking Whitman now finds this genius incarnate in the bard already described in his Preface and already evident in himself. The poet is the elect of the elect. Whitman uses his authority as spokesman for and voice of the destined American ethos, in order to appropriate to himself a still greater authority as its moral guide, enumerating as the signs of poethood those ethical qualities abundantly on display throughout the text of *Leaves of Grass*: the poet's equanimity, his familiar ease with president and

15. Emerson, *English Traits*, 67.

16. Emerson, "The American Scholar," "Self-Reliance," "Fate," in *Essays and Lectures*, 57–58, 64–71, 962.

"Cudge" alike, his universal at-homeness, his indifference to "melodious verses," his "flowing character." The notion of democracy implicit in this vision is, like that of "the Poet" himself, more than a little problematical. Whitman proposes, indirectly if not directly, an ideal America composed of justified persons who shall command but also be led forward in perfect unanimity by what amounts to the moral magnetism of the poet whose word is "decisive and final." Meanwhile, the machinery of an obedient and probably inconspicuous government is left to carry out the wishes "exurged" from the divinely inspired and poetically magnetized general conscience. Or, to paraphrase Melville, government in Whitman's regenerate America shall merely be the lawyer of the national will. *Leaves of Grass* projects a sacralized, charismatic, and essentially tribal society to which all the equipment and institutions of the modern world shall be appended as tributaries and servile adjuncts. In this society the universal soul of an untrammeled humanity will take its fullest expression, and a deviation from the attitudes of the "best" or most-awakened sensibilities will be nothing more than a proof of one's depravity. The transcendental "democracy" will have no place, because it can see no need, for political argumentation. As Whitman's 1855 Preface says of the poet, "He is no arguer ... he is judgment." The authority of intuitive revelation is above that of "parleying or struggling," of "logic and sermons," which, according to "Song of Myself," never convince (56). Whitman's ideal America will be a society with a sort of political liberty, but without any perceived use for a meaningful political dialogue.

Whitman uses his authoritative stature as "the Poet" in approximately the last quarter of *Leaves of Grass* to present, again and at its sharpest, his fundamental antithesis between the forces of liberty (exemplified in the European uprisings of 1848) and the forces of infidelism (in "A Boston Ballad"). He amplifies his authority by presenting his perfectly American origins in "There Was a Child Went Forth." The parents, the scenery, and the remembered experiences in this section are strikingly harmonious with the setting of "the justified mother of men" (in "Faces"), not to mention all the other exemplars of Whitman's desirable America. The reader is led to understand, again, that this is a poet sprung from the virtuous, rural, national yeomanry. In the penultimate section, "Who Learns My Lesson Complete," the speaker appears as the child now grown to an uncorrupted maturity: "I have become a man thirty-six years old in 1855" (141). Having struck a stance of "wonder" at the mysteries of life, he moves, in "Great Are the Myths," to his final affirmations: liberty, democracy, the self, America, "truth in man," English speech, America's imperial destiny, law and justice, and the quizzically regarded moot and final questions of the meanings of good and evil and death and life. Before an audience of genteel but essentially Romantic or transcendentalist readers, Whitman explicitly invokes the basic terms of his national mythology. The implications of that myth— among which "democracy" becomes the virtual dictatorship of a sanctified elect—remain to be realized in the thought of his readers and in subsequent bardic poems.

Whitman, then, first engages his transcendentalist or Romantic reader with appeals to the authority of "radical utterance" or poetic revelation, and he redoubles this authority by constituting himself as the voice of America's redemptive destiny. From the power to declare truths that this double appeal affords him, he is able to do, or *attempt* to do, precisely what the rhetoric of polemical sacerdotalism requires and perhaps will always require. He manages to wedge his audience away from the dominant ethos of existing society, and proposes a redeemed (and redeeming) moral identity in its place—an identity that serves, somewhat circularly, to triple his authority as not only the spokesman but also the perfect embodiment, as a God-manifesting poet, of the ethical goals toward which the regenerate American must tend. Whitman, in sum, constructs a rhetoric around the mythology of untransacted destiny, a rhetoric that has for its purpose the ethical conversion of its reader, and that rests persuasive force in a massively amplified ethical appeal. The ethical appeal, in fact, has to be massive, since it is virtually the only basis on which Whitman can command belief, within the terms of his rhetoric. In "Song of Myself" he says, "I carry the plenum of proof and everything else in my face" (53). Indeed, within the version of democracy that Whitman's rhetoric implies, no other mode of proof seems possible.

Whitman's rhetoric, of course, was not entirely successful. The nation remained far more susceptible to the orations of Abraham Lincoln, and others who were perhaps more infidelistic, than it did to the bardic imperatives of *Leaves of Grass* through all of Whitman's editions. The reasons for this outcome are apparent. Whitman's rhetoric did not and could not address the nation at large whose moral and political sense he ultimately wanted to change. Instead, that rhetoric addressed itself to an audience already sufficiently transcendentalist to read him in terms of the conventions on which his initial appeal was built—namely, those in which poetic truth came to be defined as orphic utterance out of the deep and therefore universal Self of the poet, or his Soul. Whitman's sacerdotal bard was speaking to a much more restricted audience than he claimed or wanted to claim. Whether we can say that Whitman committed a genuine blunder or not is probably moot. My own opinion is that the perhaps unmeant restriction of audience in the 1855 *Leaves of Grass* (if not in Whitman's entire canon) was built into the transcendental assumptions that underlay his rhetoric. Those assumptions allowed him to believe that he might speak both for and to a universal Self, and indeed that he might awaken that Self in others, by means of an aboriginal and orphic discourse—the language of the fundamental Self. And certainly, the appeal to an absolute ground of moral value may be the only way for an author to stand outside his reader's circle of belief and still be able to persuade, convince, or convert. The problem, however, is that the reader must see the "absolute ground" as such: the terms and conventions must be immediately comprehensible to and resonant for the rhetor's audience. The terms and conventions available to Whitman were hardly universal or natural, though he had reason to think they were, and they defined his audience in advance.

But with his actual audience, small as it was, Whitman could be extraordinarily successful. Here, for example, is Horace Traubel in *In Re Walt Whitman* (1893): "Whitman speaks in *Leaves of Grass* as would heaven, making unalterable pronouncements, oracular of the mysteries and powers that pervade and guide all life, all death, all purpose." This is what the youthful Pound would recognize in "What I Feel About Walt Whitman": Whitman speaks the language of "cosmic consciousness." Rather, he is able to convince his best (or most persuadable) audience that he does so. Perhaps we should not allow ourselves to be persuaded in this way. As Roy Harvey Pearce says of Traubel's eulogizing, "[W]e should blush." [17] Undoubtedly so. We must also admit that Traubel's response is precisely what the text of *Leaves of Grass* requires of the reader who joins with Whitman in a regenerate understanding of America, and of the nation's role in the long dialectic of history. Traubel's response is,

17. Traubel's eulogy of Whitman's orphic voice, along with Pearce's very sensible uneasiness with Traubel's style of interpretation, are taken from Roy Harvey Pearce, *The Continuity of American Poetry* (Princeton, 1977), 135.

from a basically transcendental point of view, *correct*. Whitman's rhetoric, then, was a partial success and served (with readers such as Traubel and R. M. Bucke) to advance the intermediate goals of the sacerdotal project, if not the ultimate ones. Whitman's rhetoric would not permit the direct cultivation of a national ethos, but it could—and it did—generate in the members of his actual audience the beginnings of a sacerdotal class. To Whitman's successors in the twentieth century, then, fell the problem of developing a rhetoric more adequate to the ultimate goals of the sacerdotal enterprise. Whitman had, as writers such as Van Wyck Brooks, Ezra Pound, and William Carlos Williams recognized, shown them what needed to be done without quite showing them how to do it. He gave the American poet a special untransacted destiny of his own.

III.   Some Usable Pasts

If we are a nation, we must have a national mind.
> —Ezra Pound, "The Jefferson-Adams Letters
> as a Shrine and Monument"

Unhappily," wrote Van Wyck Brooks in 1918, "the spiritual welfare of this country depends altogether upon the fate of its creative minds. If they cannot grow and ripen, where are we going to get the new ideals, the finer attitudes, that we must get if we are ever to emerge from our existing travesty of a civilization?" He went on to say:

> The present is a void, and the American writer floats in that void because the past that survives in the common mind of the present is a past without living value. . . . If we need another past so badly, is it inconceivable that we might discover one, that we might even invent one?
>
> Discover, invent a usable past we certainly can, and that is what a vital criticism always does.[1]

Needing to invent a past, or to create one's own mythic history, seems hardly Whitmanesque. The "common mind," for Whitman, bottomed out in Spirit, and thus was guaranteed direct access to all the "ideals" and "finer attitudes" required for the salvation of American culture from its rush toward urbanized industrial capitalism and ultimate "travesty." The creative mind, in that view, needed only to show the common mind the splendor latent in its depths; what could a fabricated history be, but a distraction from the timeless truth? But for the modern would-be sacerdotal literatus, who stood forlornly on the nearer side of Oppenheim's hiatus, the transcendental path to national redemption was not available. Rather, it simply could not command belief, since Emerson's Nature, which was "saturated with deity and with law," had by 1900 given way to a Spirit-less Darwinian nature of ceaseless struggle, mean-

1. Van Wyck Brooks, "On Creating a Usable Past," *Dial,* LXIV (April 11, 1918), 339.

ingless random change, and amorality. As the post-Darwinian thinkers of the late nineteenth century had come to understand with increasing and unhappy certainty, the "ideals" and "finer attitudes" that civilized life required were the products of the isolated human mind, floating upon its cultural heritage, and buffeted from beneath by the surges of a primal bestiality that had no claims to beatitude. That heritage, in turn, could not be naturally given; it was none other than the outcome of a long historical, evolutionary series of creative and poetic acts that stood *against* the primitive chaos of an essentially dead and empty, or at least unintelligent, universe. And if the would-be bardic poet was damned with an inadequate heritage, or so believed himself, then he was obliged to create or find a new one for himself, in order that he might be its voice. He was obliged, in short, to put a heritage—a memorious tradition— into the psyche out of which an orphic bard must speak.

Pound, Crane, and Williams all responded to their situation by inventing mythic histories, versions of the usable past a bard could recall and refer to in his epic poetry and make the basis of an ethical vision. A crucial point, a point to which I will return, is that the poet's mythic history is the *ground* for an act of vital, constructive imagination—the ground from which "new ideals" might rise—and not its ultimate *subject*. At least this is so in bardic rhetoric. The modern "poem including history," in other words, is not quite about the history it includes, though few have recognized this point; and yet that history is crucial. What concerns me now, however, is the mythic histories themselves, and largely as the poets invented them in their prose, their vital criticism. Pound, Crane, and Williams all chose to build upon the Whitmanesque message—the myth of untransacted or thwarted destiny—by assimilating it to the leading or fashionable thought of their generation. And by doing this, they rewrote their Whitmanesque historical myth, altering their conception of the bardic poet's rhetorical situation and possible purposes in consistent, profound, and troubling ways.

Pound's version of American history developed within a fairly conventional framework. As he maintained in "National Culture": "A national American culture existed from 1770 till at least 1861. Jefferson could not imagine an American going voluntarily to inhabit Europe. After the debacle of American culture individuals had to emigrate in order to conserve such fragments of American culture as had survived. It was perhaps no less American but it was in a distinct sense less *nationally*

American as the usurocracy came into steadily more filthy and damnable control of the union." Writers such as Mumford, Brooks, and Oppenheim by and large agreed: there was a "golden day," a lapse (into rampant capitalism) from about 1870 to "now," and the true national ethos persisting in scattered individuals who constituted, in effect, a sacerdotal unacknowledged legislature in exile, or diaspora. In "National Culture," then, Pound argued that the American ethos once visible in men such as Jefferson and Van Buren had come down to writers and artists who either lived abroad or were ignored at home, such as Henry James, Eliot, Williams, and of course himself. Clearly, their position was essentially that of Emerson's pushed-out American leaders, but worse, since the modern literati were immeasurably further from the centers of economic and political power. Pound's paranoid account of modern industrial capitalism as an international and mainly Jewish cabal of bankers and speculators—"usurocracy"—was a departure from the mainstream thought of his generation but, for all that, was derived, as was the rest of his fall-of-America tale, from widely current commonplaces. Vernon L. Parrington's *Main Currents in American Thought* (1927), for example, proposed the "Hebraic" values of Calvinism as the source of the mercantile, repressive "Yankee" ethos that had brought about the fall from the liberal democratic ideals of Jefferson's republic. Behind both Pound and Parrington stood the general modernist reaction against puritanism (which included, for the moderns, Victorian sexual mores), conflated with an unexamined anti-Semitism and the theses of Max Weber.[2]

William Carlos Williams agreed, in "Pound's Eleven New 'Cantos'" (1934) at least, with Pound's account of the "murderous business" of usury (and Jefferson's and Adams' action "here and there—alone" against it), but in his own rewriting of American history he was generally more circumspect than was Pound. In his *In the American Grain,* for example, he put forward the Parringtonesque thesis that "the result of that brave setting out of the Pilgrims has been an atavism that thwarts and destroys," an antiprogressive, Old Worldish puritanism crushing out individuality and hastening degeneration toward a present "panorama . . . of perversions" and "terrific ungoverned strength" dispersed

2. Ezra Pound, "National Culture: A Manifesto," in *Selected Prose,* 161, 164, 166; Vernon L. Parrington, *Main Currents in American Thought* (New York, 1927), I, 3–15, 81, 86, 261.

in the crude pursuit of "opportunist material advantages." In "The American Background" (1934), Williams refined his thesis to a proposition that the founding of America had established two opposed "bands of effort": the creation of a "primary" or native culture, and the suffocating persistence of an imported, secondary "culture of effigy" obsessed with materialistic accumulation, or the pursuit of appetite. Williams marked these "bands of effort" with the adjectives "true" and "false." The "true" was the suppressed and latent America; the "false" was what was everywhere dominant.[3]

Unlike Pound and Williams, Crane gave this basic topos—America versus mercantilism (or modern industrial capitalism)—no elaborate articulation, but instead simply affirmed it, as in "Sherwood Anderson" (1921) or his 1930 letter to Allen Tate, in which he defended his Whitmanism by appeal to the social criticisms in *Democratic Vistas*. (Crane's fullest and most direct expansion of the topos was probably the "Quaker Hill" section of *The Bridge*.) In sum, then, and despite the differences that clearly set them apart, Crane, Williams, and Pound agreed with each other and with the intellectual fashions of their time. They conceived American history as the *agon* of a fundamental opposition, a struggle that had thus far issued in the general suppression (or nonarticulation) of an ideal American culture fleetingly embodied, they typically thought, in the pastoral republicanism during the era before the Civil War.[4]

This redaction of the Whitmanesque mythology found its warrant in the Jefferson-Hamilton antithesis endemic to the rhetoric of national politics from 1910 through the 1940s, which, in various forms, lingers on today. Jefferson stood figurally for "the American dream," however that might be defined; Hamilton represented the dream's betrayal in federalism, centralization, industrialism, big money, banks, taxes, debt, and almost any other negative terms. A stable and significant feature of this antithesis was its attributed *eternal* quality. Claude Bowers, in his immensely successful *Jefferson and Hamilton* (1925), for

3. William Carlos Williams, "Pound's Eleven New 'Cantos'," in *Selected Essays*, 167; Williams, *In the American Grain* (1925; rpr. New York, 1956), 68; Williams, "The American Background: America and Alfred Stieglitz," in *Selected Essays*, 135, 139, 147.

4. Hart Crane, "Sherwood Anderson," in *Complete Poems and Selected Letters and Prose*, 211; Crane to Allen Tate, July 13, 1930, in *The Letters of Hart Crane, 1916–1932*, ed. Brom Weber (Berkeley, 1965), 354.

example, had declared that those "two giant antagonists" personified "elemental differences that reach back into the ages, and will continue to divide mankind far into the future." Bowers was, as Noel Stock reports, "in good odour" with Pound (Pound wrote to Bowers, and received replies, while the latter was U.S. ambassador to Spain in 1938). In "The Jefferson-Adams Letters as a Shrine and Monument" (1937–1938), Pound used John Adams as his direct authority for the same idea: "The same political parties which now agitate the United States, have existed through all time." The topos was an old and powerful one—the American *agon* as the focus, or apocalyptic fulfillment, of a universal event. It functioned for the modernist much as it had for Whitman, or for the Puritan who understood New England as a decisive confrontation between the true Israel and the forces of Gog and Magog, or who understood Boston as a New Jerusalem under siege. It gave American history a mythic depth.[5]

This general notion of eternal antagonism, expressing itself as the confrontation of a true and a false (but actual and dominant) America, was easily conflated with a mixture of Bergsonian vitalism and the popular arguments of eugenicist thought. The obvious central example is Bergson's *Creative Evolution*, which analyzed the universe into two antithetical "movements": the deterministic "torpor" of materiality (wholly governed by absolute physical laws, and wholly predictable), and the generative will-to-freedom of the life-force. The role of life, Bergson argued, was "to insert some *indetermination* into matter," by causing deviations and uncertainty ("clinamen") at the level of molecular movement and, more important, by evolving organisms of such complexity that behavior would become unpredictable, intuitive, and ultimately free. Intuition, Bergson thought, was the essence of free will, for its realizations (unlike those of rationality) did not follow from fixed principles and could not be determined in advance. Bergson had supplied a new warrant for the Emersonian or transcendentalist notion of an intuitive and inventive will contending with Fate, but with a difference. For Emerson, as for Whitman, the intuitive will was part of the aboriginal self with which every human consciousness had originally been

5. Peterson, *The Jefferson Image in the American Mind,* 332–66 (quotation of Bowers on the "elemental antithesis," 348); Noel Stock, *The Life of Ezra Pound* (San Francisco, 1982), 352; Pound, "The Jefferson-Adams Letters as a Shrine and Monument," in *Selected Prose,* 156.

endowed; for Bergson and the moderns, the intuitive potential of any human being was a function of the evolutionary advancement—the complexity—of his or her nervous system. The old Romantic notion of the genius or the superior man, or what Bergson called the "privileged person," was now regrounded on the felt scientific authority of genetics and evolutionary biology (as were the corollary notions of the "moron" and the "inferior type," which are among the major contributions, sadly, of modernist psychology). When this line of thought combined with the Whitmanesque/Jeffersonian topoi of modernism, the American self that had struggled through history toward its realization ceased to be a universal soul; it became instead a biologically determined personality type that represented (in the views of many, including Bergson) the present apex of human evolution. At the same time, the forces that stood against the vital free will and individualism of the thwarted American ethos could now be equated with—or understood in terms of—the downward drag of material nature into what Bergson described as vegetative torpor, parasitism, and the brutal unimaginative stupidity of the common mind.[6]

Personality type, or the notion of a "genetic elect," played an increasingly dominant role in Pound's version of the myth of untransacted destiny. To a large degree, this idea served as a logical (or, rather, rhetorical) patch for the early implausibility of his thinking. In *Patria Mia,* for example, Pound defined the American as a "man of the Midi" and an essential pagan awaiting a dose of "eugenic paganism" to bring him out of the doldrums of the premodern era (and into renaissance): "I see also a sign in the surging crowd on Seventh Avenue (New York). A crowd pagan as ever imperial Rome was, careless, with an animal vigour unlike that of any European crowd that I have ever looked at. . . . One knows that they are the dominant people and that they are against all delicate things." Like the empire-building Saxon identity that, in Emerson's vision in *English Traits,* had transferred itself (through the migra-

6. See Henri Bergson, *Creative Evolution,* trans. Arthur Mitchell (1907; rpr. London, 1919), 132, 263, 272–73, 278–79. On "clinamen," see Bergson, *The Philosophy of Poetry: The Genius of Lucretius,* trans. Wade Baskin (1884; rpr. New York, 1959). See also Bergson, *The Two Sources of Morality and Religion,* trans. R. Ashley Audra and Cloudesley Brereton, with the assistance of W. Horsfall Carter (Notre Dame, 1977), originally published in 1935 and first published in France in 1932. For a fascinating and disturbing discussion of American eugenics in the early twentieth century, see Stephen Jay Gould, *The Mismeasure of Man* (New York, 1981), Chap. 5.

tion of good English stock) to North America, Pound's pagan identity had (somehow) transferred itself from the Mediterranean Basin to the United States, where it could flourish again as a new Rome. However, and obviously, Pound's argument in 1913 was on weaker footing than Emerson's had been. Emerson could somewhat believably propose, for his own audience at least, that his American Saxons were the same stuff that had made England. But Pound could not expect his twentieth-century reader to readily agree that an admittedly "mongrel" national population (what Henry James in 1907 had called a "hotch-potch" that had no hope of an intelligible identity) could possibly be Greco-Roman in any but an attenuated metaphorical sense, even if one allowed for the effects of Italian and Greek immigration at the turn of the century. Pound's argument was exposed to, and deserved, dismissal as an attempt to resuscitate the Whitmanesque message through fervent wishful thinking.[7]

Pound's rhetorical resort, in 1913, was to a dredged-up version of Alexander von Humboldt's notion that civilization (or empire) takes its westward course through an "isothermal zodiac"—"New York is on the same parallel with Florence, Philadelphia is farther south than Rome"—but the argument was hopelessly creaky. Emerson had long ago dismissed it with gentle humor and skepticism in *English Traits*. Beyond this, Pound could only gesture, as would Van Wyck Brooks and Lewis Mumford, toward the obvious vitality of American business life (however chaotic) and the appearance of skyscrapers ("campaniles," for Pound) as the tokens of a disorganized national potential. By 1916, in "Psychology and Troubadours," however, he had come upon a better argument, or at least a more up-to-date one:

> I believe in a sort of permanent basis in humanity, that is to say, I believe that Greek myth arose when someone having passed through delightful psychic experience tried to communicate it to others. . . . Speaking aesthetically, the myths are explications of mood. . . . [W]e should consider carefully the history of the various cults or religions of orgy and of ecstasy, from the simpler bacchanalia to the more complicated rites of Isis or Dionysus. . . . One must consider that the types which joined these cults survived, in Provence, and survive, today—priests, maenads, and the rest—though there is in society no provision for them.

7. Pound, *Patria Mia*, in *Selected Prose*, 102–105; Henry James, *The American Scene* (1907; rpr. New York, 1947), 121. Pound was enthusiastic about this book. See his "Henry James," in *Literary Essays*, 295–338.

The gods of mythology, as Pound would say in "Religio" (1918), are eternal or recurrent states of mind. Moreover, they are states of mind peculiar to certain "types"—types he would, in "Deus est Amor" (1940), call "select individuals . . . the elect, or, you might say, the hand picked." Behind these propositions stood Bergson's notion of a religious elite, a sacerdotal tribe, as the forward edge of human evolution, and T. E. Hulme's "classical" belief that human consciousness was limited to a finite set of "attitudes" (or states of mind, or ideas) that simply recurred throughout history, being periodically discovered, forgotten, and rediscovered. Insofar as these ideas (supplemented, perhaps, by William James's concept of religious experience) were familiar and acceptable to his audience, Pound had given himself a somewhat more plausible means of arguing that the guiding ethos of pagan antiquity might be latent, though not "provided for," in certain leading types in the dominant and energetic population of the United States.[8]

Working from such an assumption, Pound fixed upon two major and, to his mind, complementary modes of pagan sensibility: the "Eleusinian" and the Confucian. Pound's Eleusinianism is fundamental to his whole project, but since Leon Surette, in *A Light From Eleusis*, has discussed it at length, it can be summarily treated here. Eleusis was, for Pound, a veneration of the creative or generative urge of the vital free will, the force that, in a Bergsonian view, underlies erotic passion, evolutionary development, divine revelation (*i.e.,* "cosmic consciousness"), artistic invention, and civilized culture. The core of this veneration was, Pound believed, a sort of higher eroticism, "a certain attitude toward; a certain understanding of, coitus, which is the mysterium." As he argued in *The Spirit of Romance* (and elsewhere), the *gai savoir* of Eleusinianism had found its characteristic expressions in archaic Venus worship, Christian Mariolatry, Provençal and Italian cults of Amor, troubadour poetry, and (outstandingly) Dante's *Commedia*. Its major ethical expressions he identified as the aristocratic and self-reliant world of Homeric epic—"a very high society without recognizable morals, the individual responsible to himself" (only insofar as he was an Odys-

8. Pound, *Patria Mia*, in *Selected Prose*, 103; von Humboldt quoted in Smith, *Virgin Land*, 37–42; Van Wyck Brooks, *America's Coming-of-Age*, in *Three Essays on America* (New York, 1934), 90–91; Lewis Mumford, *The Brown Decades*; Pound, "Psychology and Troubadours," in *The Spirit of Romance* (New York, 1968), 92, 94–95; Pound, "Religio" and "Deus est Amor," in *Selected Prose*, 47, 70; T. E. Hulme, *Speculations: Essays on Humanism and the Philosophy of Art* (London, 1924), 37, 116.

seus)—or the later and more isolated figures of vitally creative will such as Sigismundo Malatesta. Malatesta, in Pound's interpretation of him, had struggled to build a temple to love, in pagan style, amid the general drift of Renaissance civilization toward materialistic secularism (*i.e.,* infidelism), moral corruption, and political and economic chaos. Like the Bergsonian vital impulse, for which he was in fact a figure, Pound's Malatesta fought the entropic and anticreative forces of the nonvital universe. Jefferson and Adams, in their attempts to establish a civilization in the wilderness, and in their (especially Jefferson's) struggles with bankers, speculators, and Hamiltonians, became identifiable as embodiments of the same personality type. The Jefferson-Hamilton antithesis aligned itself with the "elemental" and centuries-long conflict—virtually from the fall of Rome to the present, as Pound maintained in 1931–32, 1934, 1937, and 1938—between the polyvalent (*i.e.,* nondogmatic and polytheistic) ethos of pagan Amor, and a degenerate trend toward "incult grossness" (puritanical/"Hebrew" dogmatism and taboo), the "mercantilist morale," and usury.[9]

Pound's Confucianism provided him with a code of civics corresponding, in his view, to the Eleusinian religious sense and the "volitional" (or "factive," vital, and inventive) personality type with which his mythic history was centrally concerned. As he maintained in *Jefferson and/or Mussolini* (1935), the phrase "DIRECTION OF THE WILL . . . brings us ultimately both to Confucius and Dante." Dante was concerned with the mysteries of Amor, and Confucius with training the prince in ethics according to vital principles (namely, the pursuit of inward virtue, inventive intelligence, and constant renovation). From this line of thought emerged a Confucian Jefferson, whom Pound characteristically presented as a benevolent sage presiding over an intelligent and active elite: "He governed with a limited suffrage, and by means of conversation with his more intelligent friends. Or rather he guided a limited electorate by what he wrote and said more or less privately." Pound's Jefferson had other Confucian characteristics as well—a genius for employing the talents of others, a concern with equity, and a freedom from the dogmatic fixity of verbal formulas. But Pound's admiration for the

9. Leon Surette, *A Light From Eleusis: A Study of Ezra Pound's Cantos* (Oxford, 1979); Bergson, *The Two Sources of Morality and Religion,* 40–43; Pound, "Religio," "The Jefferson-Adams Letters," "National Culture," "Terra Italica," and "Ecclesiastical History," all in *Selected Prose,* 70, 150–51, 166, 56, 61–63. See also *Guide to Kulchur* (1938; rpr. New York, 1970), 38; and Pound, *The Spirit of Romance,* Chaps. 1, 5, 6, 7.

American civilization of 1770 to 1830 centered chiefly on the notion of government by a privileged and inherently superior "limited electorate." This was especially so as the 1930s wore on, and Pound's attachment to totalitarianism grew (as did his hostility to what he called in 1938 "the total democracy bilge"). As he argued in *Jefferson and/or Mussolini*, a nation's political and economic health cannot be guaranteed by any arrangement of "administrative forms," and instead depends entirely on the "nucleus of the national mind" having the "moral force to translate knowledge into action." Similarly, he maintained in "Terra Italica" that "[c]ivilizations . . . decay from the top." Everything depends upon a vital leadership, and nothing upon democratic institutions. Pound's thought abridged the authority of the "popular superficial suffrage" much as Whitman's had, but with a greater forthrightness.[10]

This frankly nondemocratic line of thought was, after all, consistent with Pound's premises. Bergsonian (or pseudo-Bergsonian) vitalism had taught him that the advance and maintenance of civilization depended on a biologically superior type. Even Bergson, in *The Two Sources of Morality and Religion* (1935), had proposed the "democratic" and "open" world-society as an evolutionary goal toward which humanity might progress (against the torpid, antivital trend of ordinary nature and the common mind), but which it could not attain in any foreseeable actuality. Liberty for the vital intelligence conflicted, in the real present, with the futuristic ideal of an egalitarian polity; all men were not created equal. Pound ascribed the same belief to Jefferson. He wrote in 1933, "There is not the least shadow of a suspicion that T. J. ever supposed that men remained equal or were biologically equal, or had a right to equality save in opportunity and before the law." And in 1938 he wrote, "There is no more equality between men than between animals. Jefferson never thought that there was." The Jeffersonian Pound thought that all men should be at liberty to pursue just and reasonable ends, but that *not* all should enjoy political enfranchisement and the consequent liberty to determine what constitutes just and reasonable ends.[11]

Alongside the Poundian notion of an ideal American polity we may

10. Ezra Pound, *Jefferson and/or Mussolini* (1935; rpr. New York, 1970), 14–20, 112–13, 95; Pound, "Ecclesiastical History," "The Jefferson-Adams Letters," and "National Culture," all in *Selected Prose*, 55, 158, 161, 165.

11. Bergson, *The Two Sources of Morality and Religion*, Chaps. 1, 4 (for the conflict between freedom and equality, see esp. 281–83); Pound, *Jefferson and/or Mussolini*, 4; Pound, "National Culture," in *Selected Prose*, 65.

place, for comparison, the following: "All communities divide themselves into the few and the many. The first are the rich and the well born, the other the mass of the people. The voice of the people has been said to be the voice of God; and, however generally this maxim has been quoted and believed, it is not true to fact. The people are turbulent and changing; they seldom judge or determine right. Give, therefore, to the first class a distinct, permanent share in the government." These are, in the main, opinions that accord with Pound's. Even the equation of the superior few with the rich and well-born, though not quite in the Poundian style (and not Bergsonian), has an analogue in Pound's approving attitude in 1933 toward John Adams' belief in "heredity" and the notion of an "Adams dynasty" expanded in Cantos LXII through LXXI (which stand as the chronological sequel to, and formal-thematic counterpart of, the Chinese dynastic cantos). Such an equation is also implied in Pound's consistent preference for aristocratic types (Odysseus and Malatesta as paradigmatic figures) in his gallery of vitalistic heroes. In any case, the opinions just quoted, and with which Pound substantially agreed, belong to Alexander Hamilton.[12]

Pound's American mythic history was rhetorically grounded in a perplexing set of appeals. On the one hand, by defining the Jefferson-Adams ethos as the basis of a true national culture and the juncture of "Eleusis and Kung" in a reflorescence of pagan virtue, Pound effectively resuscitated Whitman's notion of the American identity as a new fusion of the ancient wisdom of East and West. Moreover, he gave this identity a prophetic, if temporary, fulfillment at the dawn of national history. On the other hand, however, Pound had managed to invent, with unintended irony, a distinctly Hamiltonian Jefferson. In view of the traditional antithesis between these two figures and its pervasiveness and potency in public discourse, Pound created a distinctly strange, unintelligible, even absurd Jefferson. In short, then, Pound's "American civilization 1770–1830" embodied—for an American audience respon-

12. Hamilton quoted in Parrington, *Main Currents in American Thought,* I, 307. Hamilton occupies the traditional anti-Jefferson position in Pound's mythic history, but chiefly on account of his fiscal policies (for which Pound endows him, in *Jefferson and/or Mussolini,* 20, with "Hebrew blood"). In mainstream versions of the Jefferson-Hamilton antithesis, however, Hamilton is the villain chiefly because of his "aristocratic" hostility to what Pound disdainfully called "demo-liberal" ideals. Pound had violated at least one fundamental assumption held by his American audience.

sive to the fundamental commonplaces of the Whitmanesque message—
the major strengths as well as the worst rhetorical blunders in his mythic
history.

Neither Williams nor Crane went quite as far toward overtly authoritarian concepts of culture and politics as did Pound, but as their thought
worked from similar premises, it ran along similar lines. Williams, for
example, displayed a version of Pound's Eleusinianism when he proposed
in "Against the Weather" that the "processes of art" like Whitman's were
the "active front [of a] Great Tradition" embodied in Hellenic culture
and the late medieval cults of Amor. However, and characteristically, he
also declared his difference from Pound, by rejecting Dante (too "restrictive" and formal) and fixing upon two Spanish epics—*Poema del Cid* and
El Libro de Buen Amor—as freer and more impulsively composed (especially *El Libro de Buen Amor,* which was "untouched by morals"), and
therefore more fully representative of true creativity. These ideas derived
from Williams' abiding concern with the "Kora principle," the prerational core of an inventive, ethical will whose central characteristic was
pursuit of an object of ideal desire, typically figured forth by Williams as
feminine and as inviolable or beyond possession. This conception of and
concern with vital will was central to Williams' poetic project from the
composition of *Kora in Hell* to the end of his career. "Choral: the Pink
Church" (1949), for example, is a celebration of coitus-as-mysterium
and virgin-worship (which, as Williams would have learned from Pound
if nowhere else, was the Catholic version of Venus worship) as a virtual
true religion: the "Church" is "the nipples of / a woman who never / bore
a / child," and Whitman, Poe, and Baudelaire appear among the "saints"
of its "calendar." Similarly, the culminating moment of *Paterson*'s "Sunday in the Park" sequence is the mountaintop vision of a persisting
ancient Venus. An old Italian woman named Mary tries to coax a group
of drunk, torpid picnickers to get up and dance. In this not-so-virginal
Mary, dancing and spilling wine, Williams' protagonist sees "the air of
the Midi / and the old cultures"—"the old, the very old, old upon old, /
the undying"—for she is one of the embodiments or guises of "Beautiful
Thing," the "Persephone gone to Hell" that he seeks throughout the text
of *Paterson.* Clearly, Williams shared with Pound a perception of Venerean sensibility or the cult of Amor as the primitive root of a vital and
inventive free will that found expression in a "Great Tradition" from
Greco-Roman times to the poetry of Whitman and the art of a sacerdotal

modernism. Williams declared in "Midas: A Proposal for a Magazine": "We proclaim the occasion of our intent to drive the program (of fertility and construction) home." [13]

This vitally pagan mode of virtue was for Williams, as it was for Pound, the defining basis of the unachieved or suppressed American ethos. In his major accounts of American history and culture—*In the American Grain* (1925), "The American Background" (1934), and "The Writers of the American Revolution" (1936)—he defined true culture as the ongoing act of realizing "the qualities of a place" and lifting them "into an ordered and utilized whole," creating an ethos in direct and true relation to its immediate world. He then identified this activity with a set of American heroes who displayed a Venerean will to enter into close sensual relation or "marriage" with a New World "land of heart's desire." This self-reliant "new relation" he thought to be the possible but thwarted "pure American addition to world culture," the achievement, thus far, of only isolated individuals (Thomas Morton, Daniel Boone, Sam Houston, Aaron Burr, Edgar Allan Poe, and others) who struggled unsuccessfully against the grossness and restrictive stupidity of a culture built on effigies of European forms. This line of thought gave Williams an American identity more autochthonous ("an Indian robbed of his world") than was Pound's, and aligned his mythic history, distinctively, with nineteenth-century precedents. Thomas Hart Benton, for example, had advanced the cause of westward expansion in about 1818 by combining the rhetoric of national destiny with his representation of East Coast cities as "an influence stifling the development of the American personality by imposing deference to [European] precedent and safe usage." But in other ways, this American nativism reduced Williams' rhetorical power. In the first place, an elemental *agon* worked out in terms of the antithetical pursuits of autochthonous/primary and imported effigy cultures deprived Williams of being able to make strong use of the Whitmanesque appeal to the notion of the American ethos as an "apex of things accomplish'd" or as a regenerative fusion of ancient wisdoms, an appeal that Pound could retain and use to great effect. The ancient Mary

13. Williams, "Against the Weather," in *Selected Essays*, 196–219; Williams, "Choral: The Pink Church," in *Selected Poems* (New York, 1969), 124; Williams, *Paterson* (New York, 1963), 57, 125; Williams, "Midas: A Proposal for a Magazine," in *Selected Essays*, 248.

of "Sunday in the Park" and her natural devotees would have to forget, and reinvent within an entirely new set of terms, the poetic "explications of mood" given her by antiquity. And in the second place, the idea of ethical renovation was hobbled. If true culture was to be created by realizing "the qualities" of a locale with which the individual had entered close sensual and imaginational contact, what was to be gained by steeping one's mind in the qualities of a place already (as Williams believed) degraded and perverted?[14]

Resort to the notion of a primitive ethical core in the deep, precultural self was, perhaps, possible; and Williams took this resort on occasion, appealing in 1927, for example, to "a certain position of the understanding anterior to all systems of thought . . . that is common to all," and in 1947 to "some rare, unblemished area of the first revelation hidden in [the] secret heart." The thought of "the age," however, ran against this. Post-Darwinian thinkers, such as Josiah Royce, Lester Ward, John Dewey, and Henri Bergson, tended to regard the natural, inner psyche as an ethical locus only insofar as it was a memory stored with codes of value developed through cultural evolution. The modernist's Nature was Spirit-less (Bergson's "vital impulse" actually opposed the laws of physical nature), and the Oversoul now was History. Pound's and Eliot's concerns with tradition proceeded from such a recognition, or an acceptance of it. Even Williams, in applying epithets to the "anterior understanding," named it "the past." Within such a frame of thought, the only way to renovate a depraved national ethos would be to provide a past not available from its own immediate experience, and the sacerdotal poet would have to do this by taking a more Poundian approach, one that violated Williams' (and Benton's) ban on effigy culture. The presentation of Mary in "Sunday in the Park" as a version of Venus, the treatment of Whitman as a saint of the calendar of the "pink church" (or as a member of the "Great Tradition" of a *gai savoir* going back to Dante and various Hellenes), and the general notion of "Kora in hell," to name only a few instances, depend entirely for their significance and rhetorical effect on appeals to non-native symbolic codes and are consequently violations. There is a grating dissonance in the internal logic of Williams' nativist

14. Williams, "The American Background," in *Selected Essays*, 143, 157. Williams, *In the American Grain*, 139; Benton quoted in Smith, *Virgin Land*, 23. See also Williams, "The Writers of the American Revolution," in *Selected Essays*, 38–54.

American mythology, and a dissonance that is central to the problematics of bardic authority in the rhetoric of *Paterson*.[15]

Despite its differences from the Poundian mythos, Williams' mythos tended also toward a strikingly nondemocratic conception of culture and politics, though he did stop short of the shrill extremes that Pound could reach. *In the American Grain,* for example, presented the strikingly un-Whitmanesque opinion that the atavistic, thwarting puritanism of the United States had resulted in "a generation universally eager to barter permanent values (*the hope of an aristocracy*) [emphasis added] in return for opportunist material advantages, a generation hating those whom it obeys." An aristocracy, as Williams explained later in the same text, was "the flower of a locality and so the *full* expression of a democracy." This is a curious and indeed a shabby-looking argument, thinly disguising the elitist preferences of vitalistic thought within the Jeffersonian rhetoric of the period. But Williams, after all, was hardly being eccentric; he could simply cite his odd opinion as something "pointed out recently." Van Wyck Brooks, in *The Literary Life in America* (1921), had pointed out that an "aristocratic tradition . . . would have kept open among us the right of way of the free individual." He had cited as his own authority William James: "The notion that a people can run itself and its affairs anonymously is now well known to be the silliest of absurdities. . . . Individuals of genius show the way, and set the pattern, which common people then adopt and follow." Pound, of course, was also a source. The "bane and hidden terror of democracy," as he had argued in 1914, was the "mediocre spirit" that failed to provide for "the outstanding personality." Williams' aristocatic democracy was, then, a fairly conventional version of the modernists' preferred American polity. Like Bergson's "open," libertarian polity, it was to be a free association of individuals, in which the creative vitality of superior types would rise naturally to the top and, as James said, "set the pattern" for the rest, who presumably would willingly obey.[16]

15. William Carlos Williams, *The Embodiment of Knowledge* (New York, 1974), 132–33; Williams, "Revelation," in *Selected Essays,* 270; Josiah Royce, Lester Ward, and John Dewey, in R. S. Wilson (ed.), *Darwinism and the American Intellectual* (Homewood, Ill., 1967); Bergson, *Creative Evolution,* 6, 48, 176; Bergson, *The Two Sources of Morality and Religion,* Chap. 4.

16. Williams, *In the American Grain,* 68, 231; Brooks, *The Literary Life in America,* in *Three Essays on America,* 203, 211; Pound, "The Renaissance," in *Literary Essays,* 224.

Williams' American mythology thus worked itself out as an antithesis between the aristocratic individual, with his creative energies, and the directionless, dangerous "headless mob"—the "great beast" in Alexander Hamilton's famous phrase, and also in *Paterson*. (The same antithesis and virtually the same terms were employed by Van Wyck Brooks in 1921.) *In the American Grain* gave the antithesis its sharpest form in the face-off between Hamilton and Aaron Burr. Williams' Burr represented the "aristocratic strain" that "a democracy must liberate," a sensibility that finds the common good "common" and refuses to yield to the degrading "tyrannical assertions [of] the herd." Burr's killing Hamilton in a duel (over which Williams rather indecorously gloated) thus figured as a blow against the "subversive force" of a restrictive, dogmatic "herd instinct" becoming manifest in federalism. Clearly, Burr's confrontation with the evil genius of antivital but soon-to-be-triumphant forces, and the ultimate failure of his own career, made him a paradigm of Williams' true-but-thwarted American ethos. Williams had rewritten the Jefferson-Hamilton antithesis by substituting Burr for Jefferson, thereby replacing commonsense rationalism and pastoral republicanism with a vitalistic and therefore elitist version of Romantic individualism. The aristocratic, "amoral" Burr of *In the American Grain* stands, then, as the counterpart (and precedent, in fact, by nearly a decade) of Pound's Eleusinian and Confucian Jefferson, embodying "a delicious sincerity . . . not a scheme, nor a system of procedure—but careless truth," which could give us, Williams actually said, "a second China." Probably, Williams did not imagine a vast bureaucracy of scholar-clerks presided over by the high society of unfettered mandarins; but his mythic history did tend, like Pound's, toward the vision of a fundamentally two-tiered society finding its leadership in a privileged class of gifted individuals.[17]

Crane's mythic history worked from similar presumptions and tended toward similar conclusions. He interpreted United States history as an *agon* between a truly American vitalistic individualism and the infidelistic powers of industrial capitalism, and he understood the national destiny as the discovery of "a new hierarchy of faith not to be developed so completely elsewhere." This inspiration stemmed from his encounter

17. Williams, *In the American Grain*, 128, 188–207; Williams, *Paterson*, 46. Hamilton's famous (or notorious) phrase is "The people!—the people is a great beast!"

in the early 1920s with Bucke's notions of "cosmic consciousness," chiefly as presented and extended in Ouspensky's *Tertium Organum*. As James E. Miller has noted, Bucke recognized three "grades" of consciousness: the unreflective consciousness of animals, the self-consciousness of humanity in general, and the cosmic consciousness of prophets such as the Buddha, Christ, and Walt Whitman. Further, these grades represented levels of biological attainment. For Bucke, species developed (mentally) upward through the accumulation of "percepts" over thousands of generations. Percepts eventually became biologically coded "recepts," potentials in the nervous system; and recepts became explicit and conscious "concepts," or "named recepts." In essence, Bucke had simplified Bergon's arguments in *Creative Evolution* into a kind of Lamarckian evolutionary psychology. The upshot, inevitably, was the wholly unequivocal notion of a "genetic elect," or what Bucke thought of as "a family sprung from, living among, but scarcely forming a part of ordinary humanity," an elect whose function was to "assist self-conscious individuals in the ascent to the higher plane." This ascent was, Bucke believed, the key factor in the transformation of global humanity (the other factors were "aerial navigation" and the abolition of private property), leading eventually to the "literal creation [of] a new heaven and a new earth" in which "religion will govern every minute of every day of all life." Insofar as Crane accepted these ideas, and apparently he did believe them, he committed himself even more than Pound or Williams had to the vision of a yet unrealized, redemptive, and religious America, an America moving toward (or creating) a world made over as a *paradiso terrestre*. And insofar as he believed the ether-voice that told him, "You have the higher consciousness," namely, "genius," as he sat in the dentist's chair in 1922, he gave himself membership in Bucke's Lamarckian elect, with all the sacerdotal duties and privileges such membership entailed.[18]

However, the sacerdotal inspiration he received from Ouspensky's appropriation of Bucke implied a reversal of the egalitarianism that Whitman, despite his implicitly authoritarian rhetoric, had wanted to advance. Bucke's cosmically conscious "family," which in essence was a new and higher species emerging from the older human stock, consti-

18. Hart Crane, "General Aims and Theories," in *Complete Poems and Selected Letters and Prose*, 219; Ouspensky, *Tertium Organum*, 284, 287–89; J. E. Miller, *The American Quest for a Supreme Fiction*, 166–68.

tuted a virtually divine aristocracy to which the rest of humanity would have to be subordinated. It was a superrace. Ouspensky realized this clearly and arrived at conclusions whose true historical significance he could not perceive in 1920:

> Man must not and cannot remain as he is now. . . . [O]nly a small part of humanity is capable of growth. . . . And the fate of the greater part of humanity which will prove incapable of growth, depends not upon itself, but upon the minority which will progress. . . . In men capable of development, new faculties are stirring into life, though not as yet manifest, because for their manifestation they require a special culture, a special education. *The new conception of humanity disposes of the idea of equality,* which after all does not exist, and it tries to establish the signs and facts of the differences between men, because humanity will soon need to divide the "progressing" from the "incapable of progress"—*the wheat from the tares,* for the tares are growing too fast, and choke the growth of the wheat.

The sacerdotal leaders, who will take humankind to a new evolutionary stage, require "special education" for those with a latent higher consciousness. There must also be a eugenic cultivation of the gene pool and a weeding of the garden. Eugenicist concerns had been advanced by such respectable authorities as Henry Herbert Goddard, the father of IQ testing in America, and a number of other hereditarian psychologists. The argument Crane was yielding to was, in essence, nothing new—with the exception, perhaps, of Ouspensky's almost complete lack of shame.[19]

It is difficult to find, in Crane, anything comparable to Pound's Confucian Jefferson or Williams' aristocratic Burr, partly because Crane wrote relatively little on the subject of American history and culture. Indeed, Crane's only concentrated treatment of the national mythology is *The Bridge* itself, and even there he does not offer a clearly articulated vision of an ideal American polity. What we find, instead, is the myth of untransacted destiny worked out in terms of Bucke's and Ouspensky's ideas of evolution toward a sacred brotherhood of the higher consciousness. We see, for example, heroes such as Columbus, Maquokeeta, Whitman, and Poe striving toward a transcendental unity or "Love" (much as the heroes of *In the American Grain* pursue "marriage" with a vision of desire). We also see this unity prevented by greed and commer-

19. Ouspensky, *Tertium Organum,* 279–80; Gould, *The Mismeasure of Man,* Chap. 5.

cial exploitation (requiring Bucke's economic revolution); it is also advanced by technological progress, namely, "aerial navigation" (the airplane sequence in "Cape Hatteras") and the symbolic fact of Brooklyn Bridge itself. Implied is a sort of polity—a socialized, high-tech theocracy—but one in which the disjunction between the cosmically conscious elect and the non-elect, degraded mass is almost complete. In effect, the sought-after unity is not attainable within the world of ordinary humanity, except as an inanimate, technological, symbolic object (the bridge), the true significance of which is available only to prophetic intelligences such as Whitman's or Crane's. If we are to identify a figure in Crane that is equivalent to Pound's Jefferson or Williams' Burr, it would be the mystic Whitman that Crane received from Bucke. This Whitman is in no sense a ruler at all, but simply a lone visionary surrounded by a world incapable of joining with him in a communion of understanding—a world apparently committed, as Crane wrote to Waldo Frank, to increasing degeneration. The tares were growing too fast. Crane, then, replaced Pound's and Williams' vital aristocrats with a mystic superrace, a race whose function was not so much to govern as it was to transcend an enclosing, suffocating, ordinary mass humanity. Where possible, the race was to transfigure those in whom election was latent or dormant—and, where necessary, if we follow Ouspensky's line, to eliminate the hopeless remainder.[20]

Crane, Williams, and Pound were probably unwilling to take a position as extreme as Ouspensky's.[21] However, Ouspensky does provide a pithy condensation of what the Whitmanesque project had become, or was tending to become. The audience for a sacerdotal poetry was no longer or even potentially "everyone," as Whitman had originally and

20. Crane to Waldo Frank, June 20, 1926, in *Complete Poems and Selected Letters and Prose,* 230–33. In another letter to Frank, of November 21, 1926, Crane mentions reading *In the American Grain* after writing (most of?) *The Bridge.* This seems to undermine J. E. Miller's belief that Crane's treatment of Columbus (and the epigraph concerning Pocahontas) are taken from Williams. What seems more likely is that both poets were working from the same or similar primary materials and with similar inspirations. For the Bridge's relation to the myth of American destiny, see Trachtenberg, *Brooklyn Bridge.*

21. But see Surette, *A Light From Eleusis,* 98–101, on Pound's interest in Remy de Gourmont's *The Natural Philosophy of Love* and in G. R. S. Mead's Gnosticism. Both Gourmont's and Mead's views are fairly close to those held by Bucke. Pound's early advocacy of a *eugenic* paganism takes on a clearer significance within this context.

perhaps naïvely hoped, nor was it to be "the citizen," as Michael Bernstein has suggested. Instead, the audience was to be "men capable of development," a latent aristocracy the sacerdotal literatus could waken to its true identity. Van Wyck Brooks had made this fairly explicit. The writer was to promote "the emergence of an aristocracy outside the creative class," an aristocracy that would subsequently serve as "a *cordon sanitaire* between the individual and the mob" and that would carry the sensibility acquired from its poetic educators into public life. Williams similarly maintained in a 1937 essay that the poet serves society by writing "in the hope that he may gather to himself others with whom he would like to see the world better populated," so that "society may be built more praiseworthily." Pound had given Whitman's concept of a sacerdotal class new meaning by proposing art "centres," creative think-tanks under civic patronage, to provide the nation ethical direction. He quickly abandoned this notion, perceiving "the hostility or inertia that is against us" and maintaining at the same time that the poet could do no "real work" with "one eye on the public." What Pound preferred but did not enjoy was the princely and liberal employment of creative individuals, as exemplified in Malatesta's recruiting artists for the Tempio (or Jefferson's search for a musical gardener) and in the "Confucian" way that totalitarianism, Mussolini's Italy, "uses the best of its human components." The sacerdotal literatus of the twentieth century, in short, turned his back on "the mob" (what Williams called the "headless beast") and addressed himself to an American aristocracy *in potentia*. This elect (if dormant) audience constituted the tribe whose tale the modernist American epic would include.[22]

This altered sense of the rhetorical situation gave the poets, perhaps, a perception of the task less naïve than the one Whitman had begun with, but it also entailed new problems. Probably the greatest of these lay in the belief (or the presumed "fact") that the American aristocracy that lay outside the creative class was indeed *in potentia*. In other words,

22. Michael Bernstein, *The Tale of the Tribe: Ezra Pound and the Modern Verse Epic* (Princeton, 1980), 14 (but see also Bernstein's remarks on p. 71, which come closer to the position taken here); Brooks, *Letters and Leadership*, in *Three Essays on America*, 211, 214; Williams, "The Basis of Faith in Art," in *Selected Essays*, 180, 194; Pound, *Patria Mia*, in *Selected Prose*, 140, 158, and "The Renaissance," in *Literary Essays*, 219–20, 224, 225. Malatesta's patronage appears in Canto VIII, and Jefferson's "musical gardener" (a *vigneron*) in Canto XXI.

it was a category of vital and intelligent types deprived of the ethical education appropriate to them. The post-Darwinian premises of Pound, Williams, and Crane required them to conceive the ethical basis of an active, aristocratic will as a memorious, *learned* sense of tradition or history, and not as an Emersonian aboriginal conscience "saturated with deity and with law." They could therefore presume little knowledge or ethical sense on the part of their audience. Clearly, the unredeemed or uncultivated reader—the latent aristocrat—was by definition a person who could have no extensive knowledge of the mythic histories from which the elements of a national ethos would derive. These histories, or what T. E. Hulme would have called the "rare type of historical intelligence" embodied in them, were necessarily the very thing that had to be provided: they were necessarily unknown, in whole or in part.[23] And to the degree that his mythos was indeed unknown, a poet could not use it, as Whitman had in 1855, as a direct source of bardic authority.

We have seen that the poets gave their histories a measure of contemporary persuasiveness by constructing them within the conventional terms, the elemental antithesis of Jeffersonian political rhetoric. We have also seen that the conflation of that rhetoric with vitalistic, pseudo-Bergsonian assumptions yielded significant and fairly bizarre distortions, such as Pound's Hamiltonian Jefferson, the frankly totalitarian Jefferson in *Jefferson and/or Mussolini,* and Williams' aristocratic Burr as a substitute for Jefferson in *In the American Grain.* These distortions left the poets holding an eccentric position, at odds with the more equalitarian tenor of mainstream demo-liberal thinking, such as may be found, for example, in Parrington. Moreover, even in appealing to the Jeffersonian topoi circulating in the American mind, the would-be bards put themselves in competition with the myriad conflicting versions of what Merrill Peterson has called "the true interpretation of the Jeffersonian scripture," which were especially various in the 1930s.[24] Insofar as their histories were truly original inventions (which they had to be, to appear believably as the products of vitally creative minds), Pound, Williams, and Crane necessarily differed from and were in competition with each other as well. The poets' histories were rhetorical constructs, and the potential aristocrat would have to be persuaded to enter them before his ethical education could occur.

23. Hulme, *Speculations,* 37.
24. Peterson, *The Jefferson Image in the American Mind,* 363.

The weakened authority of the poets' rewritten mythic histories resulted in an even greater emphasis on the conventions of poetic truth-speaking than had been necessary for Whitman. Whitman had used the authority of an orphic "radical utterance" to engage his audience from a position outside its usual beliefs. He had moved from that position to claim further authority as the voice of a national destiny in which his audience already believed, enabling himself thereby to propose or culti-vate an ethos commensurate with that destiny. The moderns, on the other hand, were obliged (insofar as they kept to the rhetoric of bardic utterance) to mount an ethical authority almost solely through voice in order to give initial validity to an original and eccentric version of the myth of untransacted destiny. Once established, that mythos could then serve its poet in Whitmanesque fashion as the basis of a redoubled ethical proof and as the ground upon which the latent aristocrat could be brought to realization of the codes of value appropriate to his true identity. The conventions of orphic utterance, then, became even more central to the problem of establishing a countercultural authority in the twentieth-century bardic poem than they had been in 1855. I want to look at those conventions—notions of how a sacerdotal bard should talk—not so much as an account of actual poetic process, but rather as a set of decorums or expectations to which the bardic poet appeals (or can appeal) as a means of establishing authority *through voice*. The poetic or the inventional process of bardic poetry is, in fact, an effort to meet and use those expectations to elicit a particular response. For the present, we may note that the needed response in the twentieth-century bardic poem is largely an exegetical one. The reader must be persuaded into acquiring the "historical intelligence" the poem depends on but often does not directly or coherently present, *before* anything else can really happen, or before the poem can really be fully experienced. Whitman had required (or requires) of his readers an exegetical posture also; but the modern poems, and the *Cantos* in particular, clearly make a greater demand. As the demand (*i.e.,* the obscurity) is greater, so is the reader's inertial resistance, and so in turn is the burden of persuasion carried by the poet's bardic voice. The twentieth-century bardic poets had set themselves a considerably more complicated and refractory rhetorical task than Whit-man had undertaken.

IV. Signs and Credentials

We see, fore-indicated . . . a language fann'd by the breath of Nature, which leaps overhead, cares mostly for impetus and effects, and for what it plants and invigorates to grow.

      —Whitman, *Democratic Vistas*

But the artist must employ the symbols in use in his day and nation to convey his enlarged sense to his fellow-men.

      —Emerson, "Art"

The question here is available means. Upon what convention of belief, what mythology, could the bardic literatus draw, in constructing for himself a sufficiently authoritative voice? For the moderns, and despite their qualifications and distancings, the available conventions stood embodied in Whitman, who was, after all, in their eyes the spiritual father of American verse. It was Whitman, moreover, who had effectively created the audience for an American epic poetry, and who had thereby generated the sort of immediate expectations that any continuation of the genre would have to meet. Even Pound, as early as his 1909 essay (when he was not fully out of his "stale creampuff" period), found what he called the Whitmanesque "maramis" necessary to "the expression of certain things related to cosmic consciousness."[1] Whitman, and the transcendentalist and Emersonian notions of poetic utterance to which *Leaves of Grass* had appealed, remained as the source for a modernist mythology of bardic utterance. Like the Whitmanesque vision of untransacted destiny, however, the source was to be reappropriated and to some extent transformed in light of the poets' vitalist assumptions. It is this reappropriation, and its consequences in terms of conventional expectations or decorums, that I want to consider now.

The place to start is with originals, with the conventions of voice that constituted Whitman's available means in *Leaves of Grass*—the topoi, that is, of the Emersonian poetic. Emerson's orphic poet was, as Harold Bloom has recognized, in essence a *sublime* poet. The poet was to redirect the reader's sensibilities toward "a point outside of our hodiernal circle" or toward "the Unattainable, the flying Perfect, around which the hands

---

1. Ezra Pound, "What I Feel About Walt Whitman," in *Selected Prose,* 145; Pound's 1965 prefatory note to *A Lume Spento and Other Early Poems* (New York, 1965).

of man can never meet." His means would be a symbolistic flux arising from the depths of his aboriginal being. The reader, in effect, was to be brought to consciousness of the golden realm of deific truth that lay beyond conventional language or the intellect's created categories. And in consequence, he would be morally liberated and transformed, or redeemed. Behind the Emersonian line of argument stood Longinus' *On the Sublime:* "Within the scope of human enterprise there lie such powers of contemplation and thought that even the whole universe cannot satisfy them, but our ideas often pass the limits that enring us. Look at life from all sides and see how in all things the extraordinary, the great, the beautiful stand supreme, and you will soon realize the object of our creation." As Emerson wrote in "The Poet," the object of our creation, or the intent of god-saturated Nature, was ascension. The role of the poet, therefore, was to reveal to us those horizon-breaking "powers of contemplation and thought" that would enable us to realize our transcendental purpose. Emerson's poetic took its warrant from a deeply rooted Hellenistic tradition, a tradition bearing all the authority of its antiquity.[2]

Emerson's poetic, however, appropriated the theory of sublimity in ways Longinus had probably not imagined. Emerson's essential departure—one the modernists followed—was to conceive "sublimity" as a generalized quality, a vague and pervasive "essence of poetic discourse," rather than a specific, localized rhetorical device. Longinus' theory of sublimity, unlike Emerson's, was embedded in and presupposed the tradition of classical rhetoric. His work was not a complete account of any literary genre, such as the oration or the lyric. He was instead concerned with those moments in a text when the author (or speaker) evokes such feeling that his audience is overmastered and swept before him. As Longinus put it: "[T]he effect of genius is not to persuade the audience [*i.e.,* by rational proof] but rather to transport them out of themselves. Invariably what inspires wonder casts a spell upon us and is always superior to what is merely convincing and pleasing. For our convictions are usually under our own control, while such [sublime] passages exercise an irresistible power of mastery and get the upper hand with every member of the audience. . . . [A] well-timed flash of sub-

2. Emerson, "Circles" and "The Poet," in *Essays and Lectures,* 403, 408, 458; Longinus, *On the Sublime* [*Peri Hypsous*], trans. W. Hamilton Fyfe (Cambridge, Mass., 1932), 225.

limity scatters everything before it and reveals the full power of the speaker at a single stroke."[3] In essence, Longinus' concern was with one of the three rhetorical purposes defined by Cicero, or, for that matter, by Horace in the *Ars Poetica*: the effective or potent discourse must teach (logically prove or demonstrate), conciliate (give pleasure), and *move*. The "well-timed flash of sublimity" was to generate such pathos that the audience would lose control, for that moment at least, over its own convictions—and would thereby be brought unquestioning within the terms or premises of an argument that would subsequently enter consciousness with irresistible power.

A modern, if unpoetic, example of the Longinian or classical sublime is Martin Luther King, Jr.'s "Letter from Birmingham Jail." The example is chosen precisely because it is *not* a version of the Emersonian sublime; therefore it offers a convenient contrast. Near the outset of his letter, King writes: "I am cognizant of the interrelatedness of all communities and states. I cannot sit idly by in Atlanta and not be concerned about what happens in Birmingham. Injustice anywhere is a threat to justice everywhere. *We are caught in an inescapable network of mutuality tied in a single garment of destiny.* Whatever affects one directly affects all indirectly. . . . Anyone who lives inside the United States can never be considered an outsider anywhere in this country."[4] The phrase emphasized is indeed a "well-timed flash of sublimity." Although it states, in essence, what the rest of the passage is simply reiterating, it puts the notion of interrelatedness in figural and transcendent terms, thereby shifting it into the realm of inarguable, absolute truth. King's intent is to *move* the reader, through the evocation of sublime emotion, into profound acceptance of the general topos underlying this passage, an acceptance that makes his reiterative claims "all true," and true without need of rational or syllogistic proof. To do this, he takes a passionate stance toward "the good and the true," a stance with which the reader is invited to join. Insofar as this succeeds, King's sublimely established general topos becomes a basis for persuasion throughout the rest of his letter. Because of our transcendental mutuality, the argument goes, we cannot idly stand aside or deny our direct responsibility while the transcendentally absolute rights of others are being violated. If we respond to that sublime flash, we are indeed overmastered. The argument of "Letter

3. Longinus, *On the Sublime*, 125.

4. Martin Luther King, Jr., "Letter from Birmingham Jail," in *Why We Can't Wait* (New York, 1963), 78–79 (emphasis added).

from Birmingham Jail" becomes virtually undeniable and inescapable. King uses the sublime in classical fashion, as a device for the sententious establishment of general principles—or, in this case, an ethical stance—upon which persuasion, and persuasion of a very powerful order, can be based.

If Longinus' account of sublimity was set within and presupposed a classical rhetoric, Emerson's was relatively detached. Emerson derived his account from a reinterpretation of classical tradition, one that brought the sublime within a view of mind and language history that made it a generalized and, eventually, ubiquitous convention for poetic language. As William Charvat and F. O. Matthiessen observed, Emerson's aesthetics developed from, and continued to incorporate, a number of major assumptions in the late neoclassical (and mainly Scottish) bellettristic theory dominant in the United States until around 1825. The key assumption, for our purposes, was the marking of a boundary between natural and cultivated mental processes, and thus between natural and artificial language. The natural processes, as eighteenth-century thought defined them, were generally reducible to a few rudimentary associational operations. These operations corresponded to what were sometimes considered primary tropes, though the number of rudimentary associations and tropes varied somewhat from one theorist to the next. The tropes and processes, moreover, were generally defined as the original language of poetry. The cultivated processes, in contrast, were built upon fossilized tropes and the supposed subsequent invention of syntactical rules and ratiocinative figures, such as the enthymeme or syllogism. In this way, neoclassical theorists divided the "language of reason" from what they sometimes called the "language of passion and imagination." The latter was supposedly the language of innocence and natural apprehension, a language that they wistfully denied themselves in the interest of pursuing cultivated Taste.[5]

5. Charvat, The Origins of American Critical Thought, Chap. 3; Matthiessen, American Renaissance, 14–24 ("Eloquence"). See also C. Carroll Hollis' expansion of Matthiessen's argument, in Language and Style in "Leaves of Grass" (Baton Rouge, 1983), 1–27. My discussion of the bellettristic thought available to Emerson's generation is drawn mainly from: Hugh Blair, Lectures on Rhetoric and Belles Lettres (London, 1783); Henry Home, Lord Kames, Elements of Criticism (Edinburgh, 1762); John Quincy Adams, Lectures on Rhetoric and Oratory (Cambridge, Mass., 1810); and Channing, Lectures Read to the Seniors in Harvard College. Adams and Channing both relied heavily on late neoclassical theory. Adams is particularly interesting for his appropriation of Locke and Priestley; Channing for his romantic interpretation of Blair (whose Lectures served as the

The presumptions that arose out of this line of thought are familiar by now, but they remain endlessly astonishing. First, "primitives" (such as Africans, American Indians, Chinese, and Arabs) spoke in languages that were "all poetry," that is, radically figurative or tropistic, emotive and "rhythmical," and of indeterminate structure or no structure at all. Second, the poetry of ancient times, such as the verse of Homer and Isaiah, was more sublime than modern verse because its inspiration was wild and convention-free. In light of modern linguistics and cultural anthropology, such presumptions are clearly absurd: there is not now, nor has there ever been, a language or a poetry that is primitive in the neoclassical sense. As we have learned, the poetic discourse of so-called primitive cultures tends to be highly ritualized and formulaic—Milman Parry, in his study of Yugoslavian oral bards, has suggested the highly and complexly conventional nature of Homeric epic. Moreover, if we assent to the contemporary argument about the biological foundation of our linguistic faculties—an argument whose strongest version is probably Noam Chomsky's—it begins to appear unlikely that there could ever be a language that is primitive in the neoclassical sense (that is, "without grammar" or logic) and still a *human* language. Quite simply, then, the eighteenth-century distinction between natural and artificial mental/linguistic faculties, or between a language of poetry and a language of reason, has collapsed.[6]

---

standard textbook in Channing's course). See also Samuel H. Monk, *The Sublime: A Study of Critical Theories in XVIII-Century England* (New York, 1935); and M. H. Abrams, *The Mirror and the Lamp: Romantic Theory and the Critical Tradition* (Oxford, 1953), 72–83.

6. The presumptions here are drawn mainly from Blair's *Lectures,* but they can be found in virtually any standard eighteenth-century treatment of "primitive" language and poetry, and in significant nineteenth-century treatments as well (for example, Coleridge's 1818 essay, "On Poesy or Art"). On the primitive literatus, especially in bardic or prophetic modes, see Albert B. Lord, *The Singer of Tales* (Cambridge, Mass., 1960); Mircea Eliade, *Shamanism: Archaic Techniques of Ecstasy* (London, 1964); and Nora Kershaw Chadwick, *Poetry and Prophecy* (Cambridge, England, 1942), esp. 58–72. A recurrent feature in all these studies is observation of the conventional and even self-consciously dramatic qualities of bardic performance.

On biologically based linguistic universals, and on the complexity of those universals, see Noam Chomsky, *Rules and Representations* (New York, 1980), and *Language and Mind* (New York, 1972). It should be noted here that we can accept these arguments concerning the biological bases of language without committing ourselves to the rather less persuasive representation of "deep structure" offered by the transformational gram-

For Emerson and Whitman, however, the distinction was still in place and was endowed with the status of indubitable fact. Emerson's transformation of the neoclassical topos lay chiefly in his redefining the primitive self, the original mind, as the locus of sublime truth in a nature "saturated with deity and with law"—as the place where deific truth was most truly perceived and spoken. Within this view, progress from primitivistic figuration and conventionlessness to the cultivated prose of civilized discourse became, inevitably, a lapse or descent from pristine truthfulness into corruption and mendacity. This line of argument was one of the major topoi in the "Language" chapter of *Nature*. In its "infancy," language was "picturesque" and "all poetry," but with the imposition of "secondary desires" caused by social competition, the will became corrupt and language fell from its original poetic state. The implication, for Emerson, was that the wise man was to restore discourse to its aboriginally truthful condition, to render it a vehicle of sublime expression by releasing it from the conventional "encrustations" of association in quotidian discourse. This argument led, in the end, to the striking claim that we could *recognize* the wise man by the "picturesqueness," the primitive, tropistic naturalness, of his language. As Emerson put it, "A man's power to connect his thought with its proper symbol, and so to utter it, depends on the simplicity of his character, that is, upon his love of truth and his desire to communicate it without loss. . . . [P]*icturesque language is at once a commanding certificate that he who employs it is a man in alliance with truth and God.*" Emerson had articulated a new decorum for poetic discourse. The poet was to signify his truthfulness by speaking in the language of primitivistic sublimity—the language in which the spiritual, transcendent facts embedded in the soul presumably took their natural embodiment. "Picturesqueness," in short, was a *credential.* And further, given Emerson's inherited belief that his account of language and language history described the true state of things (which it did not), picturesqueness should have been a credential recognizable to the natural mind of any person who was not utterly and hopelessly corrupt.[7]

---

marians—a representation from which even Chomsky appears to distance himself in his 1980 book.

    7. Emerson, "Language" chapter of *Nature,* in *Essays and Lectures,* 20–23 (emphasis added).

This credential, then, amounted to a decorum in which the figures of sublimity were *detached from the figures of rationality,* which had fallen under the sign of profane convention and artificiality. Emerson's truly orphic poet, the poet he could not find anywhere in recorded history, was in effect to prove that he spoke from the aboriginal, abysmic depths of his soul by using a voice that would be, somehow, unremittingly sublime. But what were the identifying figures of this sublimity? Aside from his discussions of the symbolistic flux of language—and the necessity that the symbolistic process not stop anywhere, but instead guide the reader toward apperception of the truth beyond linguistic codifications and fossilizations—Emerson, in typically Emersonian fashion, displayed little interest in taking up the details of the question. He did not, however, really need to do so. The figures of sublimity had received considerable discussion in the eighteenth-century bellettristic theory familiar to his generation. The fullest account, however, remained Longinus' *On the Sublime,* from which the eighteenth-century theorists had heavily drawn.[8]

The figures of sublimity, for present purposes, can be briefly summarized. They include, as local-textural devices, the conventional tropes (metaphor, metonymy, etc.) and what neoclassical theorists interpreted as imagery. The figures also include such text-structuring devices as accumulation, asyndeton (the suppression of grammatical or logical connectors), question and answer (*i.e.,* self-dialectic), apostrophe, and what might generally be called "variation." This last term, ambiguous as it is, is worth examination. For Longinus, it covers any unexpected shift in the discourse: a deviation that suddenly disrupts and reorients the pattern of response by which the audience interacts with and understands the text. Applied radically, as in the case of "inversion" or syntactic deviation, it becomes a principle of suspended coherence heightening the drama of the utterance. Longinus said that the audience becomes "terrified for the total collapse of the sentence" and is compelled "from sheer excitement to share the speaker's risk," so that when the "long-lost" element finally occurs and the sentence recovers, the speaker "astounds them all the more."[9]

8. See Monk, *The Sublime;* and Abrams, *The Mirror and the Lamp.* See also Harold Bloom, "The Sublime Crossing and the Death of Love," in *Agon: Towards a Theory of Revisionism* (Oxford, 1982), 224–45.

9. Longinus, *On the Sublime,* 195.

Variation, basically, is a principle of convention breaking, what Harold Bloom has called the "breaking of form." [10] In a poetic concerned with the convention-free primitivism and unconstraint of the abysmic self, it becomes a truly diffuse but cardinal decorum by which the poet's voice presents credentials as a locus of poetic truth. The abysmic bard is required to employ the principle of variation or deviance to destabilize patterns of expectation, thereby signifying his allegiance to a "truth and God" beyond the hodiernal circle of linguistic formulation and beyond the hobgoblin consistencies of the convention-bound "little mind" as well. This convention of convention breaking does not necessarily deny, however, the possibility of coherence, which the reader may finally attain (or glimpse), as in a revelation, and so be "astounded all the more." It does permit, or even require, the cheerful self-contradictoriness of Whitman, as well as the abrupt transitions and discontinuities of *Leaves of Grass*. Obviously, the convention of variation, in its transcendentalist appropriation, has been extended beyond its original, Longinian conception of localized sentence-level distortions of syntax, in which grammar appears momentarily to collapse, but ultimately does not. The conception of variation, in short, has varied.

Within a transcendentalist or Whitmanesque convention of unremitting sublimity, moreover, the principle of variation applies on a global scale, and in bardic discourse its consequence is the devaluing or suppressing of narrative or discursive structures. As Whitman recognized, the "great psalm of the republic" was not to be "direct or descriptive or epic." The use of "direct" narrative/discursive structures would, after all, imply the fulfillment of a preconceived and intended pattern. And that would imply the regression of the speaker into the (supposed) fixities and formalisms of the profane discourse of the non-aboriginal (*i.e.*, social) self. In consequence, then, the burden of text structuring is in principle shifted onto the figure of accumulation, resulting in what Lawrence Buell has called the "catalogue rhetoric" so characteristic of American transcendentalist literature. *Catalogic style* may be the preferable term, since a rhetoric in the fullest sense is more than a collection of figures. But whichever term we prefer, the principle is apt: from Emerson's "rhapsodic" or "Saadi-esque" stringing together of sentences from

---

10. Harold Bloom, "The Breaking of Form," in *Deconstruction and Criticism* (New York, 1979), 1–38.

his journals and commonplace books, to Whitman's paratactic additiveness, *accumulatio* remains the chief device for a sustained expression of the
aboriginal perception of sublimity. Within this convention, narrative/
discursive structures are not totally disallowed, but they do take on the
status of minor (non-governing) figures. They become, in effect, elements absorbed within a generally catalogic or accumulative pattern.[11]

Accumulatio, however, is more than mere catalog, in the sense of
"list," that is. According to Longinus, there are "ten thousand kinds."
Indeed, the number is potentially unlimited, since a technique of simple
additiveness puts no constraint on the specific principle by which the
adding-on is done. And further, as Buell has noted, the catalogic style to
be successful must maintain a certain indeterminacy or unpredictability.
Otherwise, it would be an obvious and static listing of examples, suggesting a speaker frozen into a fixed position, fossilizing rather than
progressing toward a transcendental percept continually receding over
the intellectual horizon. Longinus wrote that the simple catalog would
fall from sublimity into mere redundance, from elevation into tedious
quantification. So the catalogic style, in bardic discourse at least, must
be combined with and enlivened by the principle of variation. The
general convention, then, is one of discontinuous accumulation. The
abysmic voice must go by catalogic progression, but the reader must feel
himself presented with the catalog of an elusive x that seems suggested
by but is yet beyond all its constituent terms, and that shifts and alters as
the terms accumulate. Moreover, it may be an x eventually perceptible
or glimpsed, at or beyond the final point in the catalogic string, making
that string "astounding all the more."[12]

Such, at least, are the theoretical requirements and possibilities.
That a primitivistic language of symbolic flux and discontinuous accumulation is neither more natural nor less conventional than any other is
suggested by Whitman's failure with an audience not schooled in late
Romantic or transcendentalist assumptions. Conversely, his great success with those prepared to read him in the correct frame of mind
suggests his artfulness in managing the rhetorical means that Emersonian thought had made available to him. It is arguable, I think, that

11. Lawrence Buell, *Literary Transcendentalism: Style and Vision in the American Renaissance* (Ithaca, 1973), Chap. 6. See also Matthiessen's subchapter "Eloquence," in *American
Renaissance,* 14–24.

12. Longinus, *On the Sublime,* 161–63.

Leaves of Grass (in 1855, at least) was the first poem successfully and fully to realize the sort of primordial bardic discourse imagined by the neoclassical bellettrists and by the transcendentalists. The eighteenth century had in effect invented a curiously proscribed genre, an imaginary genre that Emerson helped to promote and that Whitman put into practice and made real. And, since Whitman's actual audience consisted of those equipped to respond in terms of the orphic conventions he worked with, it follows that the modernist neo-Whitmanians, or those who regarded him as an American Homer, composed an audience for bardic poetry in which those conventions still were viable, though partially modified.

We come, then, to the modernist appropriation and revision. The major point of revision was, as with the poets' mythic histories, the substitution of a vitalistic or Bergsonian psychology for the transcendentalist conceptions of the soul. Nature had become a chaotic and Spiritless flux, and the deep self no longer was consubstantial with Deity; rather, the deep self was conceived as a product of history, arising out of evolution and accumulated knowledge. The consequence was a distinctly psychologized conception not only of religious experience but also of the sublime processes of poetic discovery and invention. Poetic utterance, in principle at least, became the figural adumbration or projection of superior and exalted states of mind, which were grounded for the most part in "historical intelligence." The vital mind descended to the abysms of its inherited memory (a memory at once personal, cultural, and racial) and interacted with the residues of human experience. This conception was, perhaps, most clearly crystallized by Eliot, in his famous account of the poetic mind as a catalytic "platinum shred" inserted into the crucible of tradition. But even James Oppenheim, in a *Seven Arts* editorial that appeared two years before "Tradition and the Individual Talent," had arrived at a similar formulation: "The poet has only really to go to himself, to descend the inner stairway of the ages, to go down layer beneath layer of his human nature, to tap the stored heritage of the life of man." Poetic utterance, in the pervasive, commonplace view of the modernists, was the orphic embodiment of the tradition or of the spirit of the culture enshrined in the poet's memorious deep psyche.[13]

13. James Oppenheim, editorial, *Seven Arts* (January, 1917), 268. See also Bergson, *The Philosophy of Poetry, Creative Evolution*, and *The Two Sources of Morality and Religion*. For

This general topos was basic to the modernist readings (or misreadings) of Whitman, and permitted both the identifications and distancings we have observed. In essence, Whitman's twentieth-century readers were able to regard him as *actually* doing what he claimed to do—namely, giving "abysmic" utterance to the contents of a deep self. But they regarded that self as the provincially bumptious, crude, and self-satisfied spirit of mid-nineteenth-century America, rather than the God-given soul of universal humanity. As Van Wyck Brooks maintained in *America's Coming-of-Age,* Whitman had crystallized or "precipitated" the American character, but it was provided only with the ethics of an "antisocial," self-seeking or self-assertive culture. For Brooks, as for many of his contemporaries, that ethic had been the basis of a disastrous national drift into predatory capitalism, big industry, and the Gilded Age. The problem with Whitman, for the moderns, was not his "abysmic" qualities. Indeed, Pound praised Whitman as the "first honest reflex [*i.e.,* embodiment of the "spirit of the age"] in an age of papier-mache letters." The problem, rather, was what they considered his inadequate psyche. Brooks's position was that the American writer was "paralyzed by the want of a social background" or an adequate tradition. For this reason, Brooks proposed that the national literatus should improve on the Whitmanian bequest by "adding intellect to emotion," and Pound in 1909 conceived for himself the role of Whitman-in-a-collar. Pound, Williams, and Crane elaborated mythic histories that gave the poetic psyche what they could regard as a more adequate "historical intelligence" to serve as its basis of invention. Brooks, with an unmeant irony that appears when we consider his later writings, counseled going to England, which he styled as a sort of ethical greenhouse. Writers such as Pound and Eliot had taken this advice well in advance of *America's Coming-of-Age.* Whitman's aborigine was tending to become a studious aborigine, browsing amid the edifices, ruins, and libraries of civilization.[14]

Studious as he may have been, however, the American bard was still

---

additional discussion of the impact of Bergsonian and other turn-of-the-century process philosophies on modernist aesthetics, see John T. Gage, *In the Arresting Eye: The Rhetoric of Imagism* (Baton Rouge, 1981); and Sanford Schwartz, *The Matrix of Modernism: Pound, Eliot, and Early Twentieth-Century Thought* (Princeton, 1985).

14. Brooks, *America's Coming-of-Age* and *Letters and Leadership,* in *Three Essays on America,* 41, 82–85, 89, 95–96, 113–27. See also Brooks's "On Creating a Usable Past." Pound, *Patria Mia* and "What I Feel About Walt Whitman," in *Selected Prose,* 110, 145; Pound on Whitman, in *The Spirit of Romance,* 168–69.

conceived in essentially orphic and sublime terms, as one who gave utterance, *cultured* utterance, to privileged percepts, realizations, and emotions beyond the perimeter of quotidian thought and beyond the expressive powers of conventional language. (However, the percepts were frequently also to be cultured—as in Eliot's "art emotions.") In fact, with Pound, Crane, and Williams, this conception held as a commonplace in their pronouncements on poetic theory, as a workable ground upon which they could meet with and engage the sensibilities of a post-romantic audience. The commonplace was viable, moreover, on both sides of the Atlantic. As T. E. Hulme somewhat cynically said, in a rendering of the Bergsonian aesthetic, "The essence of poetry to most people is that it must lead them to a beyond of some kind. . . . So much has romanticism debauched us, that, without some form of vagueness, we deny the highest." As long as the available audience for bardic (or any other) poetry remained romantically "debauched," so would the poetics of the modernist would-be bard. [15]

Pound centered his early Imagist/Vorticist theorizing on the notion that poetry must present not only an intellectual-emotional complex but also a complex that would be a "word beyond formulated language." This "word beyond," for Pound, did not necessarily imply vagueness or imprecision. As he maintained in his key Vorticist essay (1916), the "word" embodied by the Imagist/Vorticist text *as a whole* would function as analytics' mathematical statements did, embodying abstractly the general pattern governing the particularities of psychic experience. With the *Cantos* in view, Pound's actual words on this topic are worth repeating: "The statements of 'analytics' are 'lords' over fact. They are the thrones and dominations that rule over form and recurrence. And in like manner are great works of art lords over fact, over race-long recurrent moods, and over to-morrow." A god, as Pound maintained in "Religio" (1918), was an "eternal state of mind," or the sort of powerful psychic experience that the ancient myths embodied and that the tradition of literature went on re-embodying through time. These "race-long" and godlike "recurrent moods," then, were the sublime words beyond formulated or formulable language that great art sought to embody. [16]

15. Hulme, *Speculations*, 127. See also, in this same collection, "Bergson's Theory of Art," 152–53.

16. Ezra Pound, "A Retrospect," in *Literary Essays*, 4; Pound, "Vorticism," in *The Modern Tradition*, ed. Richard Ellmann and Charles Feidelson, Jr. (New York, 1965),

This line of thought implied that the poem revealed a *mode of vision* more than it revealed any particular idea. This notion was taken up quite explicitly by Pound. In "A Few Don'ts" (1913), for example, he defined the effect of the image as "that sense of sudden liberation; that sense of freedom from time limits and space limits; that sense of sudden growth, which we experience in the presence of the greatest works of art." Such a statement takes us directly back to Longinus. The sublime transport releases our "powers of contemplation and thought," so that they "pass the limits that enring us." Our horizons are (at least momentarily) abolished, and we experience, in theory at least, "sudden growth." We need not worry here whether such early Imagist poems as "In a Station of the Metro" are *really* sublime in the way that Pound suggests. Despite Hugh Kenner's "transported" reading of that poem, it seems ridiculous to think so. We can, however, think of that poem as intending to represent a mode of perception, rather than a subway or even ideas about a subway. The point here is that sublimity, for Pound, had become a ubiquitous feature of poetic discourse and, indeed, an index of artistic quality or greatness. A poem, insofar as it was great art, was *supposed* to reveal to the reader a mode of extraordinary perception, as opposed to particular facts or ideas. In "Vorticism," Pound advanced the view that poetry was "to give people new eyes, not to make them see some new particular thing." In "How to Read" (1927–28), he declared the "function of literature as a generated prize-worthy force" to be *"nutrition of impulse,"* or the cultivation of a "sane and active ebullience," rather than the communication of specific concepts or bits of information. The recurrent idea, in short (and recurring as late as *ABC of Reading* in 1934), was that the main beneficent effect of poetry was the enlargement of mental capacities, through the liberation of sensibility from its quotidian frame of reference and the revelation of vital, noncodifiable modes of apperception. As Pound rather memorably said in 1916, "Any mind that is worth calling a mind must have needs beyond the existing categories of language."[17]

149, 152; Pound, "Religio," in *Selected Prose,* 47. See also Pound's notions of "delightful psychic experience," in *The Spirit of Romance,* 92, 94–95.

17. Pound, "A Retrospect," in *Literary Essays,* 4; Pound, "Vorticism," 148–49; Pound, "How to Read," in *Literary Essays,* 20–21; Pound, *ABC of Reading,* 75. On the "Metro" poem, see Hugh Kenner, *The Pound Era* (Berkeley, 1971), 186–87; and Gage, *In the Arresting Eye,* 47–50.

It is important to remember that this is the aesthetic frame of mind in which—or, perhaps, for which—Pound began composing the *Cantos*. Despite the recurring critical view that Pound's passage from Imagism/ Vorticism to the so-called ideogramic method marked a shift in his aesthetics or even his compositional procedures, the major topoi of his earlier poetics remained in place, and in a fairly central place at that. The ideogram itself, as George Kearns has noted, was to be an assemblage or "phalanx" of particulars, together indicating or revealing a new whole that itself would be beyond paraphrase, or that could not be adequately conveyed through direct abstract statement. In *ABC of Reading*, Pound discussed the ideogramic method in terms of what he took to be the inductive processes of science, arguing that "a general statement is valuable only in REFERENCE to the known objects or facts." The ideogram was, in effect, the means of conveying general statements in terms of the particulars that embodied them. This line of thought was a very short distance from the 1916 definition of the vortex as a "radiant node or cluster," a configuration through which a particular stream of ideation passed. In either case, the figure of ideogram/vortex was definable as the adumbration of an "analytic" pattern, and a pattern that was a "word beyond formulated language."[18]

Like the vortex, moreover, Pound's theoretical ideogram tended to adumbrate patterns that were really modes of apperception. As he said in *Guide to Kulchur* (1938), the "point of writing" was to cause the reader "suddenly to see," or to "reveal the whole subject from a new angle." This led him into one of his better-known definitions of ideogramic method: "The ideogramic method consists of presenting one facet and then another until at some point one gets off the dead and desensitized surface of the reader's mind onto a part that will register." This definition clearly implies an intention to break open the reader's conventional categories of understanding, and to cause a fresh perception. It is, in essence, not the subject itself that is to be revealed, but the *new angle* from which it may be seen. Working from this definition, Pound moved swiftly to a distinction between "information" and "knowledge." The former was what he thought was handed out in colleges (such as memorized "chronological sequences"); the latter was an "active, instant and

18. George Kearns, *Guide to Ezra Pound's Selected Cantos* (New Brunswick, 1980), 4–7; Pound, *ABC of Reading*, 4–13. See also Pound's edition of Ernest Fenollosa, *The Chinese Written Character as a Medium for Poetry* (San Francisco, 1936), 26.

present awareness [of] the process now going on." What was to be conferred was vital sensibility, or a superior state of awareness, rather than a particular collection of facts—though the facts would presumably be the means of communicating that sensibility.[19]

Pound's rationale depended on the felt need to prevent the "petrification" of ideas, or the establishment of "a koran" with its associated orthodoxy, a need he put forward as "the lesson of the Mohammedan conquest and flop." This was a characteristic position throughout his career—namely, that fixed symbologies or verbal codifications represented "mental cramps" or "arrests" of the perceptual and intellectual faculties, and that their ultimate outcome would be degeneration into torpor and corruption. Pound believed that such degeneration had been the fate of the Eleusinian "light" as it passed from paganism into Christian dogmatism and the Scholastic arguments of the Middle Ages. Underlying Pound's line of thought, as always, were Emerson's pronouncements that symbols were for "conveyance" and not for "homestead," and that the purpose of literature was therefore to liberate the will into renewed and expanded understanding—or, more simply, that books were for "nothing but to inspire." The Pound of *Guide to Kulchur* explicitly took up this position:

> Properly, we shd. read for power. Man reading shd. be intensely alive. The book should be a ball of light in one's hand.
>
> To read and be conscious of the act of reading is for some men (the writer among them) to suffer. I loathe the operation. My eyes are geared for the horizon.

The "act of reading," as Pound defined it here, meant essentially reading for information, or doing research. And reading for power, the true reading, was clearly a transformation of the familiar terms of Pound's earlier aesthetics: reading for "*nutrition of impulse,*" "ebullition," or revelation of a potent sensibility. In sum, then, the basic topoi of Pound's critical theory were fairly stable and constant from his early Imagism right through to the poetics of the ideogramic method. The poem was to reveal a "word" or position beyond usual talk and intellection, and a position that was, in essence, more a revealed angle of vision or mode of understanding than a specific fact or collection of facts. The poem would include facts, and the facts would reveal to the reader the exalted,

19. Pound, *Guide to Kulchur*, 51–53.

untranslatable position from which they were being seen. What this position amounts to is Pound's redefinition of the sublime perspective that poetic vision is supposed to reveal. To a large degree, Pound appears to have revised his critical vocabulary (making it more interesting, surely) without effecting a major change in its general concepts.[20]

Compared with Pound, Crane and Williams had relatively little to say about these commonplaces; but their positions can be aligned with his. In his key essay, "General Aims and Theories," Crane announced his belief that poetry conferred a sort of "absolute" experience, one that would approximate "a formally convincing statement of a conception or apprehension of life." That statement, moreover, would gain "our un-questioning assent." Crane appeared (in 1925) to have absorbed his terms from Pound: "It is as though a poem gave the reader as he left it a single, new *word*, never before spoken and impossible to actually enunciate, but self-evident as an active principle in the reader's consciousness hencefor-ward." Crane's theorizing returns us to the sublime and unparaphrasable word beyond, which tends to define itself as a "principle in conscious-ness" rather than a determinate idea. Again, this was a fairly stable position. In a letter to Gorham Munson, for example, Crane declared that poetry should not be "limited" to "moral classifications," "abstract tags," or "factual terms." Unlike Pound, he justified his position in terms of the emergent new-critical antithesis between "poetic" and "scientific" discourse. He apparently drew this distinction from I. A. Richards' discussion of the "pseudostatement" in *Poetries and Sciences*. In his famous 1927 letter to Yvor Winters, Crane laid claim *as a poet* to a "certain code of ethics," one that he could not put into "any exact formula" and that he declined to specify, resorting to the fantastically vague notion that "a certain decent carriage and action [was] para-mount." All the poet could do, as he told Winters, was to "approximate a true record of such moments of 'illumination' as are occasionally pos-sible." Sketchily developed as it was, Crane's critical theory resolved into the revelation of extralinguistic "words" or "principles in conscious-ness," which were undefinable but potent states of "illumination" and

20. *Ibid.*, 52, 55; Pound, "Axiomata" and "Terra Italica," in *Selected Prose*, 49, 57; Emerson, "The American Scholar" and "The Poet," in *Essays and Lectures*, 57, 463. On the continuity of Pound's "ideogramic method" with his earlier poetics, see Hugh Witemeyer, *The Poetry of Ezra Pound: Forms and Renewal, 1908–1920* (Berkeley, 1969), 36–40. See also Feidelson, *Symbolism and American Literature*, Chap. 2.

which the poet of cosmic consciousness might strive to represent by symbolistic means.[21]

Williams was less inclined than was Crane to borrow Pound's (or I. A. Richards') terminologies, but his position was not very different. As Joseph Riddel has argued, Williams' Objectivism was more a revision of than a departure from the premises of Vorticism, a revision in the direction of "structural" analysis. Williams wrote in an unpublished manuscript that the structure of a poem was to be "itself a 'word,' the most significant of all, that dominates every other word in the poem." But the "word" could also be more than a signifying structure; it could be a "metaword." In an essay for the *Yale Poetry Review* (1947), Williams defined the "objective" of poetry as revelation of "*that which is inside the man,*" suggesting that what the poem embodied was really a mode of sensibility. He defined the "inside" as the primitive deep self, in which the materials of experience and memory would appear in their prereflective (and therefore truer or more vital) condition. This sort of revelation, moreover, was antithetical to the communication of mere information and ideas, what Williams called "the claptrap of the conscious mind, the prepared thought, the rehearsed concept." Williams' structural word, in effect, was defining itself as a perceptual gestalt, a structure that gave the materials of the poem their order and that those materials were ultimately meant to reveal. Poems were to communicate not specific ideas, but the mental states in which those ideas (or things) might be known from a perspective outside the torpid, habit-ridden, quotidian intellect.[22]

This position recurred throughout Williams' critical prose, and it appeared as well in *Paterson*. In 1927, for example, he defined poetic "creations" as "situations of the soul," and in 1939 he declared that "a work of art is important only as evidence, in its structure, of a new world which it has been created to affirm." New world, for Williams, meant in this context "the world of the senses," which was at once "the only world that exists" and "the world of the artist" (as opposed to the non-artist).

21. Crane, "General Aims and Theories," Crane to Munson, March 17, 1926, Crane to Winters, May 29, 1927, all in *Complete Poems and Selected Letters and Prose*, 219, 221–22, 225, 227, 243, 247.

22. Joseph N. Riddel, *The Inverted Bell: Modernism and the Counterpoetics of William Carlos Williams* (Baton Rouge, 1974), 131; Williams, "Revelation," in *Selected Essays*, 268–69. See also Williams, *The Embodiment of Knowledge*, 132–33, for more on "*that which is inside the man*" in the years from 1928 through 1930.

The artwork was "evidence" of the artist's way of seeing the world, effectively constituting it and giving it order, and thereby providing society an ordering principle. Without that principle, the argument went, humanity would necessarily slide into self-destructive chaos. For this reason, he maintained, the poet was necessary as the fundamental educator of consciousness, as the true legislator before and above mere government. In *Paterson,* the word beyond reappeared as a "radiant gist that / resists the final crystallization," but a gist that came to be defined in Book V as "a view of what the poet is." The radiant gist, in short, was sensibility—poetic, vital, necessary, and beyond the powers of everyday language or the "claptrap" of the mind to define, describe, or name. Like Pound and Crane, then, Williams remained committed to the modernist appropriation of Emerson's orphic sublime. Poetry was to be the means of figuring forth and revealing exalted, ineffable truths, but the truths were to be *extraordinary* states of mind, moods, or modes of understanding.[23]

What does it really mean to say, even in theory, that poetry represents "states of consciousness" or "angles of vision"? It might mean, or does mean, that Pound, Crane, and Williams were committing themselves to a poetics of *stance.* As John Gage has persuasively argued, the Imagist aesthetic—from which derives the basic doctrine of the "word beyond formulated language"—implied and resulted in a poetry most effective at communicating states of emotion or "attitudes."[24] An attitude endows its object with an emotional texture; it evaluates. And that is what stance is. But to say this, in a modernist context and particularly in view of these poets' bardic ambitions, is to raise a problem. The intelligibility and power of the poet's stance depend largely on the reader's awareness or recognition of what the stance is taken toward. For the poem's organization of materials effectively to communicate a way of seeing, the reader must to some extent already know what is being organized. This fact was the basis of a serious problem for the would-be American bards. The problem derived from the very originality of their mythic histories and their inability to assume preknowledge on the part of their audience. If the modernist poem including history was to appropriate the Whitmanesque "maramis" by striking a sublime stance toward a vision of

23. William Carlos Williams, "Notes in Diary Form" and "Against the Weather: A Study of the Artist," in *Selected Essays,* 71, 196–99; Williams, *Paterson,* 109, 224.
24. Gage, *In the Arresting Eye,* esp. Chap. 5.

history and untransacted destiny—as Whitman had done—the poet would still have to find some means of communicating that history itself.

There seems to be no *necessary* reason why such communication should be precluded by an aesthetic that tends toward a conception of stance, including the sublime stance, as the preferred subject of poetry. Longinus' *On the Sublime* seems to be an account of stance figures set within a larger discursive or narrative context. The sublime transport, in essence, is a version of *apostrophe,* which Longinus puts at the head of his discussion of stylistic schemes. The forward progress of the discourse is momentarily suspended as the speaker turns aside to utter an "oath," being (seemingly) "taken with the divine afflatus" in a "sudden moment of inspiration." The other chief figures—asyndeton, self-dialectic, variation, and accumulation—are largely means of developing, amplifying, and sustaining the apostrophic moment, indeed of giving it the sublime quality. As Longinus says, the "mere swearing of an oath" is in itself not enough. Longinian or classical sublimity, in short, arises out of an argument or narrative and *turns back upon it* by providing a transcendent or simply "grand" perspective from which to see it.[25]

The difficulty for the modernists, generally, was their continued adherence to a Whitmanesque or Emersonian decorum of unremitting sublimity—a decorum that originated with the privileging of a primitivistic language of radical figuration as natural and therefore deific, and that tended to discourage the use of discursive or narrative strategies. Within this decorum, sublimity becomes a pervasive, ubiquitous "poetic quality" rather than a localized, particular device. It seems that the modernists had no absolutely compelling reason to adhere to this decorum. Vitalistic thought, after all, tended to put a premium on the evolved and cultured consciousness. Bergson, for example, in *The Two Sources of Morality and Religion* equated the primitive mind with intellectual limitation, torpor, and the antiprogressive "closed society." It seems that within the field of such beliefs, the language of a highly evolved, cultured consciousness would be superior or preferable to natural primitivism, and that the decorums of poetic language could expand to include the banished figures of rationality. A revived classicism—though not necessarily the sort of "neo-Egyptian" classicism T. E. Hulme had in mind—seems consistent with modernist premises. Why should the

25. Longinus, *On the Sublime,* 181, 183.

highly evolved mind not have access to the full range of its inherited processes and knowledges?[26]

Why not indeed? The modernist would-be bards, however, did not move to such a conclusion. Perhaps they had little motive: the linguistic premises of the early twentieth century still retained, in large measure, the eighteenth-century notion of a progress from primitivistic poetic language to a civilized language of reason made of fossil poetry. That, at least, was the basic position of Otto Jespersen in his 1922 classic, *Language, Its Nature, Development and Origin*. This survival—and Jespersen was not its sole proponent—permitted a somewhat anomalous persistence of the Symbolist (and Emersonian) notion of poetry as "original language," as a pure language of radical figuration that was virtually antithetical to the profane conventionalism of everyday public discourse. We find this commonplace taken up in such representative texts as I. A. Richards' *Poetries and Sciences* (1926; revised edition, 1935) and Owen Barfield's *Poetic Diction: A Study in Meaning* (1928). It penetrated also to the mind of the neo-Whitmanian: James Oppenheim wrote in 1917 that the "re-echo of the archaic [was] said to be the very stuff of song and literature." The post-neoclassical equation of the poetic with the primitivistic was, whatever its consistency (or inconsistency) with other available premises, well-entrenched.[27]

Pound, Crane, and Williams found no cause to significantly disagree. After all, they then had a shared assumption in terms of which they could engage an audience of contemporaries still "debauched" by Romantic thought. With Pound, and despite his intriguing gestures toward a notion of "the prose tradition in verse," the characteristic and enduring position was closest to the sort of statement made in "The Serious Artist." There, he presented a "yeowl and bark" theory of poetic creation that virtually recapitulated the eighteenth-century account of the birth of language. In *I Gather the Limbs of Osiris*, he maintained that "all the qualities which differentiate poetry from prose are things born before syntax." Poetry was primordial language "floated and tossed in the

26. Bergson, *The Two Sources of Morality and Religion*, 266–283; Hulme, "Modern Art" and "Romanticism and Classicism," in *Speculations*, 91, 125.

27. Otto Jespersen, *Language, Its Nature, Development and Origin* (London, 1922); I. A. Richards, *Poetries and Sciences* (1937; rpr. New York, 1970), originally issued as *Science and Poetry* in 1926 and revised in 1935; Owen Barfield, *Poetic Diction: A Study in Meaning* (1928; rpr. London, 1964); James Oppenheim, editorial, *Seven Arts* (January, 1917), 267.

emotional surges," and prose was a language of "conscientious formulation," born after syntax and useful only for the communication of mere information.[28]

Pound's interest in the Chinese ideogram, and ideogramic method generally, proceeded from the same line of thought. As George Kearns has said, Pound discovered in Ernest Fenollosa's *The Chinese Written Character as a Medium for Poetry* the crystallization of an aesthetic that appealed to his own "paratactic cast of mind"—that is, to a tendency toward composition by accumulative juxtaposition without explicit narrative, logical, or syntactic linkage. But we should remember also that Fenollosa's ideogram, like the paratactic cast of mind, had its warrant in the conventional association of the poetic with the primitivistic. Fenollosa was himself an admirer of Emerson, and his thought was still grounded in the nineteenth-century linguistic classification of Chinese as among the world's "primitive" languages. This assumption allowed him to maintain that Chinese was "naturally without grammar," and indeed without logic, and therefore eminently suitable to the poetic and radically figurative expression of natural and psychic process. Fenollosa wrote, and Pound agreed (in a footnote), "Poetry only does consciously what the primitive races did unconsciously." The poet was to re-create the primitivistic discourse of the deep, prerational mind, standing in effect at the fountainhead of language, thought, and culture. The figures of rationality were thereby banished, and assigned to the degenerate, antivital mentality of Scholasticism. In taking up with Fenollosa, then, Pound decisively cut himself off from conceptions of poetic discourse that might have permitted him to go significantly beyond the paratactic, accumulative "maramis" of a post-Whitmanian bardic style. He gave himself few means for the direct presentation of a mythic history— which was, after all, a matter of argumentative or narrative linkage. Such a presentation would violate the conventional decorum entailed by his own (and Fenollosa's) premises.[29]

Crane and Williams also rested their critical positions on primitivist grounds. Crane derived his from Richards, who argued in *Poetries and*

28. Ezra Pound, "The Serious Artist," in *Literary Essays*, 51–52; Pound, *I Gather the Limbs of Osiris*, in *Selected Prose*, 34.

29. Kearns, *Guide*, 5; Fenollosa, *The Chinese Written Character as a Medium for Poetry*, 8, 23. On Fenollosa and Emerson, see Van Wyck Brooks, *Fenollosa and His Circle* (New York, 1962).

Sciences that poetry was a mode of language pertaining to the "Magical View" of reality that had preceded formal philosophy and science, and that originated from the "metaphorical" or radically tropical processes of subliminal association. With Crane, this translated into what he called the "logic of metaphor," which, he maintained in 1925, "antedates our so-called pure logic, and . . . is the basis of all speech, hence consciousness and thought extension." Crane and Richards had reconstituted the eighteenth-century demarcation between the "artificial" figures of scientific reason and the "natural" figures of imagination and passion. This demarcation most probably came to Richards from Coleridge and Kames, both of whom were significant in his account of what he called "rhetoric" (which meant, in his usage, the tropistic essence of language).[30]

Williams' position was perhaps more forthrightly and conventionally Romantic, or even Emersonian, than was that of Crane. In a 1929 essay, for example, he took up the notion of ordinary language as a degraded, false currency, "enslaved, forced, raped, made a whore by the idea venders," whom he identified as, among other things, philosophers and salesmen. Ordinary *logical* language was corrupted by what Emerson had identified as "secondary desires" for personal advantage. The purpose of poetic language, or what Williams called "pure writing," was thus to break the conventional and formal patterns of degenerate language, thereby freeing its original truthfulness. As Williams put it, "There are no 'truths' that can be fixed in language. It is by the breakup of the language that the truth can be seen to exist and that it becomes operative again." By 1939, this presumption had resolved into a Stevensian notion of "the continual change without which no symbol remains permanent"; by *Paterson,* it had become the (by now) frequently noted concept of "dissonance" as the way to "discovery" or revelation of radiant gists. Poetry, then, was to be a language of radical flux, set in opposition to the nonpoetic languages of conventional pattern, logical statement, and

30. Hart Crane, "General Aims and Theories," in *Complete Poems and Selected Letters and Prose,* 221–22. See also Crane to Harriet Monroe, published in *Poetry,* October, 1926, *ibid.,* 235–36, wherein he explicitly aligns himself with Richards. Richards' relevant statements here are *Poetries and Sciences* and *The Philosophy of Rhetoric* (1936; rpr. New York, 1979). In the latter, Kames and Coleridge figure prominently as the sources for a theory of "metaphor" (see esp. Lecture V). Kames's *Elements of Criticism* contains among other things the seeds of Richards' notions of "affective alignment" through metaphor (p. 71), and also what must be the precursor for Eliot's "doctrine" of the objective correlative (p. 51).

rational persuasion. What is perhaps most striking about Williams' position is its implicit vehemence. Emerson could regard conventional language as inferior but of some utility, and Richards and Crane could redefine "science" and "poetry" as different modes of knowledge, without necessarily attributing superiority to either one. Williams, however, redefined the nonpoetic and logical as a language of lies "tricked out of meaning, hanging with as many cheap traps as an altar." In this he was fairly close to Pound, who could virtuously assure his audience in *Jefferson and/or Mussolini* that "I am not putting these sentences in mono-linear syllogistic arrangement, and I have no intention of using that old form of trickery to fool the reader." The orphic sage would not pretend to make linear sense.[31]

So the primitivistic and non-rational, or even the antirational, continued to be a conventional sign among the modernists of the poet's virtue as a man allied, like Emerson's wise man and orphic poet, with truth and God—or with the exalted psychic modes of the biological elite. The primitivistic was the language of the abysmic mind and the language of poetic truth-speaking. So the bardic poet was committed, in principle at least, to establishing his credentials by means of a Whitmanesque decorum of discontinuous accumulation and symbolistic flux. That decorum, furthermore, limited his structural alternatives and virtually disallowed the direct presentation of the mythic history out of which historical intelligence and a satisfactorily cultured ethos might arise. What the modernist appropriation of this decorum did *not* disallow, however, and what it in fact favored, was the extended presentation of stance, or attitude, or sensibility, or of what Pound called *"senso morale."* In theory, the twentieth-century bardic poem would be a catalogic display of ethos, bardic ethos, embodying a stance toward a history that the text only implied or suggested. Bardic ethos, then, would virtually have to be the poem's foregrounded subject. History would become background or context, which might eventually lead to understanding or justification of the poet's attitudinizing.

As we will see, that is approximately what does happen, with varying degrees of success or failure, in the *Cantos, The Bridge,* and *Paterson,* and

31. William Carlos Williams, "The Simplicity of Disorder," "Against the Weather," and "Notes in Diary Form," in *Selected Essays,* 96, 205–208, 71; Williams, *The Embodiment of Knowledge,* 19–20, 117; Williams, *Paterson,* 176; Pound, *Jefferson and/or Mussolini,* 28.

The Maximus Poems as well. The authors of these poems were committed to a somewhat circular rhetorical strategy. The reader was to be a genial exegete, and was to be persuaded into that posture by the poet's style, which put the sign of orphic or poetic truth over his discourse and the stance/attitude/*senso morale* it embodied. The reader, in essence, was to regard the text as revelation out of the depths of a vital and cultured psyche, and virtually subordinate himself to it, adopting the role of "understander." But if the modern poet's ethos, unlike Whitman's, was the product of a history, the backgrounded mythic history of the text had to supply a "phalanx of particulars" substantiating and underlying the text's foregrounded bardic sensibility. As Longinus and eighteenth-century theorists realized, the sublime gesture can endow a concept with only so much sublimity. Ultimately, the reader must perceive a sufficiently grand conception in the yonder toward which the poet tends; otherwise, his utterance begins to look like hot air, bombast, or hysteria. Bardic style and ethos would validate an implied vision of history, and given the reader's willingness to adopt the required interpretive posture, the history would eventually validate that style and ethos. The modernist bardic poem, in principle, was tending to become a rhetorical echo chamber.

But there was an initial point of entry into that perhaps tautologous rhetoric, and that was the bardic voice—the style and the ethical posture that the text would catalogically present, and that would serve as the primary ground of engagement between author and reader. This ethical posture or stance, however, could not even appear to be static or it would violate the decorum of discontinuous accumulation. In effect, the foregrounded stance would have to be an attitude that fluctuated as the elements of its historical vision accumulated, and that evolved toward the undisclosed final position the full vision would ultimately require. To the extent that the bardic text did present its reader with such an evolving ethos, it made the speaking poet its hero, and his progress or development its preferred subject. The text thus substituted a basically dramatistic strategy for the narrative and argumentative modes that its conventional decorums disallowed or suppressed. The reader, consequently, was to be engaged with the *agon* of a bardic figure struggling against the stupidities of the infidelistic world around him, and moving toward a realization of the *senso morale* of (his) history. But the realization could never be complete—or could not appear to be complete.

The realization enacted by the text could never be complete for two basic reasons. First, if that *senso morale* was truly a sublime state of consciousness and a "word beyond formulated language," it was to some extent an Emersonian "flying Perfect, around which the hands of man can never reach." The poet could not "arrive" at some ultimate formulation, or a definite closure, without seriously damaging his ethical claims as an abysmic bard. To reach any kind of overt and strong closure would be, for the reader who accepted the basic conventions of the modernist bardic poem, to set up a "koran" and fall victim to "mental cramps." Second, the modernist replacement of Whitman's deific self with an individual psyche grounded in historical memory gave the bardic poet a more limited perspective, for he could not, like Whitman, pretend to "include everything." The modern could only include what he had learned—history had become an unbounded field that included and largely determined the individual. The poet could not come to the end of what might be known, and therefore no ultimate position, no comprehensive stance, was possible or available within the conventions of modernist bardism.

No one could, for example, get away with a moralizing final segment like Whitman's "Great Are the Myths" in the 1855 *Leaves of Grass*. Even that, however, ends with irresolvable "moot questions" such as the "paradoxical equilibrium" of life and death. Whitman himself had come to recognize this, apparently, in his later editions. The bard of the 1892 edition deleted "Great Are the Myths," and in "Song of Myself" he announces that he will "cease not till death"—and that is what he appears to do. Whitman had defined the ultimate decorum for his successors: the bardic poet in the twentieth century was committed to enacting an ongoing and endlessly prospective engagement with the meaning of history, a process that could end only in death or psychological breakdown (as when Pound's mind "stopped"). He was to write a lifelong poem. It should be kept in mind that this decorum was largely the consequence of the anti-argument and anti-narrative conventions of bardic poetry. The historian, with different conventions of truth or validity, is under no such compulsion. His "vision of history" goes forward as an interpretive argument, and he reaches the conclusions that the premises of his scholarly community will permit. He does so even though he lacks what Michael Bernstein has called a "privileged horizon from which history can be seen clear and recorded whole," nor does that lack keep the poet from rendering intelligibly what history he does see as a matter of "epistemological honesty."[32] It is, as I have been suggesting, a matter of conventional decorum. The modernist bard's accumulative flux, discontinuity, and inconclusiveness together signify poetic truth, or the abysmic utterance of an unfolding, sublime, and therefore endless realization. Endlessness and inconclusion are, ultimately and not a little paradoxically, signs of the poet's *authority.*

Such was the mythology or set of bardic conventions that the poets found available to them and that constituted the elemental grounds of their rhetoric. The poets had taken up the Whitmanesque project for a "great psalm of the republic" that would cultivate a national ethos—or the vital will of what they imagined to be a latent aristocracy, a "true America," the necessary catalyst for creating a splendid, even world-redeeming national civilization. The ethical cultivation of this vital, aristocratic will required, the modernists believed, the communication of historical intelligence, the moral gist arising from a mythic history that "told the tale" of struggle between the agents of creative will and the antivital, torpid, and degenerate counterforces in the common mind. But the bardic poem would not tell that tale, at least not directly. Instead, it would enact the discovery of a sublime historical intelligence and would seek through the dramatic presentation of a bardic voice to involve the reader in that process. The poet's mythic history would be the *assumed ground* of rhetorical action in the bardic poem, a ground to which the reader might be brought through engagement with the overt drama of an utterance catalogically adumbrating an evolving stance. Longinus said that the reader would be compelled "from sheer excitement to share the speaker's risk" (insofar, at least, as he accepted the poet's bardic authority) and, undertaking the work of discovery for himself, would be "filled with joyful pride," as if he had himself "produced the very thing" he heard. As Whitman said, the reader would "himself or herself construct indeed the poem, argument, history, metaphysical essay—the text furnishing the hints, the clue, the start or framework." And indeed, having done so, and if everything worked, the reader would come to assume what the bard assumed, and that was ultimately the point.[33]

Thus far, we have been concerned with generally describing the

32. Bernstein, *The Tale of the Tribe,* 272, 275.

33. Longinus, *On the Sublime,* 195, 139; Walt Whitman, *Democratic Vistas,* in *Complete Poetry and Collected Prose,* 992–93.

major conventions and decorums of bardic rhetoric—a set of determining critical assumptions that the poets (and their audience) held in common. As a result, the focus has been on the ways the poets are the same. What remains to consider is how the modernist bards actually managed their available means, and what strategies they individually devised. As we will see, they work the conventions of bardic discourse in distinct ways, and with varying degrees of success. The conventions impose, however, a general constraint on the kinds of intentions the bardic poet can effectively seek to fulfill. The rhetoric of American bardism, with its accumulative style, is in many ways limiting, *except* along the path of dramatistic presentation. And yet, as *On the Sublime* has it, there are "ten thousand ways" to accumulate—or, we might add, to dramatize. We will examine the particular and differing ways discovered and employed in the *Cantos, The Bridge, Paterson,* and *The Maximus Poems*.

V.   The *Cantos*

Pity spareth so many an evil thing.
　　　—Canto XXX

Criticisms of the *Cantos* are legion, and chief among them is the oft-reiterated claim that Pound's thematic codes are incoherent. Indeed, this appears to be the belief that Pound himself arrived at toward the end of his career. He declared his poem a "botch," and announced in Canto CXVI that he could not "make it cohere." This failure is perhaps an inevitable consequence of the conventions with which Pound, as a modern bard, was virtually obliged to work. A poem that brings its themes to strong or definite closure goes a long way toward falsifying its own claims to poetic truth within a modernist aesthetic. Yet Pound's thematic failures do not necessarily defeat his purposes, nor have they led the *Cantos* to obscurity and oblivion. For example, Archibald MacLeish's *Conquistador,* another modern epic, has had a negligible impact, and few bother to discuss the poem. Clearly, the *Cantos* continues to stand as a major and even central text in the modernist canon, and has exerted a strong influence on later poets. Many of Pound's readers, in effect, have not agreed with his gloomy, sometimes bitter assessment of his enormous poem or, in spite of that assessment, have been affected profoundly by the text. In some important sense, then, the *Cantos* is and has been nothing like a failure, and the work is perhaps not even the qualified failure that, for example, Roy Harvey Pearce has judged it to be. We may with equal validity judge the *Cantos* successful within the range of intention(s) available to the rhetoric of bardic poetry. Let us begin, then, with the reasonable assumption that the *Cantos* is a qualified success.[1]

Pound's employment of the available means, or the post-Whitmanian

1. Roy Harvey Pearce, *The Continuity of American Poetry* (Princeton, 1977), 133. Actually, Pearce's phrase is "mitigated disaster." See also Barbara Herrnstein Smith, *Poetic Closure: A Study of How Poems End* (Chicago, 1968), 234–59.

conventions, of the American bardic voice strikingly reinvents the Whitmanian abysmic voice and works within (or through) the figures of primitivistic, unremitting sublimity to render a sustained presentation of stance. The foreground subject of the poem, as a result, becomes the poet's struggle. This effect opens up the dramatistic possibilities of bardic poetry and permits Pound to rescue the *Cantos* from his indisputably numerous "wrecks and errors." Pound, in short, is hardly "dammed and clogged by the mimetic."[2] Rather, the mimesis or enactment of an ongoing utterance, a process, ultimately saves him as a fictive character from his less savory opinions and from the confusions of his text. But to say this much is to anticipate the end. The discussion that leads to these conclusions begins with Pound's resuscitation of the bardic literatus.

In 1909, when Pound was discovering his Whitmanesque identity, he was also carrying on a correspondence with his mother about, as Noel Stock reports, the nature of epic and the role of the American poet. Pound's examples, in that exchange, were Dante and Whitman, and his definition of epic was "the speech of a nation through the mouth of one man." Obviously, the definition is debatable, as far as a theory of epic goes, but it is highly revealing as a description of the American bardic voice and, indeed, of the voice that Pound would eventually develop in the *Cantos*: a voice through which the multiple voice of a tribe-in-history would speak, and by which the sacerdotal poet's intended audience of latent aristocrats, or vital but uncultivated sensibilities, might be engaged and educated. The voice, moreover, would be primitivistic. As Pound continued to meditate on the problem of a modern epic, and the problem(s) of art generally, he came to the notion of the artist as a sacerdotal educator of fundamentally archaic type. The artist was a virtual shaman, or so Pound had come to assume by 1914:

> The artist has been at peace with his oppressors long enough. He has dabbled in democracy and he is now done with that folly. We turn back, we artists, to the powers of the air, to the djinns who were our allies aforetime, to the spirits of our ancestors. . . . The aristocracy of entail and of title is decayed, the aristocracy of commerce is decaying, the aristocracy of the arts is ready again for its service . . . and we who are the heirs of the witch-doctor and the voodoo, we artists who have been so long the despised are about to take over control.[3]

2. Ezra Pound, *I Gather the Limbs of Osiris*, in *Selected Prose*, 42.
3. Stock, *The Life of Ezra Pound*, 76, 158. The second quotation is from "The New Sculpture" (Gaudier-Brzeska and Epstein), in *Egoist*, XVI (February, 1914).

Vain hopes, perhaps. However, Pound was defining the sort of role for which he would invent a bardic version of himself.

Although Pound's aspirations were less democratic than those of his predecessor, he still would reappropriate Whitman's rhetoric as he understood it. Indeed, insofar as that rhetoric was one of authority, it was arguably more suitable to Pound's intentions. Like Whitman, then, he would constitute himself as the elect of the elect, the voodoo aristocrat or shaman-king, and would align himself with ancient powers and ancestral spirits. Their voices, as a nation or a tribe, would emerge from his own mouth. Through the abysmic bard, Whitman said, many long-dumb voices speak. And, like Whitman, the bardic Pound would speak in the interest of cultural, political, and economic revolution as the decayed aristocracies of the past gave way to the new/old order. The American bard would speak once more with terrible negative voice, denouncing infidelism where he found it and announcing or promoting a countervision of right conduct and right society. He would promote the ethical will of an ebullient, freely creative "eugenic paganism"—the modern version of Whitman's "savage virtue." He would promote also a revitalized society providing that will with scope for its fullest expression. The bardic Pound, in sum, would embark upon a strikingly ambitious, if not quixotic, rhetorical project.

But if he would, like Whitman, resurrect the primitive sacerdotal literatus, he would also be Whitman-in-a-collar, adding intellect to emotion, grounding his imagination in the facts of history. He would also be limited. Whitman's bardic figure speaks from a deep Self grounded in universal Spirit, the aboriginal Deity pervading nature. He can present himself as speaking from a sublime, deific knowledge already complete and contained within himself, yet beyond enclosure in verbal formulas. The speaker in "Song of Myself," significantly, tells us of his erotic soul-union and his subsequent realization of an absolute, divine truth:

Swiftly arose and spread around me the peace and joy and knowledge that pass
    all the art and argument of the earth;
And I know that the hand of God is the elderhand of my own,
And I know that the spirit of God is the eldest brother of my own.

And so on. The point here is that Whitman's realization is presented as past, and already achieved. And this complete knowledge will be the basis of his authority in the subsequent text. Such a claim is not available to Pound. The modernist psyche bottoms out in memory, which is deep (including "racial memory"), but which is also the product of learning and experience. As a product, it is never complete, and, as Bergson maintained, it undergoes continual transformation as experience accumulates. The history in which we live, the vital history, is never finished and never the same. Further, the modernist's memorious deep psyche, as a product, is not the container of history itself, or of tradition, or of what Pound called "*theos*"; it is, rather, the contained. The individual, in modernist conception, is afloat in time, knowing and possessing only the fragments that have entered his consciousness. In consequence, Pound must present his bardic speaker as a more limited identity than was Whitman's. He must speak as one whose realization is never complete and, in fact, never to be completed. Even more than his nineteenth-century predecessor, he must appear as one who pursues a fleeting vision, a "flying Perfect," and he must be endlessly on the way.[4]

What we see in the *Cantos*, then, is a collaring of the voodoo literatus within a modernist conception of the memorious deep psyche. The result is a striking reinvention of the Whitmanesque soul duet. In essence, Whitman's harmonious interplay between the abysmic Spirit-voice and a personal voice—the voice of Walter Whitman, son of Manhattan—becomes a sort of counterpoint as Pound's personal/authorial voice intrudes upon and interacts with his actually more authoritative voice-of-history. All of this is apparent in Canto I, wherein Pound, surreptitiously true to epic tradition, establishes his general argument, his Muse, and the basic figural modes of his abysmic voice, of, that is, primitivistic unremitting sublimity.

Canto I begins with a large fragment from the *nekiya* passage of Homer's *Odyssey*, in which the hero narrates (to the Phaeacians) his voyage from Circe's island into Erebus, and his consultation with the "impetuous impotent dead."[5] The style of the passage is noteworthy for its basically accumulative quality and for its anachronistic prosody and diction. *Accumulatio* in this passage is largely a result of Pound's apparent abbreviation or condensation of the original to a largely paratactic

4. Whitman, "Song of Myself," in *Complete Poetry and Collected Prose*, 30. On Pound's *theos*, see "Religio" and "Axiomata," in *Selected Prose*, 47–48, 49–52. See also Bergson, *Creative Evolution*, Chap. 1.

5. All citations refer to the New Directions edition, *The Cantos of Ezra Pound* (New York, 1981).

crowding-together of "luminous details," rendering narrative as a virtual catalog of moments:

> And then went down to the ship,
> Set keel to breakers, forth on the godly sea, and
> We set up mast and sail on that swart ship,
> Bore sheep aboard her, and our bodies also
> Heavy with weeping, and winds from sternward
> Bore us out onward with bellying canvas,
> Circe's this craft, the trim-coifed goddess.   (3)

And the fragment goes on, in like fashion, for sixty-seven lines. What Pound achieves is the same general quality that Longinus ascribes to Homer himself—"the flood of moving incidents in quick succession"—and with similar effects. In the first place, the absence of explicit logical connection between phrases, and the outright logical disjunctions, create an impression that the surge of inspiration drives the speaker onward, leaving him no chance to pause or explain. Longinus said that "upheaval of the soul demands disorder," and thus an utterance marked with syntactic dislocation, topical compression, and reduced (or absent) grammatical and logical connectives. The style indicates that the very sublimity of the subject prevents a calm, smoothly controlled exposition. And second, the omission or suppression of explicit syntactical and logical linkage invites the reader into the utterance, to make the connections himself.[6] This is relatively easy in Canto I. The reader's recognition of either the precise source of the passage or its underlying story-type provides a narrative frame within which the catalog of moments can be easily understood. In later cantos, such as the Chinese dynastic cantos, the compression is incomparably greater and the underlying narrative fairly obscure, so that reconstructive interpretation becomes a formidable task.

A further effect of the catalogic, broken treatment of the *nekiya* in Canto I—and an important one for Pound's credentials—is that it fits the concept of archaic literary utterance that prevailed from the neoclassical bellettrists to the post-Whitmanian moderns. The poet, in effect, speaks in the supposed archaic mode, without pronounced attention to syntactic or logical expectation. As Hugh Blair might have said, he speaks with a rough and negligent "wildness" (or what asks to be seen

---

6. Longinus, *On the Sublime*, 153, 189–91.

as such).[7] This "archaic" quality is underscored, strangely, by a rather anachronistic Anglo-Saxon prosody and a scattering of antique dictional features. The dictions themselves become anachronistic, for Pound combines terms such as *fosse, dreory,* and *bever* with Greek and Latin proper names (Circe, Erebus, Pluto, Proserpine, Neptune, etc.). To a certain extent, Pound's anachronism—in the *nekiya* passage as well as others throughout the *Cantos*—is to be seen as yet another gesture toward the modernist convention of convention breaking, as a sign of the poet's disregard for usual decorum. The anachronistic mixture, then, in combination with a basic accumulative structure, suggests a speaker in the archaic mode, yet archaic in a distinctly modern, educated, polyglot way.

Pound's anachronism in Canto I, however, has further and eventually large effects. Even if the reader does accept the prosody and diction of Pound's *nekiya* as aspects of a generalized modern archaism, the point of the particular anachronisms—Anglo-Saxon and Latin mixed with Greek—is unexplained. At first, it really is unexplainable, so that full or satisfactory perception of Pound's intent is deferred until the *nekiya* breaks off, and the authorial voice intrudes: "Lie quiet, Divus. I mean, that is Andreas Divus, / In officina Wecheli, 1538, out of Homer" (5). We recognize this voice as "Pound," because its modern and "American" diction ("lie quiet," "I mean") abruptly contrasts with the preceding text, and because the canto provides no suggestion of another source for the address to Divus. Considered as a figural device, Pound's intruded utterance belongs to the general category of Longinian variation—what Longinus calls the sudden change of voice, with an equally sudden shift in the apparent direction of address, as the speaker turns and changes into another character (himself, in this instance).[8] The effects of this figure in Canto I are surprisingly complex. First of all, the intrusion serves as a kind of footnote, a citation that gives us the immediate source (Andreas Divus) for the preceding passage. This marks the speaking author-figure as a scholarly knower of obscure texts, and at the same time alerts the reader to the exegetical task. We are to "go see Divus" if we wish to really understand what the author is up to. That is our homework. From the first, then, Pound invokes a master/student relationship

7. Blair, *Lectures,* 389–90.
8. Longinus, *On the Sublime,* 201–203.

between poet and reader, a relation that is one of the distinctive features of the *Cantos*.

For the reader who chooses to accept this relationship, which is a basic condition for reading the poem, further effects emerge from the authorial intrusion in Canto I. We (if "we" are the reader required by Pound) retrospectively perceive that the *nekiya* fragment was not a translation of Homer, but was a translation of a translation. We perceive a regress of nested voices, the voice of Odysseus within that of Homer within that of Divus within that of the "Anglo-Saxon" Pound. George Kearns has suggested that we see a multilayered voice, one that incorporates components from the major periods of an epic tradition leading from Homer's prehistoric materials (*i.e.,* Odysseus' account) to the present moment in English literature (as represented by Pound's appropriation of Divus).[9] In either case, this retrospective perception explains the anachronisms of diction and prosody in the *nekiya,* and establishes the abysmic counterpoint out of which virtually all subsequent cantos will be generated. We see a polyphonic voice emerging from and embodying tradition, a voice with which the personal, authorial voice of "Ezra Pound" can interact.

The nature of this interaction, as it initially appears, is also important, for we are asked to see (upon doing our homework) that Pound's intrusion and virtual dismissal of Divus correspond exactly to the action of Odysseus in Erebus. He calls forth, gives voice to, and drives away the various shades, one by one. And certainly, the purpose in Canto I is similar. Pound has descended into a modernist Erebus of ancient texts, of memorious tradition, to seek the requisite knowledge for a return to and restoration of his Ithaca. Pound's intrusion establishes, albeit implicitly, the general argument of the *Cantos.* The speaking bard will henceforth enact an instructive seance with the multiple ancestral voice, which emerges (we must assume) from the Erebus of memory and issues from his own mouth. That Pound's ancestral voice and personal, authorial voice both do issue from a single mouth (as was true in Whitman's work) is suggested by the very "translated" nature of the *nekiya,* and by the signs that this translation gives us of the mediating presence of the *"scriptor cantilenae."* There are, for example, the considerable condensation of the original narrative, and the interposition of a prosody that could not have come from any of the scriptor's antique sources. The

9. Kearns, *Guide,* 21.

ancestral voice is presented as the voice of tribal memory *as Pound knows it*. His own, historically constituted deep self is potentially endowed with great authority, a self the poet would raise to utterance.[10] Through him, as through Whitman, an ancient and long-suppressed presence will be heard.

Pound establishes his Muse by means of variation, or change of voice, as the authorial intrusion quickly gives way to another translation, from the Second Homeric Hymn to Aphrodite (via Georgius Dartona):

> Venerandam,
> In the Cretan's phrase, with the golden crown, Aphrodite,
> Cypri munimenta sortita est, mirthful, orichalchi, with golden
> Girdles and breast bands, thou with dark eyelids
> Bearing the golden bough of Argicida. So that: (5)

And thus the canto ends. That Pound begins the *Cantos* with a gesture of veneration toward an Eleusinian embodiment of the desirable—his *Venere,* indeed—requires, perhaps, no comment. He invokes this deity throughout the text, under various names and manifestations, as a Muse. More significant is the figural mode Pound adopts and its effect in establishing the rhetoric of the poem. Pound presents a convergence of the authorial and ancestral voices, signified by the citational "In the Cretan's phrase," which is the author's voice, and which suggests Pound's will to adopt the phrase of Homer and Dartona and make it his own. Pound joins with the ancestral voice as it rises toward a fervent apostrophe to the goddess. This apostrophe is crucial, for it establishes a device that recurs throughout the *Cantos,* namely, the apostrophic gesture toward the *"arcanum,"* or Pound's "tradition of the gods," which provides the religious core of his ancestral/tribal ethos. And further, we should note, the ancestral apostrophe itself is rendered through an accumulative, iterative structure—a piling-up of epithets, in the present case. This is a standard feature of the apostrophic gesture in later cantos.

Canto I, then, accomplishes a great deal with remarkable economy. The open-ended "So that" of the final line, from which all subsequent cantos will unfold, is packed with complex expectations with which the

10. Although Pound would certainly have despised the Freudian term, his abysmic or ancestral voice, an embodiment of tribal ethos or culture, presents itself as none other than the superego. I am surprised that no psychoanalytic interpretation has been built upon this point.

poem's rhetoric can work. Not only has Pound established the dramatic situation within which his bardic voice can operate—the descent into Erebus, and the counterpoint between ancestral and authorial voices. He has also established the basic figural mode within which that counterpoint can happen. The basic structure is discontinuous accumulation— that is, the juxtaposition of *nekiya*, Pound's dismissal of Divus, and the Second Homeric Hymn—in which the basic accumulata can be elements of any size or type, and indeed can themselves be built upon the figure of *accumulatio*. As key strategies for variation or the creation of discontinuities, the authorial intrusion and the ancestral apostrophe function as ways to signify the major codes of value in the text. Intrusion, in effect, indicates the personal perspective or stance of the author himself, and apostrophe usually indicates the ancestral perspective. Between these two perspectives, which can join or diverge, the events and characters in Pound's remembered/invented history, which the general accumulation adumbrates, can be understood and ultimately judged.

The result is a bardic voice with powerful credentials. Pound works within the figures of unremitting sublimity appropriate to the post-Whitmanian conception of poetic primitivism, and he casts himself in a markedly archaic role. Pound's version of the sacerdotal literatus corresponds to what N. Kershaw Chadwick has called the "mantic" poet or shaman. According to Chadwick, the Homeric *nekiya* bears "a strange resemblance" to shamanic rituals worldwide. Typically, the mantic poet enters a "trance," which, Chadwick suggests, is more often than not a consciously adopted, controlled dramatic pose. Then, in dissociation from his audience, he enacts a journey to hell or heaven (or both), there to consult with ancestral ghosts. In such performances, the dissociated mantic poet frequently speaks with or is dramatistically "possessed" by the ancestral voices. The shaman's audience overhears the consultation taking place in hell. This is, as Pound's rendition of the *nekiya* and his subsequent intrusion imply, the basic premise of the fictive action of the *Cantos*—though, of course, there are differences. Pound adopts the conceit of mantic utterance on modernist terms. His Erebus is memorious, not metaphysical, and there is no pretense of journeying to or experiencing a spirit world. To use James Oppenheim's terms, Pound appears to descend "the inner stairway of the ages," there to tap a "stored heritage." The deep-psychic entity speaks through him in a language commensurate with the decorums of primitivistic sublimity, but also displays the multilayered culture of an educated, historicized consciousness.[11]

Pound, certainly, was attracted to the ritual, sacerdotal aspect of poetry. We know, for example, that he believed the *nekiya* represented a poetic tradition antedating Homer. He also thought it was the oldest segment in the *Odyssey*, which he apparently thought of in nineteenth-century fashion as a cycle of songs that Homer had simply assembled, much as Confucius had assembled the odes of the *Shi King*. Likewise, as Leon Surette has shown, Pound considered the *nekiya* a primitive version of the Eleusinian rite. That would have given him a motive for thinking the mantic performance was both the essence of epic and the central rite of his vital tribe. The same attitude toward mantic performance is evinced in the later cantos, wherein Pound invokes the *muan bpo* ceremony of the ancient Na Khi tribe—a form of ancestor worship that involves "calling the names" of gods and spirits—as an analogue for his own activity.[12] Pound, then, reconstitutes the Whitmanesque bardic voice within a modernized version of the mantic performance. Thus he can open his poem with an implicit version of the Whitmanian claim. He locates himself at the "origin of all poems" and presents a voice that speaks with the "original energy" of archaic, ecstatic, "radical utterance" out of the abysms of consciousness.

Supporting this claim is the intended *sound* of the *Cantos*—a matter of oral interpretation that Pound's critics regularly overlook. Listening to Pound's recorded readings of his own poetry, including parts of the *Cantos*, provides ample evidence that the intended voice in virtually all his poetry is incantatory. Ezratic incantation creates a ritualistic atmosphere appropriate to the sacerdotal voice and appropriate especially to the occulted dramatism of mantic poetry. Incantation, in fact, is virtually the only mode of recitation able to absorb all the discourses that the *Cantos* includes. The humorous, the conversational, the sarcastic, and even the epistolary (as when he reads out the contents of Malatesta's postbag) are not submerged or violated by the incantation. Rather, each

11. Chadwick, *Poetry and Prophecy*, 58–72. For accounts of Central Asian shamanic rituals with uncanny resemblances (in general plot) to Dante's *Commedia*, see Eliade, *Shamanism*, 201–203.

12. Kearns, *Guide*, 18; Surette, *A Light From Eleusis*, Chap. 3 (esp. p. 55). See also Kenner, *The Pound Era*, 147–48, 520; and Eugene Paul Nassar, *The Cantos of Ezra Pound: The Lyric Mode* (Baltimore, 1976), 124–26.

discourse can actually gain in effect from the contrast between Pound's "ground bass," with its emphasis on the phrase or even the word as a tonal unit, and the actual content and the diction of what is said. This is what happens in Pound's recordings. There is no other way to read through all the discourses of the *Cantos* without reducing the mantic polyphony to a fretful, inconsistent, prosy talkiness. And that would destroy the distinctive ritualistic atmosphere the poem requires.

To force the *Cantos* into some realistic sense of spoken language, moreover, is to violate the author's sense of high poetic speech. Pound wrote, in *I Gather the Limbs of Osiris*, "There are few fallacies more common than the opinion that poetry should mimic the daily speech. Works of art attract by a resembling unlikeness." (He then raises the ideal of "dynamic acting.") In "Treatise on Metre" at the end of *ABC of Reading*, we have Pound's thoughts on "absolute rhythm." Poetic rhythm is a form cut into time, and the base rhythm of any poem must have an absolute correspondence with the psychic experience or mood underlying and preceding utterance.[13] The rhythms of the poem, therefore, must not be governed by the superficial conventions of daily speech and ordinary grammar. In short, it is not true—as has been claimed sometimes—that Pound's personae, in the *Cantos* and elsewhere, speak in conversational or otherwise naturalistic tones of voice. In the *Cantos*, Pound's mantic voice is intended as incantatory—thus the title of the work itself—as well as abysmic, polyphonic, and occult, as the disembodied voices of a textual, memorious Erebus emerge from the chanting sacerdote. When we consider what the *Cantos* is meant to sound like, we perceive a general effect that is, to say the least, unearthly.

Thus we come to the question of what Pound *does* with the mantic voice, the bardic identity he invents for himself and establishes in Canto I. First, and perhaps obviously, he does present an authoritative set of credentials, for an audience already receptive to post-Whitmanian notions of bardic poetry and abysmic utterance. If we are part of that audience, his utterance may signify to us that Pound is a true poet, or a true bard, and we may be willing to undergo the full experience that the poem intends. Of course, if we are not part of that audience, we may be

13. Pound, *I Gather the Limbs of Osiris,* in *Selected Prose,* 41; Pound, *ABC of Reading.*

tempted to regard him (at worst) as a bizarre and often incoherent poseur, or merely (at best, perhaps) as a strange phenomenon, a curiosity in the history of literary or poetic convention. The point here is that Pound begins as did Whitman—with an audience of latent aristocrats who are receptive to the sacerdotal project and its conventions, and who thus are already redeemed. And since the conventions with which the *Cantos* works are primarily literary, and have little or no validity outside what Van Wyck Brooks called "the creative class," Pound's aristocratic audience is mainly, inevitably, composed of fellow literati. This restriction may be, in some sense, Pound's actual intent. His 1914 essay does speak of the "aristocracy of the arts" and its destined leadership. Artists, in effect, and despite Pound's stated ambitions as a sociopolitical reformer, become the true America to whom the *Cantos* is directed.

We can assume, then, a preferred audience of literati, for whom Pound's rendering of the bardic voice can be persuasive. And, as we have seen, the preferred reader is invited into the text as a witness or observer of the mantic performance, and also as a student or genial exegete. This exegetical, source-finding role is assigned to the reader in part by Pound's citational gestures. In essence, the reader must know what Pound knows, assume what the bard assumes, to read or experience the poem. Enforcing this implicit command are the discontinuous, accumulative nature of the text itself, and the frequent exoticism of the materials with which Pound works. As most critics of the poem have noted, the absence of a straightforward narrative or discursive structure, paired with the initial mysteriousness of Pound's allusions and references, renders the text simply unreadable, over forbiddingly long stretches, for the reader who fails or declines to do the requisite homework. Discontinuous accumulation, then, functions powerfully as a prompt for study and exegesis. It is a demand that the reader treat the text virtually as scripture, as something primarily to be understood rather than judged, and thus to be experienced from an essentially subordinate position.

The reader must do what Whitman would have his readers do, namely, "construct indeed the poem, argument, history, metaphysical essay" out of the "hints" and "clues" the text provides. And the assumptions are that this activity is worth the genial exegete's while, and that the text is a sort of commonplace book within which true and illuminating arguments can be construed. That is the usual approach to sacred writings. And insofar as we do find Pound's mantic voice persuasive, and insofar as we do undertake the not-inconsiderable task of coming to know what he knows and building our construals, we actually become involved in the same knowledge-seeking, kingdom-restoring activity that we see the mantic Pound engaging in. We immerse ourselves in the text's tradition, thereby becoming the true companions of the bard himself, committed to the tribe of Eleusinian heroes with which he is aligned. The exegetical demand upon the reader—indeed, the mounting exegetical pressure as references accumulate—makes the *Cantos* a tribal initiation rite, in which Pound officiates and the reader undergoes induction.

For the reader who does accept this prescribed role as disciple in the *Cantos,* Pound's version of the myth of untransacted destiny does emerge from the discontinuous, accumulative "phalanx of particulars." Or, as Leon Surette has said, for the reader who undertakes a study of Pound's prose (the best available gloss of the poem's thematic codes), that mythic history is reflected in the text of the *Cantos.*[14] And in the first twelve cantos, Pound devotes himself to "preparing the palette." This palette includes, among other things: the Eleusinian, mythological locus of Cantos I–II; El Cid's kingdom-restoring struggles (Canto III); instances of Provençal *amor* and its perverse distortions, and murders during the Renaissance (Cantos IV–VI); a Waste Land vision of a devitalized London (Canto VII); and the deeds of Sigismundo Malatesta (Cantos VIII–XI). What the first eleven cantos try to show is the deflection, persistence, and occasional flickering-out of the Eleusinian light of vital intelligence as it shines from remote antiquity, through the Middle Ages, and into the Renaissance. Then it undergoes corruption and dispersal with the rise of humanism, mercantilism (hence usury), and general rascality. Malatesta's age, for Pound, is one of infidelism, of darkening sensibility. And Malatesta himself represents a late, struggling manifestation of what Pound would later call the "artifex"—the vitally creative, order-giving, love-inspired (Venerean), wily and combative (Odyssean) individual.[15] The artifex is the ideal Poundian aristo-

14. Surette, *A Light From Eleusis,* 25–26.

15. Pound used the same term in *Jefferson and/or Mussolini,* trying to explain that both men were "artifexes." And, of course, Pound declared the Malatesta cantos "openly volitionist" and called Sigismundo a "factive personality . . . an entire man" (*Guide to Kulchur,* 194).

crat. And as the Waste Land vision in Canto VII suggests, the artifex is largely absent from the modern scene.

In Canto XII the reader comes upon Americans: Baldy Bacon, who "bought all the little copper pennies in Cuba," and Jim X, who regales a bankers' meeting ("*alias* usurers in excelsis") with the obscene Tale of the Honest Sailor. Baldy, in his high-risk wheelings and dealings, has much of the volitional, "factive" quality of Pound's Malatesta, with whom he stands in immediate, contrastive juxtaposition. Likewise, Baldy is nothing like the "dry casques of departed locusts" inhabiting London, with whom Malatesta stands in immediate contrast. Baldy resembles Sigismundo more than he does his London contemporaries. In his manipulation of Cuban peons, he is one of the "dominant people" Pound had seen on the streets of New York, in *Patria Mia,* possessing an "animal vigour unlike that of any European crowd," a definitely heroic (if comically misguided) energy and wiliness. And, like the New York pagans, he is "against all delicate things":

> Sleeping with two buck niggers chained to him,
> Guardia regia, chained to his waist
> To keep 'em from slipping off in the night;
> Being by now unpopular with the Cubans.   (53)

It also seems, since Pound has complemented Baldy's story with the tale of Dos Santos the Portuguese speculator, that Baldy has the essence of a "man of the Midi." Jim X, likewise, manifests a sort of pagan consciousness with his indelicate story (in some ways a mythical burlesque), and his action resembles that of Pound in the *Cantos.* Both are telling of "honest sailors" while the locustlike, usurious bankers are "whining over their 20 p. c." (55). What is lacking in these Americans, and Baldy particularly, is the Eleusinian light. Both have will, wit, and energy, but neither is associated with the feminine (coital, Venerean) principle needed to complete them. Baldy is chained to his "Guardia regia," Jim X is alone, and the Honest Sailor is buggered by a Turk in 'Stamboul and has a son.

There are further examples, in *A Draft of XXX Cantos,* of characters embodying Pound's vision of America as an unrealized pagan civilization, thwarted by bad economics, bad politics, and the suppression of the light. In Canto XXII we come upon the story of "that man" who "sweat blood" to put through a railway but was defeated by the corporate machinations of "Warenhauser" (Weyerhauser). In Canto XXVIII is a series of prudish and unpleasant but strong-willed and resourceful American women, accompanied by another series of Baldy Bacon–like men. All these modern Americans have the dominant (or domineering) quality, but they lack the Malatestan, Eleusinian veneration of love and beauty that would make them full-fledged Poundian heroes. The women are loveless, sterilized Aphrodites, and the men (consequently?) lack civilized, civilizing purpose.

From *Eleven New Cantos* onward, however, the reader is presented with the materials, or the basis, for a modern renewal—Pound's "American civilization 1770–1830," as represented chiefly in the cultured ethos of Jefferson and Adams. Jefferson is aligned with Malatesta, through the oft-remarked device of linking (with juxtaposed quotations) Jefferson's search for a musical gardener with Malatesta's patronage of a *maestro di pentore,* and Adams is aligned with the Confucian sensibility that Pound believes to be the vital core of all successful Chinese dynasties. Indeed, both Jefferson and Adams align with Confucian civic sensibility. The reader can learn this from such texts as *Jefferson and/or Mussolini*: artifexes ran the early American republic. The critical and exegetical literature has dealt at length with this point, so nothing more need be added here. The point is that with homework and exegesis, Pound's intention comes fairly clear. In the cantos before Pisa, he lays out the ethical perspectives of "Eleusis and Kung," presents a collection of heroes and villians to be judged in terms of those perspectives, and sets up a vision of the United States as an Eleusinian and Confucian culture *in potentia.* And, beginning with *Eleven New Cantos,* he launches into an extensive demonstration of the elements of a truly American, truly aristocratic ethos embodied in the intelligence of Jefferson-Adams. There is the suggestion of an unfulfilled, yet available high destiny. But that suggestion can be discovered only by the reader who either responds to the exegetical prompt of Pound's mantic voice or yields to the exegetical pressure of a discontinuous accumulation that attains, at times, a seemingly phantasmagoric incoherence.

However, Pound's intention is not simply to disclose to his genial exegete an American mythic history, with all the information and thematic codes that history includes. His fundamental purpose is to give the reader an "angle of vision" from which that history can be seen—namely, the revealed ethical posture, the *senso morale,* the stance, of the mantic speaker. As the analysis of Canto I suggests, this revelation of ethical perspective is achieved primarily through Pound's two major uses of the Longinian figure of variation, or shift of speaker: the authorial intrusion and the ancestral apostrophe. A complete taxonomy of all Pound's uses of these two figures is impossible, since the figures of variation are in principle endlessly variable. However, a few general observations can be made about their roles in establishing stance.

Intrusion, indeed, appears in many different forms in the *Cantos*. As George Kearns has remarked, the author's voice that punctuates the text at intervals has a wide tonal range, from the whimsical and sarcastic to the reverential and elegiac.[16] Yet, the general effect is a representation of the Poundian authorial figure as a fallible, mortal, limited character. He is not omniscient, and he takes sides—and he can be wrong without violating his fictive role in the text, though he can damage his authorial credibility. To a large extent, his partisanship, volubility, and change-ability suggest a "sane and active ebullience" that serves to make the voice seem vital as well as humanly engaging. We see this in his whim-sical burlesque of slippery state-politics in the time of Sigismundo Malatesta:

> "that Messire Alessandro Sforza
>   is become lord of Pesaro
> through the *wangle* of the Illus. Sgr. *Mr.* Federicho
>   d'Orbino
> Who *worked the wangle* with Galeaz
>   through the *wiggling* of Messer Francesco,
> Who *waggled* it so that Galeaz should sell Pesaro
>   to *Alex* and Fossembrone to *Feddy*;
> and he hadn't the right to sell." (34–35; emphasis added)

Here, the Poundian voice, signaled by disruptive diction, intrudes upon a voice-from-history, in what amounts to a voice-over. And the diction clearly indicates the poet's attitude toward "Alex and . . . Feddy." They are ignoble and slightly ridiculous schemers. Others come in for the same treatment, such as the "King o' Ragona" and Pope Pio Secundo, "that monstrous swollen, swelling s.o.b." (44). Like Alex and Feddy, they are opponents of Malatesta. It may be irresponsible history, but in this case, Pound's voice and that of a ghostly source have an irrepressibly energetic interaction, making it come alive. And an exuberant attitudi-

16. Kearns, *Guide*, 14–15.

nizing gives him as a character a certain amount of comic appeal and therefore a certain amount of humanity. His "ebullience" can be engaging, and it tends to overshadow the question of conflict between "Truth and Calliope," with which the Malatesta cantos begin.

But Pound can also use the authorial intrusion for a more serious, and significant, kind of partisanship. In Canto XIII, for example, his voice intrudes upon a conversation between Confucius and several young followers. The effects, in this unusually readable canto, are subtle and complex. Pound's first intrusion occurs as the young men respond to Confucius' query about what one ought to do to "become known." One should, they say, build a temple, put the defenses in order, or put a province "in better order than it is." Pound takes the part of "Tian, the low speaking," who responds by reciting what amounts to an Imagist poem:

> "The *old swimming hole,*
> And the boys *flopping off the planks,*
> Or sitting in the underbrush playing mandolins."   (58; emphasis added)

The casual Americanisms of Tian's lyrical non sequitur reveal the intrusive author; the utterance itself proposes a sort of pastoral daydream oddly incommensurate with the more civic ambitions of the other disciples. Confucius' benevolent approval of all the disciples' responses as "natural" leaves the incommensurateness hanging, until the reader arrives at the next Americanism, in which the sage excoriates the older Yuan Jang, who "sat by the roadside pretending to be receiving wisdom": "'You old fool, *come out of it,* / Get up and do something useful'" (59; emphasis added). Confucius goes on to say that "a man of fifty who knows nothing is worthy of no respect." This obvious, direct reversal of Tian's pastoralism suggests Confucius' nondoctrinaire flexibility. It also implies a belief that Tian's attitude is "naturally" appropriate to younger poets, and older ones (like Pound) should be more "useful." The intrusive Americanism indicates a Poundian presence in the Confucian lines. We see, in sum, the authorial figure substituting his own voice for that of both Tian and Confucius. He identifies with both positions and, retrospectively, appears to accept the lesson. The Tian-like aestheticism of his early career is not repudiated, but is superseded by the more mature purposes of the epic poet. In effect, then, Pound's intrusion shows him joining the Confucian entourage.

This joining is subtly reemphasized with a pair of intrusions into

Confucius' canto-closing speech. In the first, the sage suddenly breaks from a discussion of civic virtue to announce:

> "And even I can remember
> A day when the historians left blanks in their writings,
> *I mean* for things they didn't know,
> But that time seems to be passing."   (60; emphasis added)

If this thematic break, combined with the almost imperceptible blending of Ezratic/American and Confucian voices, does constitute an instance of intrusive, discontinuity-making variation, it invokes two possible perspectives or ethical codes. First, it foregrounds a code of honesty or truth, one that may serve to interpret and organize the miscellaneous aspects of Confucian character displayed in Canto XIII. What this signifies is the canto's ultimate concern with honesty or wisdom, rather than with the historical details from Confucius' life that momentarily embody or exemplify those values. And second, the seepage of Pound's voice into the passage reminds us of the presence and activity of the poet himself. As he joins with his ancestral tradition he selects, arranges, and preserves—just as Confucius does—and honestly leaves gaps in his discourse for the things he does not know.

As exegesis reveals, Canto XIII is a collage of quotations from the *Analects,* not a single translated text as is the *nekiya* in Canto I. Pound has indeed selected, arranged, preserved. This fact, in turn, gives fuller significance to the closing lines, which are represented as Confucian utterance:

> "The blossoms of the apricot
>   blow from the east to the west,
> And I have tried to keep them from falling."   (60)

These lines constitute an Ezratic intrusion. As the studious exegete (and no one else) will realize, these lines are Pound's inventions, and have no direct source in Confucius' classics.[17] They are the *only* lines in Canto XIII originally composed by Pound. So having done our homework, we perceive an abrupt non sequitur, a shift from the characteristic didacticism of Confucius to a lyricism comparable with Tian's. The voices of the young poet, Confucius, and "Pound" (the mature poet) suddenly fuse. In effect, the Confucian ethos is absorbed or appropriated by

17. *Ibid.,* 13.

"Pound," who makes an elegiac gesture toward a fragile, vanishing past (*i.e.*, the apricot grove where Confucius supposedly taught). In sum, Canto XIII uses an accumulation of Confucian materials to illustrate a code of civic wisdom and poetic virtue, and subtly uses the device of authorial intrusion to signify Pound's alignment with that code. And that alignment serves as well to broadly signify the intentions of the mantic bard, who has set out—as both Odysseus and Confucius did—to restore order or the principles of order in the western "kingdom" that had broken in fragments after World War I.

Canto XIII also serves to interpret its immediate context, that is, the twelve preceding cantos. As we have seen, Cantos I through XII display the basic terms of Pound's mythic history: the decline and dispersal of the light, devitalized modernity, and aimless American energy. These cantos also display, wherever the light is distorted or lost, an impressive variety of human perversities, or civil and psychosexual disorder—among them are rape, incest, cannibalism, necrophilia, bondage, internecine war, murder, and political and economic trickery. What Canto XIII does, then, is evoke a retrospective and implicit *commentary* upon what has preceded. It foregrounds precisely what is lacking in the perverse and what is sought by the noble: an ethos grounded in a code of civic wisdom, personal virtue, and sane love. However, insofar as Canto XIII is also an evocation of the will-to-order inherent in Odysseus, El Cid, Malatesta, Confucius, and Pound, it constitutes a reiteration of the gesture in Canto I. Thus Pound amplifies the opening of his argument through discontinuous accumulation and authorial intrusion. And he includes some suggestion of the ideal, order-giving, civilizing knowledge the poet seeks. He would restore the kingdom, along Confucian as well as Eleusinian lines.

Authorial intrusion, then, serves to indicate the fluctuating attitudes of the authorial presence (the fictive "Ezra Pound") toward the materials of his history and also toward the ancestral perspectives of "Eleusis and Kung." It is those perspectives that are the ultimate ground of ethical value and judgment in the text. And they are implicit in the abysmic, ancestral voice with which Pound continually interacts—as in Canto XIII—but they are forcefully declared through the apostrophic moments that disrupt the text. These moments, sometimes identified as "lyric," have been frequent objects of critical attention; and they are sometimes taken to constitute virtually everything that matters in the text.[18] This view has justification, but is overly restrictive. What must be kept in mind is that the apostrophic moment is, like the Longinian oath, a means of invoking the most potent ethical authority available to Pound as a mantic bard. It comments on, evaluates, and structures the poem's accumulating vision of history. The ancestral, apostrophic oath provides an angle of vision, but there must be something that is seen. There must be a larger thematic context (a discursive or narrative context, however dispersed by the obligatory discontinuous accumulation) to give the lyrical apostrophe its full emotional power and significance.

The apostrophe, like the authorial intrusion, has a bewildering variety of specific forms in the *Cantos*. In general, however, it is marked by the use of distinctively ancestral voices, though the intrusive Pound can always join the chorus (as he does in Canto I with the apostrophe to Aphrodite). Canto XXX, for example, begins with a "compleynt" by Artemis "agaynst Pity"; Canto XXXVI opens with and is largely constituted by Guido Cavalcanti's "Donna mi priegha," which Pound believed to be an Eleusinian manifesto. In other cantos, Pound modulates into a sort of generic god-voice as he bursts through into paradisal and timeless, but markedly antique or classical, vision. Perhaps the most striking of all the apostrophic gestures in the *Cantos,* however, is Canto XLV.

What we hear in Canto XLV is neither the American voice of Pound nor any locatable translation-source such as Homer, Ovid, Confucius, or Cavalcanti. It is, instead, the generalized voice of tradition itself, bespeaking what Whitman called "the thoughts of all men in all ages and lands":

> Not by usura St. Trophime
> Not by usura Saint Hilaire,
> Usura rusteth the chisel
> It rusteth the craft and the craftsman
> It gnaweth the thread in the loom
> None learneth to weave gold in her pattern.   (230)

This voice rests upon, and gathers its authority from, all the ancestral voices that have become part of the mantic voice by this point in the text. Moreover, with its many references to fifteenth-century artists, as well as a quotation from Villon (*"Harpes et luz"* [228]), the voice establishes a resonance with the particular type of tradition it approves, even as it excoriates "usura." In the fifteenth century, Pound believed, the quality

18. See Nassar, *The Cantos of Ezra Pound.*

of art was not yet influenced by the intent to "sell and sell quickly" (p. 229), and usury had not yet become an acceptable part of public culture.[19] Or so the studious reader will discover. In effect, then, Canto XLV reveals the mantic voice speaking with all the ancestral moral force available to it, in order to mount an apostrophic denunciation of what seems to be, in Pound's mythic history, the prime corrupting force in civilization's decline toward modernity.

Canto XLV must also be considered in its context. By virtue of its clarity, this canto is an abrupt, marked contrast, for it emerges from the phantasmagorically complex historical accumulations of Cantos XLII through XLIV. In addition, the unequivocally vehement tone of Canto XLV is the product of its simple structure, which is as close as the *Cantos* ever comes to *continuous* accumulation, or to the iterative, insistent structure demanded by the traditional grand style for impassioned declaration. Canto XLV, a classically pure accumulative apostrophe, uses its authoritative, ancestral resonance, and its surprising, passionate clarity, to disrupt and then turn vision back upon the goings-on in preceding cantos. And those goings-on have generally to do with the rise of banking institutions—and usury. Canto XLV is a powerful commentary and ethical judgment on banking practices. Usurious banks are evil, and others, such as the Monte dei Paschi, are good, because of what they respectively do to or for human culture.

To say that Canto XLV raises ethical commentary and judgment on the vision of history "included" in the preceding cantos is to say that it foregrounds stance—and that, after all, is the classical function of apostrophe. Moreover, it establishes a stance with which the personal, Ezratic voice can join, as we see most clearly in Canto LI:

> Neither Ambrogio Praedis nor Angelico
> had their skill by usura
> Nor St Trophime its cloisters;
> Nor St Hilaire its proportion.
> Usury rusts the man and his chisel
> It destroys the craftsman, destroying craft;
> Azure is caught with cancer.   (250)

Pound echoes the ancestral apostrophe in Canto XLV with an authorial apostrophe of his own. The bardic speaker acquires the knowledge embodied in his tradition, and aligns himself with it. And in doing so, he

19. Kearns, *Guide*, 122.

appropriates its authority to himself—as he did in Canto XIII, by fusing his voice with that of Confucius. This is an ongoing process through the text, and Pound's personal authority is progressively enhanced. Eventually, he becomes capable of apostrophic outbursts *in propria persona,* as in Canto LXXIV:

> I don't know how humanity stands it
> with a painted paradise at the end of it
> without a painted paradise at the end of it.   (436)

Such utterances—essentially, extended authorial intrusions—rest upon and resonate with Pound's ancestral tradition, and they consequently carry great moral force.

Pound uses the basic figural modes of his mantic voice for two major purposes. First, the general pattern of discontinuous accumulation exerts an exegetical pressure, thereby initiating the studious reader into Pound's historical mythos. Second, the primary forms of variation in the text—intrusion and apostrophe—together foreground angles of vision from which that history may be seen and judged. These angles constitute the *senso morale* that the initiate is ultimately meant to discover and adopt. At the same time, Pound's figural strategy permits what amounts to the adumbration of a double perspective. We see the more permanent, authoritative, ancestral perspective of tradition, and we also see the fluctuating perspective of the personal, fallible "Ezra Pound," who is a character within his own text and a factive partisan of particular causes. He may move toward alignment with tradition, but he may also vary from it, as he struggles toward a comprehensive vision. The represented activities of this ebullient authorial figure constitute, in large part, the dramatic action of the *Cantos,* the plot of the poem. This figure, and his unstable angle of vision, are what fundamentally engage the reader. In effect, we see both history and the ancestral perspective from the variable authorial point of view, so that the *Cantos* renders history as background, and the fluctuating Poundian ethos—a life of the mind, in process over decades—as foreground.

This rhetoric has obvious potential, but it also generates problems. First of all, the pattern of accumulation and stance tends to make the historical accumulata appear to be, in retrospect, illustrative examples for the stance itself. The cantos preceding XIII, for example, become a retrospective exemplification of the absence or presence of the Confucian and Eleusinian moral code with which the Ezratic voice has joined. So, too, the cantos preceding XLV begin to resemble exemplification of usurious evils and nonusurious virtues. This problem arises particularly from the permanent perspectives of "Eleusis and Kung," the ultimate and unvarying ground of judgment in the text. The result, as Michael Bernstein has noted, is a tendency to "freeze" the text into static elaboration of what appear to be a priori theses. Exacerbating this problem is the exegetical pressure on the genial reader. Leon Surette has noted that the very impenetrability of Pound's text and the eccentricity of his mythic history together make Pound's prose the only reliable guide to the thematic codes the *Cantos* includes. The reader's experience of the text, in consequence, is often reduced to a search for manifestations of Ezratic doctrine, rather than discovery of a constantly unfolding, changing vision.[20] Insofar as this is the reader's experience, the text begins to seem more and more a massive, obsessive illustration of a relatively small number of fixed ideas. This perception is extremely damaging to Pound's credentials as an orphic sacerdote, since the decorum associated with those credentials requires that he be endlessly on the way toward an ever-receding (and ever-widening) intellectual horizon. Indeed, the potential damage of seemingly static exemplification, the very opposite of sublime accumulation, will be mitigated only for the naïve acolyte, the reader who chooses a stance so thoroughly resembling scriptural interpretation that all possibility of skepticism or critical distance is virtually prohibited.

Perceiving static exemplification becomes unavoidable in the cantos of the late 1930s, when Pound's authorial figure veers into a fairly explicit, dogmatizing fixity. The keynote of this phase is probably Canto XLV. Immediately after the ancestral denunciation of usury, Pound begins to speak *in propria persona* as a prosecuting attorney, presenting "evidence" and marshaling his spectral, textual voices as witnesses. Here, for example, is the Ezratic voice, with witnesses assembled, in Canto XLVI:

> 19 years on this case/first case. I have set down part of
> The evidence. Part/commune sepulchrum
> Aurum est commune sepulchrum. Usura, commune sepulchrum.

20. Bernstein, *The Tale of the Tribe*, Chaps. 3–4; Surette, *A Light From Eleusis*, 25–26.

helandros   kai heleptolis   kai helarxe.
Hic Geryon est. Hic hyperusura.
["statistics" presented on U.S. unemployment and crime]
CASE for the prosecution. That is one case, minor case
in the series/Eunited States of America, a.d. 1935.   (234–35)

Pound resumes this new version of himself at the beginning of Canto LII, in a sort of prefatory gesture, as he launches into the long series dealing with Chinese dynastic history and the deeds of John Adams:

And I have told you how things were under Duke
                              Leopold in Siena
        And of the true base of credit, that is
                              the abundance of nature
with the whole folk behind it.
"Goods that are needed" said Schacht (anno seidici)
commerciabili beni, deliverable things that are wanted.
                              neschek is against this, the serpent.   (257)

Whatever one thinks of this prosecution-lawyer phase of the *scriptor cantilenae,* he has clearly violated the conventions that initially established his credentials. Presentation of evidence in a "CASE for the prosecution" is by definition exemplification of a preset or fixed thesis. One assumes that the advocate has chosen his evidence because it fits what he wants to prove. Pound prefaces the cantos about China and Adams with a further gesture of prosecution. He includes references to "neschek" (*i.e.,* Hebrew usury), "a few big jews' vendetta on goyim," Adams' belief in the necessity of knowledge "ov the natr ov money," and "KUNG and ELEUSIS." He thus suggests that what follows is meant as more evidence for the next part of the author's case. Indeed, the prefatory material of Canto LII concludes with a "Know then" (258). Unlike the open-ended "So that" in Canto I, this implies that the author will now tell us what we ought to know, rather than conduct a mantic or Odyssean quest for restorative, order-giving knowledge. The bard who opens Canto LII claims to possess Truth, a Truth he will now impose. Pound, however, does not have the authority to make this claim, within a modernist aesthetic, or to impose himself in such a way. He violates the decorum applicable to a limited speaker moving within a boundary-less historical field, and in consequence he undercuts his own credentials as a modern, collared bard.

Pound's excursion into Chinese dynastic history largely confirms the damaging suggestion of obsessive static exemplification that emerges from Cantos XLVI and LII. What the studious reader learns from homework is, first, that there is virtually no original composition in this series (LII through LXI), and that Pound has not even synthesized a diverse collection of quotations (as he does in Canto XIII and in the Jefferson-Adams cantos). Instead, he has condensed de Mailla's *Histoire Générale de la Chine* (1777–83), though the condensation is unreadably diffuse. It resembles a collection of notes taken at a poorly understood lecture series. What the reader discovers, upon placing de Mailla's text and Pound's prose alongside the Chinese history cantos, is that Pound has edited de Mailla down to "luminous details." And the basis for selection, as the reader also discovers, is a belief (which is apparently not de Mailla's) that the vital continuity of Chinese civilization, with its cycles of renewal and reform, derives from adherence to Confucian principles. It is those principles with which John Adams will be implicitly aligned, by juxtaposition, in the subsequent cantos (LXII through LXXI).

As further homework reveals, particularly a reading of Pound's "Immediate Need of Confucius" (1937), the essence of these vital principles is in the *Ta Hio,* which, Pound believes, is the philosophical key to good government and economics: "Men suffer malnutrition by millions," he writes, "because their overlords dare not read the *Ta Hio.*"[21] The studious reader is bound to wonder, as he wades through the cantos of dynastic history, whether Pound has sinned against his own injunction (in *Guide to Kulchur*) against establishing any kind of "koran" or static code. What is the *Ta Hio,* in Pound's treatment of it, but a Confucian "koran"? This perception, in the Chinese history cantos, leads to an awareness that Pound has slipped into a peculiar sort of reductive pedantry. He creates little or nothing, while forcing historical narrative into the scheme of a rather dogmatically fixed idea. That process, if we judge from his unreadable condensation of de Mailla, has produced more distortion than illumination. Pound's activity at this point in the text, then, bears little resemblance to that of a vital artifex, and he hardly seems to be enacting the sort of onward-to-the-horizon passage expected of an American bard. He is, if anything, using his obsessive attraction to

21. Ezra Pound, "Immediate Need of Confucius," in *Selected Prose,* 75–80 (quotation, p. 80). Similar statements can be found in *Guide to Kulchur* and *Jefferson and/or Mussolini.*

Confucius—or to the fixed perspectives of "Kung and Eleusis"—to *set* horizons, and he has degenerated into dogmatic fixity.

This erosion of credentials reduces the validity of Pound's authorial perspective and, at the same time, distances the reader from the historical vision the case-making, obsessive, and sometimes strident poet seems to force upon the available facts. Also, the Ezratic vision, which the diligent reader finds so insistently illustrated in the *Cantos*, emerges as unacceptable. This becomes increasingly true in the cantos of the 1930s as the poet's anti-Semitism reaches the peak of its virulence, and his abiding attraction to authoritarian politics and the charismatic leader graduates to utterly uncritical fascination with Mussolini and the Fascist state. And this development is clearly reflected in the poem—as in Canto LII, where the references to "jews, real jews, chazims, and *neschek*" are dated "anno seidici" of the Fascist era (257). The fundamental *rhetorical* problem, however, is not simply the emergent ugliness of Pound's ideas and ethics. It is that Pound's version of history must be measured against the reader's own knowledge. As the reader diligently undertakes a study of Pound's sources, Pound has no direct means of controlling the reader's interpretation. History, after all, is an independent entity: it contains the limited bard, and it cannot be known in its totality. And the ancestral perspective, the ultimate ethical authority in the text, must be independently grounded in the facts of history, and embody a sense of history or tradition persuasive to the reader on its own terms. Pound's bardic authority must *derive from* that independent historical ground. In consequence, he cannot turn around and attempt to create it by sacerdotal fiat, without falling into a hopelessly circular argument. In effect, then, the reader is brought, through homework, to the textual grounds of a larger History, however he may construe it. Alongside is Pound's history, which tends to suffer (as Bernstein has amply demonstrated) in comparison.[22]

The authorial figure veers off into a rather strident, obsessive fixity, which undermines his claim to bardic status (for all but the most uncritical acolyte), and an eccentric and not especially persuasive mythic history grows into what has euphemistically been called Pound's

22. See Bernstein, *The Tale of the Tribe*. Pound's circular argument would go something like this: "My authority derives from X, which I declare to be true by reason of my authority that derives from X, which . . ."

"wrongheadedness." We can interpret this in a number of ways. Pound was falling victim to mental illness, or to paranoid delusion—he believed in a Jewish conspiracy, "a few big jews' vendetta on goyim," as a major cause of the decline of Western civilization. Or he was the naïve and apparently not-so-bright dupe of Fascist propaganda abetted by the lack of reliable information in Rapallo. Or he simply was bigoted and vicious. All these views have found support, as have various combinations of them. Nevertheless, one perception remains: as a character within his own poem, Pound has become difficult to like and impossible to admire. He has fallen into a terrible error, and he is either responsible for his bad judgment or unworthy of serious consideration as the voice of an ethical vision, or any other kind of vision.

The text, however, does not leave us with that perception. There is, from the *Pisan Cantos* on, a major shift in Pound's voice, and it rehabilitates his ethos and substantially alters the impact of the *Cantos* as a whole. In essence, Pound exploits the license for mortal fallibility given him by the initial conventions within which he established his voice. From the collapse of Fascist Italy and his former hopes, he emerges in the guise of a chastened survivor. Instead of the strident and often tedious "case-maker," he presents the reader with "a man on whom the sun has gone down" (Canto LXXIV, pp. 430, 431), "a lone ant from a broken ant-hill / from the wreckage of Europe, ego scriptor" (Canto LXXVI, p. 458), "old Ez," folding his blankets and musing on his losses (488). This retrospective and sad musing presents the reader with an extended inside view of the poet. The authorial figure is brought dramatically into the foreground, and in more personal, humane terms, to elicit sympathy or pity for the fate he suffers.

That attempt is based on a number of appeals. One of the most powerful occurs in the much-praised "What thou lovest well" apostrophe in Canto LXXXI:

> What thou lovest well remains,
> > the rest is dross
> What thou lovest well shall not be reft from thee
> What thou lovest well is thy true heritage
> Whose world, or mine or theirs
> > or is it of none?

. . . .
The ant's a centaur in his dragon world.
Pull down thy vanity, it is not man
Made courage, or made order, or made grace,
            Pull down thy vanity, I say pull down.
Learn of the green world what can be thy place
In scaled invention or true artistry,
Pull down thy vanity,
                        Paquin pull down!
The green casque has outdone your elegance.
"Master thyself, then others shall thee beare"
. . . .
Pull down thy vanity
            how mean thy hates
Fostered in falsity,
            Pull down thy vanity,
Rathe to destroy, niggard in charity,
Pull down thy vanity,
            I say pull down.   (520–21)

In this passage, Pound revives the ancestral voice of tradition, no longer forcing it to make a prosecutor's case, but instead allowing the authority of that voice to denounce his own personal failures and excesses. He turns the judgment formerly reserved for others upon himself, and appears to learn at last the lessons of humility. This gesture allows Pound to admit wrong while restoring his tradition as the ground of some sort of acceptable moral authority. The antique voice of history returns as a chastising conscience, to which he apparently submits.

At the same time, however, Pound continues to affirm the basic purpose of his epic enterprise, namely, the sacerdotal will to restore the tradition(s) and the sensibility necessary to high civilization. He goes on to say, at the close of his apostrophe in Canto LXXXI,

            To have gathered from the air a live tradition
        or from a fine old eye the unconquered flame
        This is not vanity.
            Here error is all in the not done,
        all in the diffidence that faltered.   (521)

In effect, the authorial voice replies to the chastising conscience of his "true heritage." The error is in his vanities, his hatreds, and (as he says on page 460) his lack of pity or compassion—all "fostered in falsity"—and his consequent "faltering" or failure to do what conscience requires. But the error is *not,* Pound here affirms, in the attempt itself, however much he may have failed. A similar reaffirmation of the motive for the bardic project is in the poet's repeated gestures toward the vision of a *paradiso terrestre,* which now seems impossible in historical existence, and yet still stands as an object of dedication:

> I surrender neither the empire nor the temples
> > plural
> nor the constitution nor yet the city of Dioce.   (Canto LXXIV, p. 434)

"Constitution" here refers to the American document, which Adams defended in earlier cantos; the "city of Dioce," as a *paradiso terrestre* associated with "the constitution," becomes in effect the *Theopolis Americana,* the untransacted destiny of the true America. In the *Pisan Cantos,* it is a city that the author holds "now in the mind indestructible" (under various mythological guises), though the city is lost to him as a present possibility. He keeps the faith. Pound balances self-recrimination with assertions of the worth of his thwarted effort—a gesture grounded in appeals to the Whitmanesque and Jeffersonian mythology that underlies his own conception of apocalyptic history. And these appeals are to endow the poet's basic desire with nobility or virtue. What is wrong, after all, with desiring a splendid civilization, however misguided the pursuit? Or so Pound's rhetoric suggests.

Alongside these self-ennobling gestures of keeping the faith despite adversity and the apparent self-recriminations, there are the many plaintive and personal moments of "old Ez" himself, as in Canto LXXVI:

> O white-chested martin, God damn it,
> > as no one else will carry a message,
> say to La Cara: amo.   (459)

We also see him, through the *Pisan Cantos,* experiencing the fear of death, feeling cold at night, observing insects, thinking of absent friends, and considering the ways of the U.S. Army—to name only a few of the phases in which he appears. All such moments are authorial intrusions, sometimes extended. But they take stances mainly toward direct, personal experience rather than toward historical figures. We see Pound lonely, aging, conscious of failure, and cut off from his desire, which is now largely purified of its former ugly attachments. The general effect is to reduce the distance between the reader and the authorial voice. Pound creates for himself a frail and fallible, and therefore *forgiveable,* ethos. It is the ethos of a man who admits his wrongs and who struggles to retain integrity amid the calamities befalling him. He begins to reinvent himself as a tragic hero—as a man caught up in and defeated by the disasters of history (or who suffers what the opening lines of the *Pisan Cantos* call "the enormous tragedy of the dream in the peasant's bent / shoulders"), and who nevertheless survives with purged and melancholy dignity.

This posture of tragic-heroic persistence, or faith amid disaster, is maintained through to the final cantos. Indeed, through the ongoing accumulation in *Rock-Drill* and *Thrones,* we see Pound extending and enlarging his characteristic themes. Although they are the object of his retrospective faith, those themes have become essentially static. Pound is adding new examples for his old ideas. There is a distinct (and unintended) irony in all this, for Pound is actually compelled, in these cantos, to go on as if his subject is endless, as if he is still in pursuit of a coherent vision of history, in order to maintain his credentials as a bard. He must pretend that he cannot come to the end of his subject, that he cannot "make it cohere," when in fact it has been essentially complete (as a basic scheme) and coherent in his own mind for decades. In consequence, the later cantos tend toward a puttering miscellaneousness. Pound presents a loose collection of bits and pieces from Byzantine codexes, Na Khi rituals, Coke's *Institutes,* and so forth, most of which— no matter what their inherent interest—do not advance or alter the basic historical vision of the poem. Ultimately, Pound can only justify this material as curios for the "specialist," or as "further study" for the faithful reader-student who has stayed with him in the later cantos: "If we never write anything save what is already understood, the field of understanding will never be extended. One demands the right, now and again, to write for a few people with special interests and whose curiosity reaches into greater detail" (Canto XCVI, p. 659). This authorial intrusion constitutes a clear admission that Pound is now writing exclusively for an audience of the faithful. It is also an implicit admission that *Rock-Drill* and *Thrones* are in essence "graduate courses" for the reader who has undergone the initiation. The sacerdotal bard will now take "a few people" into "greater detail."

But if Pound's historical scheme has become static, the energy and interest of the authorial figure can still keep the few engaged and carry them along. For *Pound* is not static. Indeed, his intrusive attitudinizing is ever present and pervasive. The later cantos effectively continue the extended inside view of the authorial figure that the *Pisan Cantos* began. The subject of history now becomes secondary to the activity of the poet beholding history. We see this especially as Pound begins to foreground a "personal" awareness—or a pretense—that history is chaotic and tragic, and that it cannot be forced into the coherence that one might individually desire. For example, he fastens upon "*hilaritas*" (most likely, a later version of "sane ebullience") and strikes whimsical attitudes toward his own inability to make sense. In Canto XCVIII the authorial voice intrudes upon a largely "Hellenistic" accumulation dealing with "the sacred" and says, "Patience, I will come to the Commissioner of Salt Works / in due course." Neither the identity nor the significance of the Commissioner (discoverable, of course, through homework) will be revealed in subsequent text. And there is no reason to expect (impatiently or otherwise) the Commissioner's appearance. This gesture is an inside joke to the faithful exegete: "You and I, dear reader, know what I mean, though to others all of this is crazily incoherent, isn't it?" Pound's *hilaritas* is a means of bonding the faithful reader to the personable, whimsical, and outwardly nonsensical author.

This whimsical stance, however, does more. It also feeds directly into the pervasive tragic mode of the later cantos. For history, as Pound has come to see it, is now "All neath the moon, under Fortuna" (Canto XCVII, p. 676). Seen from this perspective, which *is* the tragic perspective, history (or "time") is necessarily a locus where all attempts at a redeeming order are doomed to failure. In consequence, Pound's own attempt to "write paradise" (as he says in Canto CXX) and his dreams' failing to materialize are absorbed into this perspective. Like the characteristic tribal heroes with whom he has aligned himself, Pound has struggled to bring light against darkness. Like Malatesta, he has been largely thwarted, leaving behind not a realized *paradiso* or even a finished Tempio, but an eccentric, ramshackle compendium that only suggests what it cannot attain. Pound thus gives himself the Aristotelian image of the tragic hero. He is, in his role as a sacerdotal bard contending with the infidelisms of his time, a character who is "a head above" the ordinary run of men. He is pursuing a noble goal. He suffers inevitable defeat, through a combination of his own mistakes and the arbitrary decrees of

Fate. Moreover, his fall and subsequent purgation come about through sudden reversal, or what Aristotle calls "peripeteia," with the defeat of Fascist Italy and his incarceration at Pisa. In Pound's mantic drama, we retrospectively discover the materials of tragic plot.

In the guise of a tragic hero, then, Pound exits from his poem and, indeed, from the debacle of history. This is, in essence, the governing stance of the final *Drafts and Fragments,* and particularly of Canto CXVI, which is the last completed canto in the text. A striking feature of this canto is that it seems to be almost entirely set in the authorial voice. In effect, the poet turns aside from his mantic performance and addresses his reader, confessing that, at the end, there is no conclusion:

> Litterae nihil sanantes
> Justinian's,
> a tangle of works unfinished.
> I have brought the great ball of crystal;
> who can lift it?
> Can you enter the great acorn of light?
> But the beauty is not the madness
> Tho' my errors and wrecks lie about me.
> And I am not a demigod,
> I cannot make it cohere.   (795–96)

This plaintive, personal apostrophe, which occupies all of Canto CXVI, has a profound effect on the reader's perception of the *Cantos* as a whole, and on the kind of response ultimately asked for. In the first place, the distance between poet and reader is reduced to a minimum. The faithful, exegetical reader, the bard's longtime "camerado" by now, is invited into this act of pathos-laden, contrite admission. At the same time, Pound's repudiation of his "errors and wrecks" exploits the license for fallibility with which his limited perspective is endowed. Pound's specific, personal opinions are now largely dismissed, and the charges of "wrongheadedness" and invalidity that might arise are disarmed (or sidetracked). Insofar as those opinions partake of the "madness," they are not the "beauty" that Pound has intended. He "confesses wrong," he says, "without losing rightness" (797). So the reader, in judging the poem, is to edit out the wrong and to look for what Pound now calls "the gold thread in the pattern" (797). Further, this reader—engaged and cultivated as a tribal companion, and one of "the few"—is to take up the sacerdotal quest, to lift "the great ball of crystal" and enter "the great acorn of light," if he can. Pound ends the *Cantos* by abandoning his failed opinions. He foregrounds the tragic pathos of his effort to "write paradise" and enjoins the reader to take up the noble but difficult (perhaps impossible) quest.

Certainly, Pound suggests, the "light" is "there" to be entered, even if he himself has largely failed—rising (as the lark) "so high toward the sun and then falling" (802). He offers encouraging advice for the next sacerdote, or whoever will "copy this palimpsest":

> but about that terzo
>   third heaven,
>   that Venere,
> again is all "paradiso"
>   a nice quiet paradise
>   over the shambles,
> and some climbing
>   before the take-off,
> to "see again,"
> the verb is "see," not "walk on"
> i.e. it coheres all right
>   even if my notes do not cohere.   (796–97)

In this, Pound is not far from a passage near the end of "Song of Myself": "Do you see O my brothers and sisters? / It is not chaos or death . . . . it is form and union and plan . . . . it is eternal life . . . . it is happiness." Nor is he far from a passage of his own, written for *Guide to Kulchur* (1938): "Truth is not untrue'd by reason of our failing to fix it on paper. Certain objects are communicable to a man or woman only 'with proper lighting,' they are perceptible in our own minds with proper 'lighting,' fitfully and by instants." [23] Canto CXVI thus presents the tragic Pound admitting his failures and enjoining his faithful reader to carry on. At the same time, it makes a strong appeal to the post-Whitmanian (or post-transcendentalist) conventions of sublime poetic truth. And that appeal, ultimately, constitutes the basis for an ethical proof that justifies and even aggrandizes his apparent failure to "make it cohere." Pound, we are meant to see, has not sacrificed the integrity of his utterance for a specious, formal closure. He refuses, or makes a gesture of refusing, to pretend that truth is not fleeting and fitful, or to pretend that limited,

23. Whitman, "Song of Myself," in *Complete Poetry and Collected Prose*, 87; Pound, *Guide to Kulchur*, 295.

dogmatic formulas can pose as whole truth. We are thus to understand—insofar, that is, as "we" are the studious tribe of neophyte sacerdotes whom Pound now addresses—that Pound has attempted what Emerson said the orphic bard must always attempt. He has tried to go "by a way strange and new" and has challenged Fate. He has striven toward a noble purpose, namely, to utter the unutterable or "lead back to splendour" (797), in a time when the situation interdicts that purpose. And so he fails with splendid grandeur, as every tragic hero must fail; in that state, he exits from his poem. This is true only if the reader accepts the conventions of belief to which Pound directs his closing gestures. Consequently, Pound's confession in Canto CXVI appears not only as an act of sincerity, contrition, and enjoinment to the faithful but also as an astonishingly cagey act of self-dramatization worthy of Whitman at his most audacious.

Whether Pound's chastened integrity, sincerity, and contrition in the *Cantos* are real will probably remain a moot question. Certainly, J. Fuller Torrey's biography raises strong suspicions that Pound never did abandon his Fascist preferences. He simply disguised his views because that was politically expedient. And if he did feel actual remorse, it was not until the last few years of his life, when he had already stopped writing. Even then, Torrey suggests, the remorse may have been for failure to live up to his views. Perhaps he repudiated them out of fear of retribution, and pretended to be insane so as to avoid trial.[24] Certainly, if we are skeptical, there is the man who writes (in Canto XXX), in the voice of Artemis, that the world goes awry when pity prevents "foulnesse" from being "cleane slayne," and who later decides to embrace pity, compassion, and humility—and denounces capital punishment from that perspective—when he is under indictment for a capital crime. Indeed, Aristotle notes, pity for a fallen, noble hero is precisely the emotion that tragedy means to generate in its audience (the other emotion being fear of random Fate and unavoidable death). It is possible to regard Pound's tragic pose from Pisa onwards as a strategy to save his skin or, worse, as an expression of cowardice by a man who cannot face the consequences of his own actions. But such a view is likely to receive a passionate rebuttal, though not necessarily a persuasive one.

In the end, perhaps, we must remember that the *Cantos* is fiction,

24. J. Fuller Torrey, *The Roots of Treason: Ezra Pound and the Secret of St. Elizabeths* (New York, 1984).

despite the Whitmanesque claim of the mantic bard, in Canto XCIX, that "This is not a work of fiction / nor yet of one man" (708). The *Cantos* presents the imitation, the mimesis, of an extended mantic performance. The modernized voodoo literatus strives to speak with the voice of all men in all ages and lands, or at least all men who belong to his tribe. And the point is this: Pound, like Whitman, has invented a version of himself that is better than the probable reality. Moreover, by ultimately relegating to the category of "wrecks and errors" most of his specific political and economic enthusiasms—and, by implication, the eccentric view of history that generated them—Pound leaves us with his fictive, tragic ethos as the foreground subject of his poem. On this basis, the poem succeeds; it even attains a kind of dramatic (if not thematic or formal) coherence and persuasiveness. For the reader who stays to the final gestures of *Drafts and Fragments,* the recognition of a tragic plot permits an intelligible perception of the poem as a whole. Pound sets out as a sort of mantic Odysseus, degenerates into an obsessive Ahab, crashes, and then floats up as a purged, chastened Ishmael. This perceived dramatic action finally permits an overall response that goes beyond the miscellaneous searching out of Pound's sources and taxonomically locating his many particular themes. In the *Cantos,* then, as in most tales, the hero's fate—Pound's fate—elicits pathos, so that the text not only teaches or initiates but also moves. The startling fact is that Pound, the actual author, seems not to have begun with a tragic plot, or any plot, clearly in mind; he has capitalized on circumstance and the means available to him to rescue his failed poem. The *Cantos* as we finally see it is, as Pound said in 1938, "a record of struggle." Rather, it fictively enacts a struggle.[25] Insofar as it succeeds, it displays an amazing artistic and indeed rhetorical resourcefulness.

But what does this tale teach? Even if Pound does rescue the *Cantos* (and himself) by exploiting the tragic possibilities in self-dramatizing rhetoric, his success is only partial—from the viewpoint of his original motives. Pound's rhetoric ends by rendering his mythic history as mere decor (what Browning called "historical decoration" in his introduction to *Sordello*). The reader is asked to admire the bard's virtuous doomed effort, but not necessarily the actual opinions through which that effort moves, and frequently runs aground. Moreover, the poem's exegetical pressure produces a situation wherein the reader, constructing the

25. Pound, *Guide to Kulchur,* 135.

poem's thematic codes, may come up with a view of history, and a "paideuma," rather different from what Pound intends. Indeed, this is what Canto CXVI specifically invites the reader to do. Ultimately, the reader is asked to see in the *Cantos* the history and ancestral tradition he likes best, and to assume that *that* is what Pound is really gesturing toward. This leaves the reader, most probably, with a highly generalized notion of a virtuous strife for an infusion of "pagan beauty," whatever that may be, into the modern (American) world. It may be true that to overlook or relegate to background Pound's historico-political-economic theories is to deprive the *Cantos* of much potential significance, and thereby to render much of the poet's effort trivial.[26] The fact, however, is that such a relegation—trivializing or not—is exactly what Pound's rhetoric asks for, in the end, from his faithful reader.

Where, then, does this leave the Poundian rhetoric and its audience? To a large extent, it leaves both on square one of the bardic project, though the square itself may be enlarged. Pound has addressed himself, in the first place, to a restricted audience—namely, his "aristocracy of the arts" and, more specifically, those who already hold the conventions and expectations relevant to bardic poetry. This is, basically, the audience created for Pound by Whitman. But the audience is not necessarily small. Indeed, as Whitman continues to be read, and continues to be an object of study in English departments, an audience "with proper lighting" for bardic poetry will continue to exist, and may even proliferate. But what Pound does with this audience, in the end, is limited. The faithful reader comes to a generalized affirmation of the virtues of "bringing light against darkness" or of infusing an exhausted modernity with restorative pagan virtue. Pound thus merely reaffirms the virtue of the sacerdotal project itself. It is good, the *Cantos* suggests, to attempt, as Whitman did, a "great psalm of the republic." Pound, then, continues to cultivate a sacerdotal class, and thereby serves the first goal of the bardic project. But he does not serve the second and ultimate goal, to actually transform the national sensibility.

Beyond this, Pound's rhetoric also impresses upon the reader the virtue of his own attempt, and his own status as a failed but true bard. Even as he cultivates a modern sacerdotal community, he establishes himself as one of its canonic (tragic) heroes—as one of its ancestral figures, along with Whitman. The tale the *Cantos* tells the tribe is the

26. Bernstein, for example, makes this point in *The Tale of the Tribe,* 105.

tragedy of Ezra Pound. It is no wonder, perhaps, that Pound criticism has tended at one extreme toward hero worship. In sum, then, the success of Pound's rhetoric is to generate an inner circle of sacerdotal literati, with himself presiding as a patriarchal figure; but he does not provide the sacerdote with anything more than a general purpose, the purpose inherited from Whitman. Like Whitman, he offers no rhetoric by which the sacerdote can directly engage the public mind. Such a rhetoric, of course, may be impossible for anything still recognizable as poetry. In any case, Pound has successfully persuaded his true, inner audience of would-be bards to carry on, whatever the improbabilities.

One such attempt—inspired partly by Pound, but more directly by the millennial Whitmanism of the early modernist years—is Hart Crane's *The Bridge*. Crane develops a rhetoric in some ways distinctly different from Pound's, but no more successful. The interest of *The Bridge* is largely in the retrospective light it casts on Pound's rhetorical sagacity—his sensitivity to the available means or conventions, and what they permit or require.

VI.   *The Bridge*

Arouse! for you must justify me.
         —Whitman, "Poets to Come"

The primary consideration here is the power of conventional expectation—that is, the constraints imposed upon the would-be epic bard by
the governing mythologies of his genre. *The Bridge* is an attempt at
American epic verse that largely goes its own way, toward a more accessible and less imperious (and less ethically and politically disturbing)
poem than Pound's. *The Bridge,* too, attains moments of real brilliance,
as all its readers recognize. And yet, for all its genius and originality, *The
Bridge* somehow has been more a failure. While the *Cantos* is the canonic
text for American modern epic verse, establishing Pound as a modern
(though tragically faulted) bard, both *The Bridge* and Crane have comparatively minor status, and with some critics, their status is marginal.
The *Cantos* is a qualified success; *The Bridge,* a qualified failure. As we
will see, these differing receptions are a consequence of Crane's eccentricity, his difference. He did not take full account of his rhetorical
situation, and the poetic means it makes available or unavailable for the
poet who wants to play the role of American epic bard.

The sources of Crane's trouble have been variously identified, but a
focal point might be his statement, to Gorham Munson in 1923, when
he was already thinking toward *The Bridge,* that he thought he could be a
"Pindar" for American modernity. Crane's motive for this statement
was, in large part, the indeed Pindaric urge to praise, and to present a
truly affirmative vision that would counter the post-Edwardian enerva-
tion in *The Waste Land.* In this desire to "present a positive" (as Pound
once put it), Crane was coming close to Whitman's notion of a "great
psalm of the republic," or of the true, apocalyptic republic lying latent
in the actual one. The machine-age, industrial-capitalist world in 1920
may have been the dead-end of an elder European civilization, but its
American version could be seen as an "acme of things accomplish'd" and

an energetic, new world in the process of emergence from the old. All this was betokened in the splendor of Brooklyn Bridge. Or so Crane hoped to show, around 1923, when he was writing what would become his perorative poem "Atlantis," and beginning to plan the epic that "Atlantis" would conclude.[1]

In itself, Pindaric praise is not a source of trouble, though it does suggest a revision of the polemical urges that surface in the 1855 *Leaves of Grass* and again in the bardism of Ezra Pound. We can argue that, as the tradition of American bardic discourse has developed, the will-to-praise has fallen to the status of an invalid intention, at least in a poem that offers judgment on modernity and on the city. Of "Finale" (the 1923 poem that became the 1929 "Atlantis"), for example, Edward Brunner has said that Crane "refuses to be critical and . . . praises his culture . . . as though it could be loved." Brunner's "as though" emerges from a well-established topos that permeates the discourse of and about the American bardic literatus, and says *of course, it can't really be loved, as is.* Whitman said, "Do you suppose I could be content with all if I thought them their own finale?" To praise modernity, then, is to become uncritical and, by implication, false. It can be argued that a poem of Pindaric praise would truly realize the sort of national panegyric that Whitman hoped would eventually appear. He gestured toward it in his prefaces, though he himself did not in fact achieve it. Such poems as "Passage to India" and the praise of Lincoln in "When Lilacs Last in the Door-Yard Bloom'd" were efforts in that direction. However, for any would-be American epic bard since Whitman, the topos implied by Brunner's "as though" and Whitman's "Do you suppose" has indeed become pervasive, even fundamental. It must be directly confronted and overcome, if not simply absorbed as an integral, naturalized assumption in bardic discourse. Pindaric praise, in short, has been more obliged to bear the burden of proof than has its opposite.[2]

1. Edward Brunner, *Splendid Failure: Hart Crane and the Making of The Bridge* (Urbana, 1985), 22–25; Crane to Munson, March 2, 1923, in *Letters,* 129. For a discussion of Crane's panegyric motives, see Tom Chaffin, "Toward a Poetics of Technology: Hart Crane and the American Sublime," *Southern Review,* XX : 1 (January, 1984), 68–81.

2. Brunner, *Splendid Failure,* 22; Whitman, "Faces," in *Complete Poetry and Collected Prose,* 125. Crane was aware of the polemical Whitman of *Democratic Vistas* (see Crane to Tate, July 13, 1930, in *Complete Poems and Selected Letters and Prose,* 257–59). However, and perhaps significantly, Crane did not cite Whitman's poetry in relation to this point.

Crane's evocation of Pindar points not only to revisionary rhetorical motives but also to revisionary rhetorical methods for post-Whitmanian bardic discourse, and hence to a further and ultimately greater source of difficulty. Pindarism suggests the rhetoric of the Pindaric ode, the measured, highly cultured, prosodically and stylistically convoluted panegyric sung or declaimed by an authoritative spokesman (solo or in chorus) for the values and mythologies of public culture. Pindarism also suggests the rhetoric of proleptic "digression," that is, the strategic use of mythical narrative to create homologies and/or metonymic links between the figures of myth and the actual thing or person to be praised, and to frame the present in "the timeless" to reveal it as a moment of beatitude and grace. Digression thus serves, ultimately, the interests of strong closure, for it provides the grounds for an emphatic and resounding gesture of celebration in the final strophes of the ode. Pindar was enormously successful and achieved precisely the sort of culture-wide reception and pervasive influence that Whitman hoped for. Moreover, his poetry "included" history and myth while dramatically presenting an extended, danced mimesis of the *senso morale* commensurate with the poet's memorious vision. But Crane's Pindaric rhetoric is largely inconsistent with the dominant ideal of orphic, abysmic utterance in American epic discourse.[3]

The Bridge has a double problem. In rhetorical method as well as general intention, it runs against the grain of generic expectation in post-Whitmanian bardic poetry, and thus against the basic pattern of responsiveness in its available audience. Crane has an intention that needs, in his rhetorical situation, defense or justification; and his method cannot easily establish his credentials as a twentieth-century American bard, thereby making justification that much harder. Perhaps Crane moved to a kind of bardic poetry that differed from Pound's or even Whitman's. Perhaps he reinvented Whitman's sacerdotal literatus in a distinctive and original way. Undeniably, he did. Indeed, Crane's Pindarism is potentially conducive to a rhetoric far preferable to Pound's and, in the long run, more consistent with the goals of Whitman's sacerdotal project. But the problem of audience and generic expectation

3. See E. L. Bundy, *Studia Pindarica, I–II,* in *University of California Publications in Classical Philology,* No. 18 (Berkeley, 1962); Christopher Carey, *A Commentary on Five Odes of Pindar* (New York, 1981); and William Mullen, *Choreia: Pindar and Dance* (Princeton, 1982).

stands. No poet or rhetor can ignore the major expectations of his available audience, or fail to meet and overturn them if he runs against the grain. Otherwise, he will be blindsided by the pattern of response those expectations generate. And that is what has happened to *The Bridge.*

Ever since its publication in 1930, critical opinion regarding *The Bridge* has been essentially unfavorable, even among Crane's friendlier critics. Yvor Winters, Allen Tate, and R. P. Blackmur, in their classic and disastrous early essays on *The Bridge,* stepped up to the poem and declared it incoherent, both thematically and formally. Crane was a lyric poet out of his depth in an epic undertaking, they said, a poet in the tradition of Rimbaud and Baudelaire who was ruined by his Whitmanesque aspirations and bardic pretensions. Winters even went so far as to declare *The Bridge* "a form of hysteria" and Crane's Whitmanism the cause of his emotional problems and eventual suicide. More recently, Margaret Dickie and Edward Brunner have extended the "misguided lyricist" account of Crane's failure. In their studies of the poem's compositional history, they point out that Crane committed himself to writing epic before he was prepared to write it; the centrifugal, digressive, "exploratory" energies of lyrical invention conflicted with the centripetal pressures of structure and closure in the outline Crane projected for his poem and tried to stick to; and the result was a "blurred and vague" poem that suppressed and falsified Crane's true genius.[4]

However, as the example of Pindar shows, there is no necessary reason why Crane's centrifugal and centripetal energies should be in conflict or should falsify each other—unless we assume from the start that the centrifugal is poetically genuine, and the centripetal somehow poetically fake (too much like public oratory, with which the Pindaric ode in fact has much in common). Moreover, much of what is said about Crane could be, and repeatedly has been, said about Pound. He committed himself to writing epic before he was fully clear about what he was doing, the *Cantos* is an attempt to write epic in a lyric mode, and the

4. Yvor Winters, "The Progress of Hart Crane," in *Uncollected Essays and Reviews,* ed. Francis Murphy (Chicago, 1973); Winters, "The Significance of *The Bridge* by Hart Crane, Or What Are We To Think Of Professor X?" in *In Defense of Reason* (Chicago, 1947); Allen Tate, "Hart Crane," in *Essays of Four Decades* (Chicago, 1968); R. P. Blackmur, "New Thresholds, New Anatomies: Notes on a Text of Hart Crane," in *Language as Gesture* (New York, 1952); Margaret Dickie, "*The Bridge,*" in *On the Modernist Long Poem* (Iowa City, 1986); Brunner, *Splendid Failure,* 219–24, 232, 243–44.

Cantos does not cohere (even though Pound has a core of fixed ideas). We could also say that Pound gave the *Cantos* a form of closure—admittedly, a dramatistic rather than thematic closure, the only kind that Pound could find available by the time he wrote *Drafts and Fragments*. Pound's closure is not Crane's closure, at least not obviously. And that is the point: the ultimate cause of Crane's failure, with his audience of critics, is his "failure" to follow Pound dramatistically.

Allen Tate's comments are a case in point. Tate could dismiss *The Bridge* as "incoherent," even though he also had no trouble locating and castigating what he believed were the poem's major themes and symbolisms. At the same time, however, he could praise the *Cantos* for being "about nothing." The *Cantos* was incoherent also, but in a more interesting way. The source of this seeming inconsistency can be found in Tate's unstinting praise (in 1931) for the bardic Pound. Tate finds "Mr. Pound's poetic character" the "very heart" of the *Cantos,* and he treats the poem's "ostensible subjects" as "only the materials around which Mr. Pound's mind plays constantly." These "subjects," for Tate, are merely a background against which the author has enacted an extended, dramatistic display of poetic sensibility prospectively searching through the materials of memory. Alongside Tate, we should put Blackmur's declaration (in 1935) that the "doctrines" in poems—such as Dante's *Commedia*—"do not matter" and are only "guides and props." "What does matter," Blackmur writes, "is the experience, the life represented and the value discovered, and both dramatized or enacted under the banner of doctrine." One suspects that Dante would view this as a truly astonishing critical stance. It does suggest, however, the difference between the *Cantos* and *The Bridge,* and the causes of the relative success and failure these two poems have had among their available and primary audience of fellow literati. The notion of poetry as dramatized experience—as an enactment of the *agon* of the speaking poet—is the ground upon which the *Cantos* has mainly succeeded. On that basis, recent criticism faults *The Bridge* for "suppressing" the prospective, exploratory motives and the personalism of Crane's "true" poetic impulse. Crane has not persuasively enacted, for his audience, the *agon* of an abysmic bard. The cost of Pound's success is his resort to a rhetoric that relinquishes the chance to persuade his reader into the specific vision of history, politics, and ethics he originally had wanted to promote. In the end, and perhaps luckily for Pound, the *Cantos* asks to be read in the way that Allen Tate has read it. *The Bridge* does not; and that is a major source of trouble between the would-be bardic Crane and the tribe that he has had to write for.[5]

My focus will be on the failure of *The Bridge* to sustain the pressure of conventional expectation, at least within its immediate rhetorical context. There are, however, passages of brilliance, moments and signs of genius that make *The Bridge* a qualified and not a total failure. As even his harshest critics agree, Crane was a poet of astonishing abilities. The problems of *The Bridge* are rhetorical. They have to do with the relation of the poet to his audience, not with his inherent gifts, not with his poem's features considered *in vacuo* or in terms of some aesthetic "standard." These problems appear at all three of the traditional levels of rhetoric—namely, argument, or *inventio*; structure, or *dispositio*; and style, or *elocutio*. And from the more global rhetoric of argument down to the local rhetoric of style, the problems affect and exacerbate one another.

Central to Crane's trouble is the argument unfolded through the digressive movements of *The Bridge,* for his argument, which relates mythic, historical, and present time, is what provides the Pindaric bard with grounds for praise. The problem is not that Crane's argument is "incoherent," as Tate, Winters, and others have charged, and as more recent critics have tried variously to deny.[6] The problem is, paradoxically perhaps, that the argument presented through *The Bridge* is relatively easy of access, much more so than is the argument presented through the *Cantos.* Crane's argument stands open to the reader's direct inspection, reflection, and judgment. Obviously, this could be a virtue, especially in a literary rhetoric whose ultimate goal is to cultivate the ethical will of more than an inner tribe of fellow sacerdotes, neophyte bards, and professional exegetes and critics. But this openness and this coherence

5. Allen Tate, "Hart Crane," "Ezra Pound and the Bollingen Prize," "Ezra Pound," and "To Whom Is the Poet Responsible?" in *Essays of Four Decades,* 310–16, 510, 366, 367, 17–30; R. P. Blackmur, "A Critic's Job of Work," in *Language as Gesture,* 372–99 (quotation on 374–75).

6. See, for example, Paul Giles, *Hart Crane: The Contexts of The Bridge* (Cambridge, England, 1986); Helga Normann Nilsen, *Hart Crane's Divided Vision: An Analysis of The Bridge* (Oslo, 1980); Sherman Paul, *Hart's Bridge* (Urbana, 1972); and L. S. Dembo, *Hart Crane's Sanskrit Charge: A Study of The Bridge* (Ithaca, 1960).

lead Crane into trouble, for they leave the weaknesses of his argument exposed, and finally put him in an indefensible position.

Crane's argument, as it unfolds through the digressive movements of *The Bridge,* rests upon a basic antithesis, which first arises in the proem-ode "To Brooklyn Bridge." Crane begins with a gesture toward the "seagull's wings" aloft and "Shedding white rings of tumult, building high / Over the chained bay waters Liberty."[7] The gesture is clearly toward a sense of possibility and freedom that is, literally, in the air—though its antithetical counterpart is present in the *chained* bay waters. If the gull in flight represents freedom and free play in the blue, the industrial harbor city represents, and disturbingly so, something else. In Crane's opening lines, this sense of opposition is only incipient; in the second stanza, however, the opposition moves more emphatically into the foreground of the poem's concerns, and then is amplified through most of the remaining stanzas:

> Then, with inviolate curve, forsake our eyes
> As apparitional as sails that cross
> Some page of figures to be filed away;
> —Till elevators drop us from our day.   (1)

We are, that is, "dropped" from the purity of the sky—the flying gull forsakes us like a vanishing apparition, or like the daydreams that beguile us in our dreary office-jobs as we pore over "Some page of figures." We are likewise "dropped" by elevator, alarmingly and as if we are falling, into the confusions of urban modernity. This modernity, as the proem accumulates, reveals itself as a scene of tumultuous power and activity, including "cinemas, panoramic sleights / With multitudes bent toward some flashing scene" as well as "cloud-flown derricks," Wall Street, and traffic lights. But it also is a scene of destructive madness:

> Out of some subway scuttle, cell or loft
> A bedlamite speeds to thy parapets,
> Tilting there momently, shrill shirt ballooning,
> A jest falls from the speechless caravan.   (1)

A city where such things happen, for all its energetic and machine-made vistas, is also a "bedlam," where the distinctive deed or *geste* is also a

7. *The Bridge: A Poem by Hart Crane* (1933; rpr. New York, 1970), 1. All subsequent references to and citations of the poem are from this edition.

crazily self-destructive jest, before an automated caravan to nowhere in particular.[8] The mere circulation of traffic, perpetual movement without a perceptible *telos,* displaces, or is the current version of, the ancient routes of trade and pilgrimage. Here the numb speechlessness of the caravan contrasts, obliquely and implicitly, with the vital loquaciousness of a caravan like Chaucer's. Moreover, rendering a suicide leap as a "shrill" and falling jest/*geste,* and the bridge traffic seemingly indifferent or in any case voiceless, serves by contrast to make the "sane" inhabitants of bedlam seem dehumanized, at least emotionally paralyzed. The city itself appears a confining place, with its inhabitants emerging from subway scuttles, from cells and lofts, or crowding into cinemas. Most human energies have apparently been reduced to what Pound would have called the "mere dynamic" of the economic process under industrial capitalism. In consequence the shrill suicide has performed the only act of free will, and perhaps the only possible one, in the entire opening panorama—a self-obliterating leap back into the freedom of open possibility. The modern city, then, appears in Crane's ode "To Brooklyn Bridge" as energetic, impressive, and unbearable all at once. The reader, with the poet, regards it from the airy heights, and from a distance, and then descends or "drops" to bridge- and street-level.

The antithesis that Crane develops is constituted in the sense of ideal possibility (flight, liberty, the open space of the sky) confronted with a real actuality (modernity, urbanity, the chained bay waters) that emphatically falls short of ideality. Perhaps we have a parodic distortion (as in the "speechless caravan"), perhaps a negation (the will-to-freedom is suicidal). Crane locates the resolution of this antithesis—or the redemption of modern actuality—in the unspoken and "obscure" significance of Brooklyn Bridge:

> And obscure as that Heaven of the Jews,
> Thy guerdon . . . Accolade thou dost bestow
> Of anonymity time cannot raise:
> Vibrant reprieve and pardon thou dost show.   (2)

In effect, the bridge itself gestures in Pindaric praise, its "accolade," which Crane describes, in subsequent lines, as harplike with "choiring strings." Through that gesture, the "guerdon" of its higher meaning is

8. See Giles, *Hart Crane,* on Crane's propensities for punning, and the elaborate puns in *The Bridge.*

revealed. The accolade reprieves and pardons all the failures, confinements, and distortions of desire and will in modern actuality. The meaning of this accolade, however, is "obscure," though in fact not wholly so; nor has Crane wishfully willed it upon the bridge. As Alan Trachtenberg has shown, Brooklyn Bridge had been surrounded by the rhetoric of American destiny from its inception to its actual creation.[9] The architect intended it to signify the apocalyptic national ideal in terms of the real—the technological, the mechanistic, and the modern. Crane thus grounds his poem upon an available commonplace, though perhaps an excessively local one. The notion of a bridge (or Brooklyn Bridge in particular) as modernity transfigured has and has had little national currency, though it does resonate with the Whitmanesque embrace of science and globe-encircling technologies in "Passage to India." And for virtually everyone, there is something inspiring in the sight of a beautiful bridge, especially a large, impressive suspension bridge with its mixture of monumentality and delicacy. If bedlamite industrial modernity can *also* produce an object as sublimely beautiful as Brooklyn Bridge, America's untransacted destiny may still be in the process of transaction. The "guerdon" the bridge bestows, then, is the speaking poet's renewed and hopeful sense of redeeming possibility in the turbulent, disturbing urban scene that faces him.

And yet, as Crane presents it, the redemptive meaning of the bridge *is* obscure, "obscure as that heaven of the Jews," and therefore beyond clear knowing or telling—or so the proem seems to declare. In the closing stanzas, which are set not in daylight but in darkness, Crane must ask the bridge to render up its meaning, to grant that meaning to himself, his audience, and the benighted unconscious city:

> O sleepless as the river under thee,
> Vaulting the sea, the prairie's dreaming sod,
> Unto us lowliest sometime sweep, descend
> And of the curveship lend a myth to God.   (2)

Thus Crane completes his version of epic invocation, placing a city-lighted nighttime Brooklyn Bridge in the role of Muse, and establishing with his reader the contractual expectations under which the rest of his epic ode will necessarily go forward. The bridge is now no longer the physical bridge of masonry and steel, but is instead the "choiring" harp

9. Trachtenberg, *Brooklyn Bridge*.

of a gigantic presence, at once betokening and embodying a mythic ideal that "vaults" not only the sea but the prairie as well. Mysteriously, spectacularly, the vaulting, reprieving, and divinely obscure myth the poet perceives in the choiring bridge/harp arches the continent and corresponds to the path of American westward movement, which is, mythically, the passage to India and more. The subsequent text, as the invocation thus implicitly promises, shall be the partial revelation of this visionary and hopeful ideal.

Crane begins, then, with an argument consisting of three essential terms: the sense of a mythic and sublimely obscure ideal; the opposed sense of an actuality unequal to the ideal, or that (at worst) negates it; and the hopeful sense of a possible redeeming, transfiguring fusion of the two antithetical terms. In short, modern actuality itself may be a bridge, a passage, to more-than-India. As Crane's modernist reader is going to see, however, the text considerably expands upon these terms, yet does not convincingly advance Crane's argument beyond this opening position. Rather, the argument fails to demonstrate persuasively the redemptive possibility suggested in his vision of the bridge/harp, so Crane can merely assert the possibility as an article of faith. This outcome follows from the way Crane develops, and probably must develop, his basic opposition between ideal and real.

The ideal side of Crane's antithesis appears most fully in "Ave Maria" and "Powhatan's Daughter," the first two sections of the poem. In "Ave Maria," Columbus brings back from the New World an "incognizable Word" that embodies aspiration or desire, an "inmost sob, half-heard" that "dissuades the abyss" of doubt and despair (6, 7). Columbus hears or perceives the divine meaning of America, or of the passage to an imaginary Cathay that is still "one shore beyond desire" (8). He senses high destiny and thus repeats or echoes the vision of the proem. However, Columbus cannot clearly fathom or articulate what that destiny is. The Word is "incognizable," and the holy purpose of which he is the instrument is an inspiring but veiled mystery. There is, at the same time, an irony in Columbus' situation that appears through his allusions to the difficulties with his crew, and through his musings on the reception he anticipates in Spain. As Crane and Crane's reader cannot fail to know, Columbus has misidentified his discovery. Even if he is the instrument of an inscrutable deific intent, he has misinterpreted the nature of his role, and he is heading toward a future of wangles and betrayals that will leave him ruined. Moreover, and as Crane's reader well knows (and as Crane must also know), Columbus' actual main purpose was personal enrichment, not redemption. If Columbus' "heralding" of the New World is an analogue for Crane's action in *The Bridge,* the gap between idealist perception and reality bodes ill. Nevertheless, Crane's intention in "Ave Maria" is fairly clear. The significance of the New World, or America, is involved with a passage toward holy desire, and the object of that desire is sublimely "incognizable." Its name, in effect, is a word beyond formulated language.

In "Powhatan's Daughter," Crane renders this sublime ideal, the holy object of desire, in the primitivistic and coital (or Venerean) terms of modernist vitalism. It is the mysterious "woman in the dawn" with whom the waking protagonist of "The Harbor Dawn" would "merge his seed." It is the continental "body under the wide rain" referred to as "her" that, in "The River," is "known" by wandering hoboes, and across which the "river of time" (the Mississippi) flows, absorbing all and carrying all to a single conclusion (in the Gulf or, symbolically, in oceanic eternity). And, most significant, it is Pocahontas, with whom the medicine man Maquokeeta achieves a mystical union and apotheosis through a Dionysiac sacrifice (or perhaps a murder by whites) in "The Dance." Maquokeeta, in fact, is the only hero figure in *The Bridge* in actual union with the object of desire, or *genius loci,* represented by Pocahontas. He stands as a native ethos in right relation with the spiritual essence of America, whereas the poet and Columbus, like most of the characters in the text, are seeking the objects of their desire(s). As the whites advance upon the Indian and encroach upon his freedom, he retreats beyond "beyond their farms" (26), taking with him the "tribal morn" (24) they desire for themselves but can never possess. The right ethos, somewhat disturbingly for Crane's American mythology, is embodied in the vanished or vanishing Indian, who persists mainly as a ghostly presence in "old gods of the rain" submerged in pools (19) or brooding in the forest shade. By means of "The Dance," then, *The Bridge* decisively locates value in the natural or primitive—in the truly "aboriginal mind" as the locus of a properly Venerean, Dionysian, self-sacrificing or self-yielding ethical will. At the same time, value is beyond the circumference of the created America that has displaced it.

The object of this will, its Venere, Crane can represent synecdochically as a beloved (in "The Harbor Dawn"), or as Pocahontas, or as the continental body-in-the-rain across which hoboes stray. But if he even appears to define it, what is supposed to be "incognizable," he will falsify his poetic credentials in the eyes of a modernist audience. All he can do, in the end, is gesture toward a generalized but probably Bergsonian (or Buckean and Ouspenskian) notion of self-effacing universal Love as the essential act of vital and ethically enlightened will, and therefore as the destined terminus of history (in "Atlantis"):

> Migrations that must needs void memory,
> Inventions that cobblestone the heart,—
> Unspeakable Thou Bridge to Thee, O Love.   (76)

Crane's modernist reader, however, has a number of definitions available, and these cannot be entirely predicted or controlled—though Crane's synecdochic representatives of Love do, to a certain degree, restrain the interpretive possibilities. Still, it is on Love that Crane's argument goes necessarily vague, and the reader is invited to read in, as a number of Crane's critical readers have actually done, their favorite definitions. We might, for example, use the "universal love" that Bergson ascribed to the visionary mind, or that Bucke ascribed to "cosmic consciousness." We could as well use Pound's notion of Venus-worshiping Eleusinianism, or Malatesta's struggle against the downward drag of history and the "river of time"—which, finally, in "The River," appears to wash away, along with the "humpty-dumpty" hoboes straggling along the railroad lines, the "Sheriff, Brakeman and Authority" who ride the Twentieth Century Limited (20). And we might perhaps use Christian *caritas,* eroticism, free love, or some other kind of love, or various mixtures.

Yet even if Crane's Love *is* defined (by the reader's assumptions and/or by synecdoche), it supplies no definite vision of its ultimate object, which would be the apocalyptic City, the *Theopolis Americana,* in which the passage toward desire completes itself. The City of Love, in fact, is never envisioned anywhere in *The Bridge;* it too must be sublime and past imagining. Even Bergson, in *The Two Sources of Morality and Religion,* could not say with any precision what the ideal civilization of perfect freedom and realized love would be like. By his own definition, after all, such a society must be free from the restraints of systematic principle, constitutionality, and law. Those "torpid" things are unnecessary and even opposed to the higher consciousness.[10] The main feature of Bergson's future society of universal love is indeterminacy. Given such lines of thought, then, Crane can only declare the redeeming essence of an

10. Bergson, *The Two Sources of Morality and Religion,* Chap. 4.

achieved "American aboriginal" mind to be "Love," by which he most probably means the venerative, self-sacrificial will of the primitive sachem. But he must leave the actual ethics (not to mention the politics) of that will to be worked out, or guessed at, by the reader.

The mythic ideal *The Bridge* proposes—the American experience as passage toward a sublime, incognizable state of sacramental and vitalistic Love—is, for the most part, in strong accord with Crane's available modernist mythologies. And yet, those mythologies being what they are, and Crane's handling of them being what it is, his obscure guerdon gives him little ground for praise, reprieve, or pardon. Bergson's society of love is beyond and completely different from the civilization that now is. Bucke's and Ouspensky's high-tech theocracies, which are possibly more "cognizable," are nevertheless utterly beyond the present civilization, and must await the evolution of a new superrace from the smothering weediness of ordinary people. Maquokeeta, the one definite index of a possible society in *The Bridge*, exists beyond the bounds of Western civilization and history. In every case, the available mythic ideal requires the erasure of actual modernity for its realization—thus the suicide leap presented in the proem.

As the speaking poet of *The Bridge* moves on to the "real" side of his basic antithesis, in the segments after "Powhatan's Daughter," his problems deepen and finally become insoluble. In his characterization of American history, from the westward movement glimpsed in "Indiana" to the modernity viewed at length from "Cape Hatteras" onward, Crane brings forward no example, other than Whitman and perhaps Poe, of an American who really perceives or consciously pursues the mythic national ideal.

The pioneer mother in "Indiana," for example, displaces Pocahontas (seen as a homeless, "halfbreed" squaw with her papoose, stumbling or retreating west) and ushers in a scene of prodigal wandering. She herself returns defeated and widowed from the gold rush, and her last surviving son takes to the sea. Eldorado, or a generalized urge for adventurous fortune-seeking, has replaced Cathay. In "Cutty Sark," similarly, Crane evokes the nineteenth-century romance of the clipper ships, but also the world of Melville and Melville's Ahab, by means of an encounter with an alcoholic old sailor. This sailor is at once the prodigal son from "Indiana" and a debilitated, debauched version of Columbus, his mind possessed by hallucinations of Atlantis, and with his mind dispersed, like the bygone ships themselves, to all points of the compass. Indeed, as Crane presents the ships, their mission appears to be quixotic and finally tragic. They virtually sail off the map and disappear in the final lines of "Cutty Sark."

Crane rather ironically presents the original promise of the New World, or the American vision of unaccomplished destiny, as splintered, deflected, and distorted in the pursuit of global commerce. Yet it persists all the same, in isolated instances, as a "submerged" dream (*i.e.,* Atlantis) or as a mirage (Eldorado) that haunts the mind. In what is roughly the first half of *The Bridge,* it is a dream for the most part displaced, distorted, falsified, and gone awry in actual history. Or so Crane represents the years before the twentieth century.

In "Cape Hatteras," Crane returns to the direct consideration of modernity. The modern world is presented almost exclusively in terms of machinery, or its emergence as a central fact of life—the "nasal whine of power whips a new universe" and dynamos whirl in "oilrinsed circles of blind ecstasy" (41). Some elements of the proem also reappear, such as the stock exchange and the clearly claustrophobic "prison crypt / Of canyoned traffic" (41). But presiding over this industrial-capitalist scene, as a "new cipher" from the "prophetic script" of technological wizardry, is the airplane. As Bucke's readers if no one else will instantly recognize, it is one of the three developments required for the advent of a millennial and theocratic new civilization (the other two are socialism and cosmic consciousness). In *The Bridge,* however, the airplane seems more an avatar of the clipper ships, or an extension of their quixotic, entrepreneurial energies into a new and aerial frontier. It seems to be as much a perversion as a fulfillment of the poet's redemptive ideal. Crane must *tell* the "skygak" in his airplane that his purpose is a noble one:

> Remember, Falcon-Ace,
> Thou hast there in thy wrist a Sanskrit charge
> To conjugate infinity's dim marge—
> Anew . . !   (43)

The gesture is clearly Emersonian. The pilot must see himself as a breaker and extender of horizons, literally, figuratively, and spiritually. Further, and in a more Whitmanesque sense, he must understand this conjugation as a "Sanskrit charge," a destined purpose or duty given from the ancient and sacred origins of history, and bequeathed to him through his blood. However, the pilot has obviously not heard or understood the incognizable Word that should be pulsing through his arteries. The airplanes in "Cape Hatteras" are warplanes bent upon destruction—"the dragon's covey"—and the pilot himself is shot from the sky,

> down gravitation's
> vortex into crashed
> . . . . dispersion . . . into mashed and shapeless debris.   (44)

If the pilot's crash and "dispersion" are part of some deific purpose, there is nothing in the poem to signify that fact but Crane's insistence, which, without an evident warrant in historical fact, begins to look like wistful hope.

Crane thus still has to redeem or justify technological, capitalistic, urban American modernity, or he has to pardon it as a passage toward sublime desire and universal love. All he can really say of American actuality, in "Cape Hatteras," is "Towards what?" And the answer seems to be crashed dispersion. This is, in fact, the general fate of almost everybody in the poem but Maquokeeta. Crane's solution is to invoke an "elegiac" Whitman, who serves to redeem "fraternal massacre" and "man's perversity"—"all that sum / That then from Appomattox stretched to Somme." This Whitman also declares for Crane the redeeming myth:

> Our Meistersinger, thou breath set in steel;
> And it was thou who on the boldest heel
> Stood up and flung the span on even wing
> Of that great Bridge, our Myth, whereof I sing!
>
> . . . .
>
> Vast engines outward veering with seraphic grace
> On clarion cylinders pass out of sight
> To course that span of consciousness thou'st named
> The Open Road—thy vision is reclaimed!   (46)

Whitman perceives what Columbus could not, and what everyone but Maquokeeta fatally, delusively fails to see properly or see at all. In Crane's rhetorical situation, this is shaky argument indeed. The reader is asked to believe—contrary not only to the overt evidence in the text but also to the gist of established modernist mythology—that a divine but obscure purpose redeems mechanized modernity *because Whitman said so.* The reader is asked also to believe that the airplane or warplane reclaims

Whitman's vision because the poet has chosen to so believe. Beyond the late Romantic world of Bucke's mystical Whitmanism, however, most of Crane's audience thought of Whitman as a true poet who faithfully but too uncritically "crystallized" the bumptious culture of shallow self-interest and ignorant posturing responsible for everything that was wrong in America. In Crane's immediate situation, consequently, he could hardly invoke Whitman as an authority figure to justify that very culture and its excesses. Moreover, even if Whitman is not the naïve celebrator of industrial-capitalist social Darwinism and bourgeois pretension, he still cannot make available a transcendental myth of inevitable progress that the modernist (and postmodern) epistemology now renders invalid. Crane's Whitman thus appears, like Crane, to be holding out for a visionary hope, one the facts of history and modern actuality will not justify. He declares for Crane a faith that is in doubt, and that the poem has put in doubt virtually from the start.

And yet, if the audience does accept Whitman as the source of a justifying, pardoning, reprieving gospel, Crane's argument is further weakened by the following declaration:

> O, something green,
> Beyond all sesames of science was thy choice
> Wherewith to bind us throbbing with one voice,
> New integers of Roman, Viking, Celt—
> Thou, Vedic Caesar, to the greensward knelt!   (46)

The crucial problem here, from a rhetorical point of view, is that Whitman, as Crane's "Vedic Caesar," is placed "beyond all sesames of science" and is devoted to the natural, living "greensward." Crane uses Whitman to value the natural above (and "beyond") the artificial and technological, which by implication are little more than "sesames," tricks and gadgets. There is the possibility that this gesture may portray Crane to his modernist readers as a naïve romantic. However, the more damaging perception, which has been building throughout *The Bridge*, is that Crane's mythic ideal is beyond the boundaries of American history and actuality, and indeed requires the erasure of that actuality for its fulfillment. "Sesames," like the airplane or like Brooklyn Bridge itself, can only be justified insofar as they lead beyond themselves, to something "green," and then cancel themselves. But that is not what they appear to do. Instead, they lead to crashed dispersion, they proliferate, and their "blind ecstasy" is an ecstasy of self-annihilation.

Crane's argument has reached an impasse. He has, by the time the reader gets through "Cape Hatteras," built up a neo-Romantic version of the modernist antithesis between mythic ideality and fallen, historical actuality. The opposed terms cannot be reconciled, because they are mutually exclusive, and because Crane privileges one side of the antithesis. Unavoidably, actuality/modernity becomes the not-ideal, and it appears consistently as not-ideal throughout the text. We should remember that in Whitman's 1855 rhetoric, after all, much the same sort of antithesis occurs. The mythic ideal is invoked to allow the poet to speak with "terrible negative voice," to denounce and negate the infidelisms of his time. In "Passage to India," Whitman affects an optimistic ebullience, but his purpose is to invoke a future toward which the present *ought* to be directed, and emphatically is not. Likewise, in Williams' *In the American Grain,* the true native ethos does not grant to the landscape-smothering "culture of effigy" a pardon and reprieve; it opposes and subverts. And in the *Cantos,* Pound invokes his vital tradition largely to judge and denounce the inadequacies of present civilization, and to advance a "new paideuma" by which modernity can be put right. In the long run, Crane cannot use his mythic ideal to redeem or bless the present, or cannot do so within a modernist reprise of Whitmanesque rhetoric. The rhetorical function of the mythic is to criticize, to judge, to suggest reform. Invoking the mythic emphasizes the gap between it and a fallen actuality.

This gap widens as Crane continues beyond "Cape Hatteras." In "Three Songs," he presents three contemporary versions of the American Venere: the prostitute in "Southern Cross," a "simian Venus" in whom the ideal of Love seems to persist, despite exploitation and abuse; the striptease dancer in "National Winter Garden," who with snake rings and "turquoise fakes" appears to be a tinsel version of Pocahontas, and who performs "the burlesque of our lust"; and the Mary in "Virginia," who seems to be the only acceptable alternative, but who also seems to be a sanitized and relatively insipid representative of Venerean desire. Cathedral Mary is certainly not, or is not yet, the protagonist's mysterious woman in the dawn; she is someone to eat popcorn with, and, as the speaker says, "I'm still waiting you." In sum, the modern scene provides no fully adequate embodiment, in female flesh, of the *genius loci*— Pocahontas is degraded or sterilized. In "Quaker Hill," we find the land (*i.e.,* the "body of America") unloved, and bought and sold by speculative developers: "This was the Promised Land, and still it is / To the persuasive suburban land agent" (60). The dream, the poet's ideal, seems to be entirely betrayed; he comes to look upon himself as "a guest who knows himself too late, / His news already told" (61). As the poem goes on, the sense of modernity as deviation from or perversion of the true national purpose is intensified, and intensified to the point of despair.

This despair brings Crane, at the end of "Quaker Hill," to ask "Must we descend," belated as we are, and still ask entry into our imagined "Promised Land." His answer is yes. The penultimate section of *The Bridge*, "The Tunnel," presents that descent, and under an epigraph from Blake: "To Find the Western path / Right thro' the Gates of Wrath." The nightmarish subway journey presented in "The Tunnel" renders modernity as a subterranean and purgatorial passage over which "the Daemon" presides. The traveler emerges as one who has passed over (or, rather, under) Lethe: "Here by the river that is East— / Here at the waters' edge the hands drop memory" (70). Crane has brought his argument, again, to a declaration of faith. Although the present in itself is unredeemable, he now seems to say, it leads to a redeeming future. However, since that future exists where "the hands drop memory," it appears to be (as it has always been) outside time and history. Here the present, or modernity, or history itself, is something to be endured, because history leads, despite appearances, toward some incognizable apocalypse in which the urge toward Love may be fulfilled. This, ultimately, is the basic perorative stance in "Atlantis": the bridge, as in the proem, embodies an untranslatable "multitudinous Verb" that sustains, justifies, and leads us "from time's realm" (75). If we are patient, and if we believe, we will get there, because the myth of untransacted destiny—the Whitmanesque gospel—has told us so.

Crane's argument is hardly incoherent. Indeed, it is actually more accessible than is the argument of the *Cantos*. We might also note that Crane's argument, in substance, at least partially resembles the final position in Pound's self-dramatizing progress: history is largely unredeemable, a debacle, but a debacle that can be endured, transcended, and perhaps (if only momentarily) overcome by faith in some sustaining and saving myth, even if the believer alone is saved. Yet Crane's argument, accessible and open to inspection as it is, reveals itself as indefensible. It develops no evidence that gives his modernist reader reason to believe that Crane's (and Whitman's) faith in a providential and evolutionary progress toward apocalyptic Love is justified. Nor is there evidence that those who believe in that progress are engaged in anything but wishful or deluded thinking. The argument of the *Cantos,* after all, would have us resist the course of history, not pardon and bless it as a purgatorial passage that eventually will end in an Elysium of heart's desire. And Pound, in not assuming a providential progress, while focusing attention on the virtues of the vital struggle, is closer than is Crane to the paradigmatic mythic histories of American modernism. Indeed, it is the inability to overturn or escape the paradigmatic mythos, which creeps into and virtually becomes the mythos of *The Bridge,* that renders Crane's argument so visibly untenable. The would-be Pindaric bard of *The Bridge,* in sum, is at odds with the fundamental assumptions he must work with, and he has not discovered a poetic means for directly confronting and/or transforming them. In consequence, the affirmative faith embodied in his urge to praise has little logological ground to stand on.

The persuasive force of Crane's affirmative faith depends almost entirely on his authority, as a sacerdotal bard, to command or inspire the reader's acceptance of it by simple declaration. But Crane's authority is weak, and for several reasons. The obvious and primary reason in the reliance on Whitman in "Cape Hatteras," the barely implicit suggestion that "I am justified in my faith because Whitman embraced it." Not only did most of Crane's modernist audience see Whitman as crude and "nauseating"— with the exception of the mystical Whitmanians, such as Waldo Frank—but also, and more significant, this gesture shifts the basis of authority away from Crane. The conventions of Whitmanesque bardism require the poet to embody in himself "the origin of all poems," to be the locus through which a sublime identity speaks, be it Spirit or Tradition. The bardic poet must repossess the mythic vision and make it original with himself, as Pound does in the *Cantos.* Or, as Whitman himself suggested, the perfect sacerdote must overcome, and perhaps even abandon, his master (*i.e.,* his master/precursor). Crane's stance toward Whitman, however, is that of a disciple, reverential and subordinate:

> My hand
>   in yours,
>   Walt Whitman—
>   so—   (47)

For the kind of poetry Crane attempts in *The Bridge,* this gesture is fatal. Crane effectively sends his reader back to Whitman: *Leaves of Grass* is the definitive statement, the "koran" with which *The Bridge* aligns itself and which it does not supersede. Crane constitutes himself as the belated companion and follower of a former bard, not as a bard in his own right. He does not stand at "the origin of all poems," for his vision is avowedly derivative.

This lack of bardic authority is evident throughout the poem, and most pervasively in the kind of utterance that Crane fictively enacts. The two key aspects of this act are the dramatistic unfolding or development of his voice, and the dominant textural features of his style.

We should, perhaps, first clear away what has become a critical commonplace regarding *The Bridge*—namely, that Crane's poem is structured as "a day in the life." The "protagonist" (sometimes identified as the poet himself, sometimes not) awakens, goes by subway or commuter train to work, passes the day in New York City, and returns home again by subway. This interpretation is motivated by four segments in the poem: "The Harbor Dawn" (awakening), "Van Winkle" and "The River" (going to work), and "The Tunnel" (the subway home). However, nothing else in the poem supports the narrative line those sections seem to hint at, and there is much that completely undermines it. In "The River," for example, the train the speaker envisions is no commuter train or subway but "the 20th Century Limited," a figural railroad that is transcontinental and that seems to be mainly westward-bound: "You have a half-hour's wait at Siskiyou, / Or stay the night and take the next train through" (19). And after "The River," the protagonist and his day disappear—Crane evokes the aboriginal past of Pocahontas and Maquokeeta, as well as the historical past of pioneers and clipper ships. These digressions are followed, in "Cutty Sark," by a midnight walk home across the bridge. If the poem does present a single protagonist and a single day, he leaves home once, goes home twice, and disappears in the meantime. We never do see him, in fact, going about his day in the city; we are taken to Cape Hatteras, the suburbs in "Quaker Hill," and the Caribbean (most likely Cuba) in "Southern Cross." The only city scenes outside the morning sequence in "The Harbor Dawn" and "Van Winkle" are the South Street sailors' dive in "Cutty Sark," Bleecker Street in "Virginia," and possibly the skin show in "National Winter Garden." There are, of course, the beholdings of the bridge in the proem and in

"Atlantis." Aside, then, from his not arriving at work, his leaving home once, going home twice, and appearing in scenic contexts that would more than fill a single day, Crane's speaker seems to spend his actual city-time just loitering—under the bridge, and in bars, and mostly at night. It is possible, of course, that Crane wants to suggest the narrative framework of "a day in the life," but his poem violates that framework so extensively that it is untenable as either a fictive device or a useful principle of interpretation.

A more coherent interpretation is available if the poem is considered not so much as a narrative, or as a *Ulysses*-like odyssey through one day, but instead as an act of speaking—the mimesis of an utterance—set within a scene of speaking. What establishes this scene is Crane's initial conceit, which is elegantly simple. Crane locates himself, in the proem, as one gazing toward Brooklyn Bridge—which, as he speaks, is "across the harbor"; at the end, in "Atlantis," he reappears in this position, allowing his gaze to pass over the moonlit shape of the bridge, as he "floats" in mind around and under it. This situation frames the entirety of the discourse. The reader is asked to imagine a scene of speaking, in which the poet looks toward the bridge. As he speaks he mentally digresses from the immediate object of his vision, and into a range of associated reveries that constitute his argument. These, finally, bring the speaker back to himself as the object of his literal sight becomes again the object of his contemplation. Insofar as he speaks out of this proleptic mental drifting, which might be construed as a "visionary dream," Crane plays the role that he names for himself in the penultimate stanza of *The Bridge*: he is, indeed, a "floating singer."

Clearly, this Pindaric conceit is Crane's invention from within the bases of abysmic utterance, for the poet's utterance emerges from, and to a large extent is engaged with, an inward experience. Crane's handling of this conceit, however, compounds the problems generated by his untenable argument. Most obviously, the "frame" created by the proem and "Atlantis" give *The Bridge* a formal and, for his audience, a rather artificial-looking closure. Instead of enacting an "endless utterance" or ceaseless, horizon-breaking process, Crane seems to force a "conclusion" upon his dramatistic action. This testament of faith is, as we have seen, little more than a simple, unsupported assertion. His concluding "testament," moreover, is really only a restatement, in more elaborate terms, of his opening position in the proem. The bridge, or the myth behind it, somehow justifies, pardons, reprieves the perversions of modernity and history. The reader, then, is invited to see that Crane has started from, and written toward, a preconceived conclusion (what intensifies this impression is the reader's learning from external sources that Crane wrote "Atlantis" first). With dramatic emphasis, he ends at his point of departure. There is, of course, nothing inherently wrong with frame devices, strong thematic closures, or fixed argumentative positions; indeed, these are among the most powerful resources of the Pindaric ode. However, and unfortunately, the governing decorums of bardic discourse disallow these virtues. Crane violates generic expectation. He is, or appears to be, trapped within a fixed stasis, or what Pound would have called dogmas and mental cramps.

A second and perhaps more crucial problem in Crane's handling of the "floating singer" conceit is his general failure to constitute his voice in any but personal terms. The speaker of the proem and "Atlantis" is an "I" who cannot be identified as anything but the individual voice of an authorial figure, one who beholds and imagines. Unlike the "mantic" speaker Pound establishes in Canto I, Crane himself speaks through Crane. This holds true for virtually all sections in the poem, the only clear exceptions being "Ave Maria" and "Indiana," which present the "voices" of Columbus and the pioneer mother. But in these two sections, and in the "Powhatan's Daughter" sequence as a whole, Crane introduces a device that serves to separate these voices from himself, and that contributes to the seeming fragmentation of the poem's dramatic action—namely, the marginal commentary. This development requires discussion.

Crane's commentary first appears alongside the opening lines of "Ave Maria": "Columbus, alone, gazing toward Spain, invokes the presence of two faithful partisans of his quest." At the same time, the reader "hears" the voice of Columbus: "Be with me, Luis de San Angel, now—" (5). Crane's marginal comment effectively moves the authorial voice, which spoke in the proem, to the border of the discourse. From this position, he seems to address the reader, and to behold Columbus just as the reader does. Certainly, his own voice does not interact or conflate in any way with that of the speaking historical figure. At the same time, the question of where Columbus' voice is coming from (in a dramatistic sense) becomes extremely problematic. Crane's standing apart, and the simultaneity of his and Columbus' voices, suggests separation. More important, there is nothing in Crane's basic conceit, as established in the proem, that invites the reader to assume that both voices emerge from a single mouth. We have no seance in a memorious Erebus of texts. Columbus' voice, then, does not appear to rise from the abysms of the speaker's psyche, and not even as a dream image that the speaker somehow witnesses. Instead, it appears to come from an unspecified (and unspecifiable) "elsewhere," and to be inserted as though it were a cinematic cut. The speaking poet, meanwhile, stands offscreen, or sits with the audience, watching and listening to Columbus and whispering explanatory comments.

A crucial fact in "Ave Maria" is that the authorial/marginal voice through which Crane represents himself is not inside the history he beholds; nor is the history inside the voice. And, since he begins his presentation this way, he establishes a pattern of expectancy—a contract—within which he must and usually does operate. As a floating singer, he generally hovers above, outside, or apart from the figures of his vision. This permits an interesting if puzzling effect in the opening sections of "Powhatan's Daughter." In "The Harbor Dawn," for example, Crane's authorial/marginal voice appears alongside another voice, which seems to be his also. The onscreen voice reflects upon the "tide of voices" that "meet you listening midway in your dream," upon the morning, and upon "you beside me," all of which sounds like good modernist reference to the polyphony of deep-down memory that vital desire calls forth. The "tide of voices," however, is never actually presented; it is only mentioned or thought of. There is instead a meditative and "poetic" soliloquy, spoken most probably but not necessarily by the author. The authorial voice in the margin reflects: "Who is the woman with us in the dawn?" (12). Is the Pindaric bard of *The Bridge* reflecting upon an image of himself from another time or upon some wholly impersonal dramatis persona? Or does "The Harbor Dawn" present a moment of extreme and multilayered self-consciousness? The text provides no way to decide. What is certain, however, is that Crane's authorial voice, in the margin, is distanced from the scene. He reflects upon someone reflecting upon his situation. The floating singer is kept apart.

Essentially the same situation obtains throughout "Powhatan's Daughter." A succession of onscreen speakers, who may or may not be Crane, generally face toward or muse on a scene, whether remembrance or history, which does not speak through them. The authorial voice continues to hover (flickeringly) in the margin. Whether all these onscreen voices belong to the bardic Crane, or are simply a series of monologuists in different contexts, remains essentially ambiguous until the reader reaches "Indiana." At that point, Crane introduces the pioneer mother's "speech" to her son Larry, along with the marginal commentary "and read her [Pocahontas and/or the woman in the dawn, presumably] in a mother's farewell gaze" (27). As he has done with Columbus, Crane separates the mother's voice from his own. At the same time, he thereby creates the retrospective impression that "Powhatan's Daughter" is a series of disconnected vignettes featuring different speakers, since that is certainly what has happened in the jump from "The Dance" to "Indiana." The reader is now invited to see that the only reliable ground of continuity from "Ave Maria" to "Indiana" is, or has been, the marginal voice of the author, which has kept up a running discourse, a virtually continuous sentence, as the other speakers have come and gone. The voice that spoke in the proem has continued in the margins; the speaker witnesses or imagines, in his digressive reverie, a sequence of thematically related but dramatically discontinuous episodes.

The pattern of expectancies thus created is generally fatal to the subsequent and overall dramatic structure of *The Bridge*. After "Powhatan's Daughter," the marginal voice disappears. Yet Crane continues with his disconnected scenes as the text progresses through "Cutty Sark," "Cape Hatteras," "Three Songs," "Quaker Hill," and "The Tunnel." Since the speaker is an "I," and since the marginal commentary has disappeared, the reader is invited or required to see this "I" as representing the authorial voice, speaking from different contexts, in a broken sequence. The effect, in other words, is that the reader is encouraged to perceive *The Bridge* as Winters, Tate, Blackmur, and others have perceived it. The work is a loose collection of thematically related but formally and dramatistically independent lyrics. Possibly, the work is a series of apostrophes without the intervening and connecting accumulata the *Cantos* provides and, for that matter, without the relatively strong discursive linkages a classical ode would give its proleptic digressions. Reinforcing this general impression is the insertion of the "Three Songs" section, clearly, as the title suggests, in the lyric mode, parallel, and separate. Thus Crane's American epic ode as a continuous, exploratory, horizon-bound utterance, or as a continuous prospective *agon* with an unfolding vision, becomes dramatistically untenable, at least for his modernist reader. The text breaks up, taking on the look of a series of lyrical gestures, a set of reflections within a static, preplanned arrangement. The reader will not call such a text "epic" at all, nor recognize it as bardic either. This perception does no good to Crane's credentials.

As *The Bridge* begins to resemble a lyric sequence, the "personal" quality of Crane's voice becomes correspondingly emphasized. The reader is led to see that, aside from the voices of Columbus and the pioneer mother, which are distanced from Crane's authorial voice (rather than being absorbed into it), no other "voice from history" emerges. The only other voices that issue from the speaker are the reported voices of contemporaries: snips of bar-car conversation and hobo talk in "The River," the old salt's alcoholic muttering in "Cutty Sark," and the random phrases of fellow travelers in "The Tunnel." These voices, and particularly those in "The Tunnel," are more than a little reminiscent of the low-class dialogue amid nightmare cityscapes in *The Waste Land*:

> The phonographs of hades in the brain
> Are tunnels that re-wind themselves, and love
> A burnt match skating in a urinal—
> Somewhere above Fourteenth TAKE THE EXPRESS
> To brush some new presentiment of pain—
>
> "But I want service in this office SERVICE
> I said—after
> the show she cried a little afterwards but—"   (67)

What Crane's audience is shown, in general, is a poetic consciousness whose abysms seem not to contain a sublime vision of history, or even a polyphonic "tide of voices" speaking out of the historical depths, though he does *mention* one in "The Harbor Dawn." What the reader sees is more an isolate personal identity, a lyric self, constituted by an Eliotic, unpleasing contemporaneity. This textually represented "Crane" looks toward Whitman to provide a vision he seems not to possess in his own right. And further, as the reader cannot fail to notice, the American history upon which Crane has tried to force a Whitmanesque affirmation really consists of the most obvious of figures—Columbus, Indians, pioneers, clipper ships, and technological modernity. This is the stuff of grade-school primers or, as Edward Brunner has said, of chamber-of-commerce pageants. Those images could be quite suitable in a Pindaric rhetoric aiming toward a popular audience; but "the popular," in a modernist context, is generally beneath respectability. (Crane's businessman father liked the American panoramas of "The River," and Brunner, revealingly, takes that as proof of that poem's "folksy" shallowness and compromised integrity.)[11] The "abysms" of Crane's poetic psyche begin to look somewhat commonplace and secondhand. Such an image matches poorly with the standard modernist conception of the true sacerdotal literatus, the sublime epic bard.

Together, Crane's "argument" and the dramatistic structure of his poem put him in a weak position. He insists, without evidence and through pure assertion, upon a redeeming, sublime ideal, an incognizable Love toward which the purgatorial miseries of history must be moving us, as an article of faith. But his voice acquires no persuasive ground of authority; it tends toward a personal and lyric mode, revealing an ethos more discipular than visionary, grounded more in contemporary commonplace than in deep memorious many-voiced Tradition. What makes this situation worse, moreover, is Crane's characteristic style, which violates the conventional decorums for bardic utterance at almost every point. The style and the argument and dramatistic structure ultimately motivate the Yvor Winters school of judgment that *The Bridge* presents the reader with "a form of hysteria," or in general with the image of a would-be Pindaric bard desperately declaring for a false position.

In the first place, cluttering the style of *The Bridge* are conventionally "poetic" locutions or seemingly decorative artificialities that break the illusion of sublimity. Most obtrusive are the archaisms, particularly *thee* and *thou,* expressed by Crane's personal voice, and the frequently regular, sometimes prominent rhythm-rhyme schemes throughout the poem. Since Crane's voice is personal and apparently issues from a modern psyche—as are most of his onscreen voices in "Powhatan's Daughter"— the *thee*s and *thou*s can have no justification. This usage, given the conditions of Crane's presented voice, appears as mere decorative conventionality or, worse, amateur contrivance. We should remember that in the *Cantos,* Pound's "mantic" voice allows him to speak as the channel of a voice-from-history that is, at least dramatically, of ancient origins and

11. Brunner, *Splendid Failure,* 117, 221–22.

that therefore ought to use archaic diction. Archaism functions rhetorically in the *Cantos,* because it signifies the tradition voice and distinguishes that identity from Pound's personal voice, which has a consistent and identifiably modern (and sometimes exaggeratedly "American") diction. In *The Bridge,* however, the only really justifiable use of archaism occurs in "Ave Maria," when Columbus speaks. Otherwise, Crane's archaism takes on the unfortunate look of ornament or an overdone attempt to be "poetic" or reverential.

The prosody of *The Bridge* is probably more damaging to Crane's credentials than is its archaism. This is a matter of well-established convention. According to Longinus and his eighteenth- and nineteenth-century redactors, meter and rhyme are most appropriate to "the beautiful" or the merely pretty, rather than the sublime. Such features bespeak preoccupation with artifice and formal proportion, rather than the wild, impulsive burst of inspiration. They resemble flower gardens and hothouse orchids, rather than a mighty mountain's craggy spires, glaciers, and shaggy forests. Emerson used this contrast in "The Poet," to distinguish between the mere "lyrist" and the real thing. More significant for the problems of *The Bridge* is the Longinian dictum that the "over-rhythmical" or too-musical passage distracts the listener from the sublime idea the words are meant to suggest. The sound of the language claims too much attention for itself, the passage "jingles," and the utterance loses grandeur.[12] *The Bridge* can hardly be called a "jingle," but at its moments of stylistic excess or infelicity, Crane's strongly metered prosody creates effects—or appears to create effects—that are less than conducive to sublime grandeur. Consider, for example, this passage from "The Dance":

> I heard the hush of lava wrestling your arms,
> And stag teeth foam about the raven throat;
> Flame cataracts of heaven in seething swarms
> Fled down your anklets to the sunset's moat.   (24–25)

Here, the dominant prosodic impression is one of metronomic tick-tockiness. The passage jogs along from end-stopped line to end-stopped line, and from rhyme to rhyme. And there are a number of specific problems. The phrase "the sunset's moat," for example, seems motivated

12. See, for example, Blair, *Lectures,* 57, 69–76; and Longinus, *On the Sublime,* 241.

primarily and possibly only by the need to complete a rhyme. The reader has a sense of uncertain reference and a question whether "sunset's moat" is anything but a "poetic" and decorative circumlocution for "sunset" (and why a "moat"?). The same could be said of "seething swarms." Does a cataract "swarm," like bees? Do swarms flee down anklets? Does "swarms" have any purpose other than rhyming (and not very well) with "arms"? It seems unlikely. Further, the reader can ask why "anklets" rather than "ankles," which would make more sense. Apparently, "anklets" has a longer second syllable, permitting some stress to fall on "to," thereby preserving the general iambic quality of the line. The same motive probably accounts for "foam," in the second line (can teeth foam?). Crane wants, it seems, a weakened stress, or even an unstress, on "teeth," so he needs to follow it with a heavily stressed word—though the image/idea would be conveyed by "stag teeth about the raven throat." Of course, there are many other problems, among them, the question whether one can *hear* stag teeth. Crane has shifted to visual imagery without changing his verb. But the apparent cause of all or most of the confusion in this passage is the poet's attempt to force a preset prosodic scheme, one that insistently draws attention to itself, onto whatever it is he wants his voice to say. The prosody in this passage seems to be controlling the poet's invention, even impeding it.

One could cite a great many examples of prosodic success and failure in *The Bridge* ("Cutty Sark," probably, is most successful, at least in terms of bardic convention), but this one example from "The Dance" is symptomatic. Not frequently, but still too often, *The Bridge* verges toward what Pound would have called "composition in sequence of the metronome." That studied artificiality is inconsistent with Longinian grandeur, and seems to force semantic and syntactic distortion on the text. This distortion, at its worst, clearly has little to do with the struggle to utter ineffable, extralinguistic truth. It does have a lot to do with spinning out verbiage to fill an arbitrary pattern—Crane's profusely overwritten style begins to look like mere poetic ornament, and ornament unsteadily controlled. At such moments, obviously, he departs from the ways of the bardic literatus. His prosody presents to the reader an air of fretful contrivance, of meter and rhyme at odds with perception and discovery, rather than the open-ended, impulsive-looking, accumulative surge of Pound or Whitman.

We could point to Milton's epic iambic as a preset, consistent metrical scheme that does achieve sufficient grandeur; and we could with the classicists point to Pindar's prosodic and stylistic complexities, which Horace celebrated as a "mighty flood [of] daring dithyrambs bearing words in measures freed from rule." [13] However, neither Milton nor Pindar falls as dramatically as does Crane into the appearance of forced prosodic scheme, and both poets remain essentially within the "normal" syntactic and dictional conventions of their languages. Milton is more likely to distort his pentameter to accommodate a phrase than to do the opposite; it is Pindar's measures that seem to Horace potently "freed from rule." The "unforced" appearance of the Miltonic or Pindaric surge, then, keeps it within the bounds of Longinian grandeur. The true sublime requires a kind of simplicity, or what the neoclassical and Romantic redactors of Longinus thought of as the negligent, hardy roughness of true poetic genius. This remains basically true for the sublimity of modernist bards as well. An uneven accumulation of phrase on phrase, clause on clause, is most consistent with the image of primitivistic and abysmic spontaneity, of vital and inspired wild-speaking from the aboriginal layers of the psyche. A tortured, elaborate syntax and diction set to an apparently forced (or imposed) metric and rhyme scheme is a poor credential for a would-be American bard to be presenting.

Crane's prosodic habits in *The Bridge,* moreover, seem closely related to his tendency toward a tropological profusion that often looks too much like fake or overdone intensity. Even Waldo Frank, undoubtedly Crane's most fervent defender, could see in *The Bridge* a figural "inflation," suggesting a "febrile, false ebullience," which for Frank embodied the frantic mood of the years just preceding the crash of 1929. Edward Brunner finds "a superficial, exotic glitter" and "patently laborious writing" that now and then appear. In fact, however, the tendency is basic to Crane's poetic style, from the poems of *White Buildings* onward. Perhaps the most outstanding single instance is "corymbulous formations of mechanics," which occurs in "For the Marriage of Faustus and Helen," Part III. Crane wrote to Yvor Winters in 1927 that the phrase signifies, "as plain as day," war and airplanes. And he added sarcastically that perhaps he should have told his literal-minded readers

13. Horace, *Odes and Epodes,* trans. C. E. Bennett (Cambridge, Mass., 1978), IV: 2.

that the corymbulous formations were "Fokker planes." Crane's defense for this kind of diction is well known. He ostentatiously referred his critics to I. A. Richards' concepts of the poetic "pseudostatement" and the semantic "interanimation of words," which Crane renamed the "logic of metaphor." Crane claimed, essentially, that he was pursuing a sort of linguistic alchemy, generating new concepts by arranging words in novel and sometimes bizarre collocations.[14]

Yet Crane's assignment of a simple, literal referent to his corymbulous formations of mechanics neatly belies his own defense. What the reader perceives in such locutions is neither a new, "unspoken word" being forged in the crucible of pseudostatement, nor a sublime, horizon-bursting percept or ineffable mood struggling toward articulation through the inadequate medium of human speech. What the reader perceives, instead, is the attempt, through high-flown, periphrastic figuration, to endow an ordinary, real-world object—a squadron of warplanes—with a meaning that would not otherwise emerge from the thing itself. Of course, we can say that such endowing is the essential function of tropological diction. Aristotle theorized that the trope or "poetic word" (meaning, in the *Rhetoric* and *Poetics,* virtually any deviant locution) tends to function as an epithet, through which the author predicates his attitude toward the thing he is also naming.[15] Crane's characteristic diction, in *The Bridge,* becomes so hyperbolic that the words interfere with one another, and the "plain" meaning to which they stand as epithet begins to disappear, and sometimes does disappear, beneath the piled-up endowed meaning. Creating a semantic buzz might be appropriate in the context of (and with the expectations appropriate to) a Symbolist lyric, but not in the context of the bardic. Consider this example, from "Cape Hatteras" (warplanes again):

> This tournament of space, the threshed and chiselled height,
> Is baited by marauding circles, bludgeon flail
> Of rancorous grenades whose screaming petals carve us
> Wounds that we wrap with theorems sharp as hail!   (42)

14. Waldo Frank, Introduction (1932) to *The Bridge,* xxxv; Brunner, *Splendid Failure,* 28, 229; Crane to Yvor Winters, May 29, 1927, in *Complete Poems and Selected Letters and Prose,* 246.

15. Aristotle, *The Rhetoric and the Poetics of Aristotle,* trans. W. Rhys Roberts and Ingram Bywater (New York, 1954), esp. *Rhetoric,* Bk. III, and *Poetics,* Chaps. 21–22.

This appears to be a dogfight, but the description is considerably inflated. As Longinus would say—and does say, of an overblown passage from Aeschylus' *Oreithyia*—"the phrasing is turbid, while the images make for confusion rather than intensity." Here, for the sake of comparison (insofar as translation will permit), is the passage Longinus takes to task:

> [says Boreas:]
> Yea, though they check the chimney's towering flame.
> For, if I spy one hearthholder alone,
> I'll weave one torrent coronal of flame
> And fire the steading to a heap of ash.
> But not yet have I blown the noble strain.

According to Longinus, the turbid and confused phraseology in this comparatively clear passage, with its "torrent coronal" and so on, creates the impression of an overstrained attempt at eloquence. In consequence, the utterance falls from the dignified high sublimity expected in a tragedy, and down into ridiculous bathos.[16] If Crane's reader applies this standard of judgment and the expectations and decorums for the bardic to his "tournament of space" passage, there indeed are turbidity and confusion, and the floating singer descends from the empyrean. What, for example, is the reader to make of "threshed and chiselled height"? How far is it possible to think of anything (and especially the sky) as simultaneously "threshed" and "chiselled" without just forgetting what the words mean? And if the passage is evoking the fearful violence of modern warfare, what is the point of shrapnel as "petals"? How can a tournament be "baited" by circles that are also the "bludgeon flail" of grenade bursts? What is a theorem "sharp as hail," and how does one wrap a shrapnel-inflicted wound with it? Crane might be praised, perhaps, for deconstructing the illusion of referentiality. But he is not creating a concise, potent image of modern war, or any war; the effect is vagueness and confusion.

Crane's tournament of space is, in the context of bardic sublimity, a major blunder. Warfare has been, from the eighteenth century onward, a standard object of sublime description. Consider Whitman's more effectively bardic handling of a sea battle in the 1855 *Leaves of Grass*, the John Paul Jones sequence:

16. Longinus, *On the Sublime*, 129.

> Along the lowered eve he came, horribly raking us.
> We closed with him . . . . the yards entangled . . . the
>   cannon touched,
> My captain lashed fast with his own hands.   (67–68)

Or consider Pound's battle imagery in the Malatesta sequence in Canto XI:

> And we beat the papishes and fought
> them back through the tents
> And he came up to the dyke again
> And fought through the dyke-gate
> And it went on from dawn to sunset
> And we broke them and took their baggage.   (48)

In both these passages, short and fragmentary as they are (each from a page-long description), Whitman and Pound are sublime in the traditional sense. Each fully conveys the scope and heroism amid violence of a martial engagement, and a good deal of specific detail. Moreover, each communicates a definite sense of the chaos and confusion of warfare, but neither is confused or confusing. We should also note that both rely on simple and paratactic accumulation.

Here, we might refer once more to Milton. Despite his unpopularity with the modernists, and despite his voice generally not arising from the abysm, Milton also makes good use of catalogic amplification to convey at once the literal detail and the grandeur of the tale he tells. Consider his description of the infernal army mustering in Hell:

> All in a moment through the gloom were seen
> Ten thousand Banners rise into the Air
> With Orient Colours waving: with them rose
> A Forrest huge of Spears: and thronging Helms
> Appear'd, and serried Shields in thick array
> Of depth immeasurable: Anon they move
> In perfect *Phalanx* to the *Dorian* mood
> Of Flutes and soft Recorders; such as rais'd
> To highth of noblest temper Hero's old
> Arming to Battel, and in stead of rage
> Deliberate valour breath'd, firm and unmov'd
> With dread of death to flight or foul retreat,
> Nor wanting power to mitigate and swage
> With solemn touches, troubl'd thoughts, and chase

> Anguish and doubt and fear and sorrow and pain
> From mortal or immortal minds. Thus they
> Breathing united force with fixed thought
> Mov'd on in silence to soft Pipes that charm'd
> Thir painful steps o're the burnt soyl. [17]

Bardic sublimity requires, as most theorists of sublimity have recognized, and as the martial passages from Whitman, Pound, and Milton suggest, a certain degree of rough literality, a simplicity and directness of statement. The swelling, paratactic accumulation of elements in unstable catalog suggests, or adumbrates, the sublime percept. This is not what happens in Crane's "tournament of space" passage, nor is it what happens generally in *The Bridge.*

What the style of *The Bridge* falls into is an apparent tendency toward an overelaborated, figural periphrasis—the "fault" that Longinus called "*parenthyrson.*" As "turbid" diction diffuses and distorts the literal statement it builds upon, the "endowed" or attitudinal meaning begins to seem excessive for its occasion, or (worse) unnecessary or just irrelevant. As Longinus puts it, the poet or speaker indulges in an overdone and seemingly inappropriate emotion: he "subjectively" emotes while the audience, confused by the turbidity of his language, observes but cannot easily understand or share the passion. In consequence, the strain to be "uncommon and exquisite" founders on "the tinsel reefs of affectation." [18] Insofar as Crane's diction in *The Bridge* produces *parenthyrson,* or appears to be strained and willed—insofar, that is, as Crane's tropological excess communicates "febrile, false ebullience" (Frank) or "superficial, exotic glitter" (Brunner)—Crane the would-be Pindaric floating singer has created a disaster. Like Aeschylus in the *Oreithyia,* Crane in *The Bridge* descends from the sublime to something less.

Parenthyrson, in conjunction with the argument and dramatistic structure of *The Bridge,* is the ground of Yvor Winters' view that the poem embodies a "form of hysteria." What the text presents, in the context of Longinian expectations or the governing decorums for bardic discourse, is a speaker who tries to insist upon a tenuous, wishful faith that neither his argument nor the authority of his voice can justify. Further, the speaker knows he has no justification, and resorts (in conse-

17. *Paradise Lost,* I, 544–62, in *The Complete Poetry of John Milton,* ed. John T. Shawcross (Garden City, N.Y., 1971), 265.

18. Longinus, *On the Sublime,* 131–33.

quence) to a feverish, artificial intensity as the means of enforcing what he himself cannot believe. Febrile inflation is the proof to which *The Bridge* resorts. The poet enacts for his available audience a psychic state resembling, or approaching, hysteria fending off disillusion. And if the audience is still sufficiently romantic (as Winters was) to read a poem as an expression of a poet's actual emotions, then *The Bridge* does not enact or represent hysteria. More alarmingly—and Winters was alarmed—it *is* hysteria.

Crane was a poet of major powers; and in the concept of a Pindaric rhetoric, he raises a distinctive possibility for bardic discourse. But the would-be Pindaric bard of *The Bridge* has not succeeded very well with his available audience, because he has failed to take full account of his rhetorical situation. The outcome of that failure demonstrates the real power of generic expectations. *The Bridge* does not sustain or overcome (and perhaps does not even meet) those expectations and, in consequence, develops a disastrous rhetoric that cannot present its readers with a convincing mimesis of bardic utterance, that cannot persuasively achieve bardic authority. *The Bridge,* in sum, is a scene of miscues. Crane's floating singer, viewed through the conventions that the poem does invoke, cannot, as can the bard in Emerson's "Merlin," strike his instrument rudely and hard. All he can do is play more frantically, and in a minor key.

Williams, as we will see, confronts a rhetorical problem that in some respects is like Crane's. The bard of *Paterson* wants to validate a native ethos grounded in a *genius loci,* an ethos fundamentally cut off from the authority in a Poundian or Eliotic tradition. Williams, however, more skillfully works the available stylistic and dramatistic conventions of bardic sublimity. In consequence, he attains a rhetoric more authoritative and more potent than that of Crane. At the same time, Williams' rhetoric distinctly differs from Pound's and opens up a different line of possibility—a counterrhetoric, in fact. Deciding what that counterrhetoric is and what it suggests, of course, must wait upon analysis. However, the rhetoric of American bardism, if it would accomplish a "great psalm of the republic," must advance beyond the partial success of Pound's mantic tragedy, and must avoid Crane's catastrophic floating lyricism. The ultimate question, perhaps, is what you can accomplish—in the context of the modernist conventions for bardic/epic discourse—with a Whitmanian inspiration.

VII.   *Paterson*

Such is the mystery of his one two, one two.
                    —*Paterson,* Book I

Paterson, beginning with Robert Lowell's enthusiastic review in 1947, has frequently been approached not only as a polemical "answer" to Eliot and *The Waste Land* but also as an "anti-*Cantos.*" More specifically, Michael Bernstein sees it as a text designed "to *contest* the fundamental priorities, the entire hierarchy of values" that Pound "celebrates" in his epic poem.[1] This latter view needs substantial revision. The question to ask is *in what way* does Williams' version of the bardic constitute a counterstatement to the Poundian and Eliotic voice of tradition.

In order to define the bardic controversy in which *Paterson* engages Williams' rivals, and to identify the rhetorical *means* of that engagement, we need to consider, first, the general preoccupations and intentions surrounding the invention of *Paterson,* as well as the conventions out of which the Patersonian voice and rhetoric are generated. *Paterson* represents a striking yet problematic effort to speak *through* one rhetoric, or a system of conventions, in order to question or alter the system itself. The bard of *Paterson* meets an audience of fellow literati on its own ground, which is largely Pound's, and attempts to shift it toward another. What this effort implies, ultimately, is a redefinition of the rhetorical means of the sacerdotal enterprise, a means perhaps more commensurate with its ends. And for this reason, the text of *Paterson* is of no little interest.

A place to start is Williams' opinion in a 1932 letter to Kay Boyle that the *Cantos* is the product of "a medieval inspiration" and, as such, no

1. Robert Lowell, "Thomas, Bishop and Williams," *Sewanee Review,* LV (1947), 500–503; Bernstein, *The Tale of the Tribe,* 200.

more than "a pre-composition for us . . . which when later (perhaps) packaged and realized in living, breathing stuff will (in its changed form) be the thing." In this statement, Williams is not, as Bernstein has suggested, talking about *values*; rather, he is talking about *prosody*, Pound's "line," and the problematics of form in modern versification. Williams said to Boyle, "I believe that Pound's line in his *Cantos* . . . is something *like* what we shall achieve." But that line is not what the age requires. The overwhelming concern in the letter—which concludes in a discussion of the "foot" as a "minimal requisite"—is the need to create a poetry commensurate with the age, a poetry "pliable with speech, for speech, for thought, for the intricacies of new thought." And "poetry," Williams insists, is "creation of new form."[2] Insofar as Pound has developed a poetic form that is "something like" the new form for the age, but is not the new form itself, he takes on the sort of status accorded Whitman: he has made a rough but inadequate beginning, and stands as a figure to be at once acknowledged and surpassed. What all this suggests about Williams' stance toward the *Cantos* is a will to contest the form or rhetoric of the bardic undertaking, and not necessarily the central mythologies or codes of value that Pound includes and celebrates.

Williams' early and highly sympathetic reviews of the *Cantos*, written in approximately the same period as the letter to Kay Boyle, reveal what the would-be bard of *Paterson* would not contest. In his 1931 review of *A Draft of XXX Cantos*, and later in his 1935 review of Pound's *Eleven New Cantos*, Williams dramatistically reads the *Cantos* as the representation of an *agon* of sublime consciousness, or of a "movement of the intelligence which is special, beyond usual thought and action." The "basic theme" of this *agon* is, in Williams' view in 1931, the Manichaean struggle of vital "intelligence" against the torpid "closed mind which clings to its power." In 1935 that struggle becomes "Love versus usury, the living hell-sink of today" as embodied in the virtuous struggle of Jefferson and Adams against "blackguards" and "corrupters." Then Williams offers a pseudo-Poundian celebration of C. H. Douglas' economic theories and the Social Credit movement: "When a light breaks and penetrates the binding chaos in which we are sweltering—a name

2. Williams to Kay Boyle, n.d. [1932], in *Selected Letters*, ed. J. C. Thirlwall (New York, 1957), 129–36.

such as that of Douglas in England—it is poetry and Pound hails it not from a spirit of partisanship but as it is, a light from heaven." We should probably note that Williams' hailing of that light has deeper motivations than its appearance in the *Cantos*. As Mike Weaver has pointed out, Williams was intimately involved with the Social Credit movement from its stirrings in 1934 until well beyond its official demise in 1943, and he was familiar with Douglas' writings when Pound first mentioned them to him in 1933. The point is that Williams recognizes and approves of Pound's essential dramatistic strategy in the *Cantos*. Williams sees in Pound's *agon* the same basic oppositions that govern the argument of *In the American Grain*. Further, Pound works out that *agon* through a historical and economic thesis that Williams entirely and enthusiastically agrees with.[3]

Williams, then, has no quarrel with either of the fundamental mythologies that form the ground of Pound's bardic effort. He accepts Pound's historical vision—in its basic terms, at least—as well as Pound's analysis of and prescription for the ills of modern civilization. And he accepts the dramatistically represented struggle of an "intelligence which is special" as the means of bringing the reader into contact with the mythic history the poem includes. Where he differs from Pound is his insistence on a more local or nativistic ground for the memorious historical intelligence commensurate with a truly American ethos. The counterpart to that insistence is his rejection of foreign or "medieval" models for the poetic language and the form in which the bardic struggle should be represented. Indeed, Williams' primary and virtually only criticism of the *Cantos* in his 1931 review is precisely that Pound is stuck within an artificial prosody and diction that run against "the principal move in writing today—that away from the word as symbol toward the word as reality." Pound's language, Williams believes, is forced to strain "with too much violence" toward "slang effects," or toward direct expression of "modernity," because it is trapped in a system of "classic similes and modes," or references and allusions that are essentially antique. Williams writes, "You cannot *easily* switch from Orteum to Peoria without violence (to the language)"—though he does give Pound credit

3. Williams, "Excerpts from a Critical Sketch—*A Draft of XXX Cantos by Ezra Pound*," "Pound's Eleven New 'Cantos,'" in *Selected Essays*, 105–12, 167–69; Mike Weaver, *William Carlos Williams: The American Background* (Cambridge, England, 1971), 103–14.

for sometimes achieving the difficult fusion of "classical beauty" with the "normal accent" of modern American speech.[4]

These observations return us, by and large, to the concerns expressed in the letter to Kay Boyle. The issue, as Williams sees it, is essentially one of poetic technique. Similar concerns appear, and with direct reference to *Paterson*, in subsequent letters. In a letter of 1945, for example, Williams claims that *Paterson* will be his "detailed reply" to the notion—prevalent among his critics, he believes—that art should be a sort of "metaphysics" or the creation of philosophical and symbolic systems. The real objective, as the "Author's Introduction" (1944) in *The Wedge* suggests, is "formal invention" or an original appropriation of the language available in the poet's own world, to achieve an exact, authentic, and intense "expression of . . . perceptions and ardors." These lines of interest resolve, with a certain amount of oversimplification perhaps, in a 1947 letter to Kenneth Burke: "I am trying in *Paterson* to work out the problems of a new prosody—but I am doing it by writing poetry rather than 'logic' which might castrate me, since I have no ability in that medium (of logic)."[5]

We cannot assume that *Paterson*—especially the final text of *Paterson* I through V—is really "all about" prosody, simply because Williams said so in a letter of 1947. Moreover, the question of prosody or poetic technique, for Williams, involves issues that run much deeper than a merely formalistic concern with versification, "measure," or the "variable foot." As Linda Wagner has noted, Williams' technical concerns were grounded on an urge to "reach a public, a public at least partly comprised of actual people"—to create, that is, a poetry that would be high art and, at the same time, would be accessible and communicative for an audience beyond the cloistered circle of a literary priesthood. The audience, however, might still be restricted to vital men of affairs, or latent aristocrats outside Van Wyck Brooks' "creative class." These concerns appear, for example, in Williams' "Caviar and Bread Again"

4. Williams, "Excerpts from a Critical Sketch," in *Selected Essays*, 107. In the 1935 review, however, Williams has nothing but praise for the "technique" of Pound's *Eleven New Cantos*. He saw in Pound's massive transcription of the sentences of Jefferson and Adams a "poetic line" based upon authentic American speech.

5. Williams to Norman McLeod, July 25, 1945, in *Selected Letters*, 238–39; Williams, "Author's Introduction," *The Wedge*, in *Selected Essays*, 257; Williams to Kenneth Burke, n.d., in *Selected Letters*, 257–58.

(1930), wherein he asserts—against the formalism of contemporaries who want to "play tiddlywinks with the syllables"—that technique must be understood as the means of articulating "substance" to an actual world. This assertion accompanies Williams' forthrightly sacerdotal concept of the poet as "leader of the race" when it has "gone astray." As counterpoint is the despairing recognition that modern poetry, a poetry of tiddlywinks, is in general not up to the task. Williams says, "And yet we moderns expect people to actually read us—even to buy our magazines and pay for them with money." Modern poetry, Williams implies, deserves and has no public audience.[6]

This concern appears throughout Williams' career. In a 1939 "interview" with the *Partisan Review*, for example, we find him hoping, perhaps too fondly, that people from "my own suburb" will "surreptitiously" read his works in the public library and "snicker and chortle to themselves in their closets over what I have written saying . . . By God, that's true!" And in an interview on *Paterson*, reprinted in *New Directions* 17 (1961), we see this urge toward an audience raised against what Williams takes to be Pound's aesthetics:

> I've always wanted to fit poetry into the life around us. . . . I want to use the words we speak and to describe the things we see, as far as it can be done. I abandoned the rare world of H. D. and Ezra Pound. Poetry should be brought into the world where we live and not be so recondite, so removed from the people. To bring poetry out of the clouds and down to earth I still believe possible. Using common words in a rare manner will advance the cause of the Poem infinitely. The world will be brought to share the wonders of the Poem. Poetry can be used to dignify life, which is so crass and vulgar.

Reflected here is a concern for audience, or for communication with "the world," in which questions of poetic technique become questions of rhetorical means. By means of a "not . . . recondite" poetry using the world's language, the world will be "brought to" the "wonders of the Poem," or what Williams calls the poet's revealed "perceptions and ardors."[7]

This rhetorical concern is, ultimately, the ground of Williams' criti-

---

6. Linda Wagner, Introduction to *Interviews with William Carlos Williams*, ed. Wagner (New York, 1976), xv; Williams, "Caviar and Bread Again: A Warning to the New Writer," in *Selected Essays*, 102–104.

7. Wagner (ed.), *Interviews with William Carlos Williams*, 62–63. See also Williams, "The Situation in American Writing," *Partisan Review*, IV:4 (Summer, 1939), 41–44; and Williams, "Appendix IV," *New Directions* 17 (1961), 307–10.

cisms of Pound and the *Cantos*. Pound's rhetoric belongs to a hermetic literary world, and for that reason, it is impotent, or "sterile," or ineffective as a vehicle for acting upon the world we actually live in. A version of this concern appears sharply in a 1946 "letter" for the *Briarcliff Quarterly*. Williams attacks the Poundian notion that "the mere environment is just putty," and that the poet-artifex must work from within a tradition—a tradition that presumably will provide conceptions of order, or beautiful designs, to be imposed upon the indifferent "putty." Instead, Williams says, "there may be another literary source continuing the greatness of the past which does not develop androgynetically from the past itself mind to mind but from the present, from the hurley-burley of political encounters which determine or may determine it, direct. . . . We must acknowledge that the origin of the new *is* society, that each society not only originates but fertilizes its whole life, of a piece. . . . If a man in his fatuous dreams cuts himself off from that supplying female [*i.e.,* society], he dries up his sources—as Pound did in the end heading straight for literary sterility." [8] Whatever was vital in the past, Williams here suggests, must still be vital, but in a different form resulting from the dialectic or the politics of actual experience through time. The true source, then, is not Pound's or Eliot's Tradition but the immediate social context, or what Williams calls "that supplying female." The problem of the *Cantos,* to use the language of *Paterson,* is "divorce" and impotence as the bard withdraws from "that supplying female" to his "rare world," followed by the tribe of initiates, exegetes, and students that the *Cantos* requires and creates. What Williams wants, in essence, is a poetry grounded in and commensurate with the actual, sometimes vulgar world the poet inhabits—a poetry that will engage that world's concerns and speak its language, and that will therefore have the power to affect and change it. This concern goes far beyond a simple-minded localism that would merely apply a modernist technique to provincial or suburban subjects. It also goes well beyond a formalistic preoccupation with structures and measures able to accommodate "modern materials." Ultimately, Williams' concern reflects (or reveals) the radically Whitmanesque desire at the root of the bardic project itself: to formulate a public voice, and a public rhetoric, by which the poet may engage and shape the ethical will of "thirty millions of live and electric

8. Williams, "Letter to an Australian Editor," *Briarcliff Quarterly,* III : 2 (October, 1946), 207–208.

men," or "the people," or even an elite of aristocratic vital leaders. In this way, the poet might lead the nation—or "the race"—when it "goes astray."

In sum, then, there seems to be little warrant for the belief that Williams' intent in *Paterson* is to contest the "entire hierarchy of values" that the *Cantos* celebrates. What is truly at issue in Williams' approach to Pound and to the *Cantos* is the question of rhetoric: discovering the means by which the would-be epic bard can engage "the world" and bring it into the vision of "the Poem." As Williams said in 1937, "The poet has to serve and the reader has to—be met and won—without compromise." [9] The bardic poet's job is ethical persuasion, not a "compromised" playing to the audience's uninstructed tastes (*i.e.,* mere entertainment), and not the induction of acolytes into an alienated, yet imperious "rare world" of literature. This latter activity, however, is also a form of persuasion and, as practiced by Pound, a fairly effective one. The fundamental question, perhaps, is what kind of persuasion to pursue. Or, what is at issue between Williams and Pound, in life and in *Paterson,* resolves into how to be an American literatus committed to Whitman's original goals. From this perspective, then, *Paterson* is an "anti-*Cantos,*" or a riposte to the rhetoric of Ezra Pound.

At the root of Williams' revisionary appropriation of the bardic rhetoric, and his reinvention of the bardic voice, is an abiding, dramatistic conception of poetic discourse—the sort of conception that underlies his perceptive and enthusiastic reading of *A Draft of XXX Cantos.* But Williams' dramatism has its own, somewhat un-Poundian inspirations. In 1928, for example, we find him elaborating a Kenneth Burkean theory of invention: "Creations:—they are situations of the soul . . . but so closely (subjectively) identified with life that they become people. They are offshoots of an intensely simple mind. . . . The drama is the identification of the character with the man himself (Shakespeare—and his sphere of knowledge, close to him). As it flares in himself the drama is completed and the back kick of it is the other characters, created as the reflex of the first, so the dramatist 'lives,' himself in his world." [10] Williams, as ever, is none too clear; but in this description of "creations," the general features of an abysmic and indeed polyphonic voice

9. Williams, "The Basis of Faith in Art," in *Selected Essays,* 183.
10. Williams, "entry" for November 24, *The Descent of Winter,* in *Imaginations,* ed. Webster Schott (New York, 1970), 261.

are visible. In the poet's deep self, constituted as his "sphere of knowledge" (the inward image of "his world"), subjective identifications "with life" generate characters or voices who are projections of the poet's sensibility. But the characters are also generated, by an internal necessity, out of one another. The drama's "back kick," Williams says, is the different characters arising as the "reflex of the first." This permits, in theory at least, oppositions and conflicts within the resulting polyphony, and it implies as well the appearance of characters or voices who are not mere projections of the poet's ego. The poet thus can argue with himself as he follows out the (presumably unforeseeable) articulations of an internal dialectic. What he "creates" or adumbrates, ultimately, is a general perception of the world as constituted in his deep, prerational psyche. Because of divisions and complexities, this perception is beyond direct rational statement (*i.e.,* by logicians and philosophers) and therefore is sublime.

This is remarkably close to Kenneth Burke's contemporary notion of "the symbol as a generating principle" in *Counter-Statement.* All of this, as well, is Theory. We need not assume that Burke's or Williams' pictures of the psychic processes of poetic creation actually describe what Williams, Shakespeare, or any other poet really does. Indeed, we need not even assume that Williams strictly believes or disbelieves this picture. The essential point is that Williams identifies and embraces what are, in modernist thought and practice, circulating ideas of the dramatistic, and of dialectical invention. What Williams finds is an available convention for the creation of a dissociated or multivocal deep-psychic voice in a poetic text. Most distinctive is Williams' persistent recognition of and emphasis upon the inherently oppositional or differential nature of the dialectical process. In "Danse Pseudomacabre" (1920), for example, Williams writes, "Everything that varies a hair's breadth from another is an invitation to the dance. Either dance or annihilation. There can only be the dance of ONE." Variations or differences are, Williams suggests, implicitly antagonistic: either they join in "dance," or they annihilate each other. The implied dialectic is a "dance of differences," in which opposed elements preserve their independent qualities, even as they are reconciled in the "oneness" of the dance itself.[11]

11. Kenneth Burke, *Counter-Statement* (1931; rpr. Berkeley, 1968), esp. "The Poetic Process" (45–62) and "Lexicon Rhetoricae" (123–83); Williams, "Danse Pseudomacabre," in *The Farmers' Daughters* (New York, 1961), 210. One wonders how much of the theory in *Counter-Statement* was communicated to Williams, or received from him,

This notion resurfaces, in a new guise, in Williams' *Novelette and Other Prose* (1932), as "conversation as design." This process, he finds, is at work in the paintings of Juan Gris, and he suggests it might be a solution to the problems of the modern novel. A novel based on that principle would be freed from the constraints of conventional narrative and plot and also from what Williams calls, somewhat enigmatically, "a single monotonous repetition like the one hill of Eze [*sic*] continuously repeated without wit." One suspects that the "one hill of Eze" is the *Cantos,* which Williams would eventually criticize as "repetitious, tiresomely the same or positively decayed." In any event, the notion of conversation as design, or of a dialectical dance of difference, provides at least a potential alternative to the basically iterative structure of the Poundian voice—particularly the "case-making" voice of the cantos of the 1930s and 1940s, in which Pound increasingly uses his multiple "voice of tradition" to supply him with "witnesses for the prosecution." Williams' alternative to both conventional narration and the repetitive "one hill of Eze," then, is a rhetoric based on dialectical invention, a rhetoric yielding what *A Novelette and Other Prose* calls "a novel that is pure design." [12]

An urge toward conversation as design is not restricted to Williams' interest in the novel. It is manifest throughout his career—from his early and continuing experiments in drama to the frequent dialogic structures of his prose and the widely noted use of oppositional "tensions" in his lyrics. It is not surprising, then, to learn from Margaret Glynne Lloyd's study of *Paterson* that in Williams' early drafts, the poem begins with a conversation between two figures named Doc and Willie. They represent the poet's internal divisions and the image of the world that constitutes his psyche. Willie is, the drafts suggest, a figure for Paterson and a local Everyman. The subject of their conversation, also not surprisingly, is Doc's "economic thesis." It is probably fortunate, for

---

during their many exchanges (by mail, and over cider at Burke's farm). Burke notes, in a 1953 postscript to *Counter-Statement,* that the original 1931 edition arose from ideas that developed in the late 1920s. Williams' high opinion of Burke is recorded in such early essays as "Yours, O Youth" (1921, in *Selected Essays*) and "Kenneth Burke" (1929, in *Imaginations*). Their friendly association was lifelong.

12. Williams, *A Novelette and Other Prose,* in *Imaginations,* 286–89; Williams, "A Study of Ezra Pound's Present Position," *Massachusetts Review,* XIV:1 (Winter, 1973), 118.

Paterson, that Williams chose to eliminate this passage from the finished text. The naming of the characters is rather heavy-handed, and one suspects that Doc and Willie would have been a disastrous opening for a text meant to rival the *Cantos*. Williams' wise decision to delete, however, does not reflect a fundamental change of plan; if anything, it reflects the author's clarifying what he is up to. The intention and generally dramatistic strategy revealed in the "Doc and Willie" passage are the governing principles of Williams' rhetoric in *Paterson*.[13]

The conventions of dialectical, dissociated voice out of the prerational self are at work in *Paterson,* and the text itself directly appeals to them. In the first place, the notion of the poet's deep psyche as the ground of inventional energy is part of virtually the entire text, if one reads it faithfully as the quest after "rigor of beauty locked in the mind past all remonstrance," which the Preface proposes. The appeal is most explicit in the famous "descent" passage in Book II:3, from which I partially quote:

> No defeat is made up entirely of defeat—since
> the world it opens is always a place
>   formerly
>   unsuspected. A
> world lost,
>   a world unsuspected
>   beckons to new places
> and no whiteness (lost) is so white as the memory
> of whiteness   .
>
> .   .   .   .   .   .
>
> The descent
>   made up of despairs
>   and without accomplishment
> realizes a new awakening   :
>   which is a reversal
> of despair.[14]

13. See James Breslin, *William Carlos Williams: An American Artist* (New York: 1970), 50, 132, 137; and Margaret Glynne Lloyd, *William Carlos Williams' Paterson: A Critical Reappraisal* (London, 1980), 138, and Chap. 4. For another view of Williams' experiments with "conversation as design," see Ezra Pound on the "dialectical ladies" of *A Voyage to Pagany,* in "Dr. Williams' Position," *Literary Essays,* 398.

14. Williams' *Paterson* (New York, 1963), 78. All subsequent references to *Paterson* are to this text.

The poet is to redeem himself, in the "defeat" that his fallen world imposes on him, through retrieval of what abides in buried memory—or what a 1947 essay called the "rare, unblemished area of the first revelation [*i.e.*, of experience] hidden in the secret heart."[15] The "awakening" that results from a descent into memory, then, is the means of discovery. The descent opens up "unsuspected worlds," or what Williams subsequently calls "unrealized hordes" and "new objectives" (77–78). The poet retrieves his vision of desire and, with it, his conceptions of a possible world.

In the next sequence, the poet-hero emerges from his self-communion with the promptings, heard or felt apparently for the first time, of an inner voice:

> Her belly   her belly is like
> a cloud   a cloud
>   at evening   (85)

This is a Venerean urge, what modernist psychology would recognize as the essence of vitally creative will. Significantly, the voice sends the poet-hero "obscurely / in to scribble," and with "a war won," as he sets about revising a "previously written" and somewhat conventional or stale-looking "song" (85–86). If we return to Emerson's account of orphic poetry as "ejaculation of logos in solitude," we can see that Williams' poet-hero has indeed found the way to true poethood. He has, in Emerson's phrase, left the world and come to know his Muse. And if the reader is to accept the dramatic action in *Paterson* II : 3 as a poetic baptism and rebirth, then the reader must, for the sake of the fiction, also accept the premises of this passage. A descent to memory and the release of deep psychic energies, we are asked to believe, is the way to poetic invention. The "descent" passage stands as the authoritative warrant and explanation for what follows it.

According to *Paterson,* the theoretical means of releasing deep psychic energies, the "radiant gist" of the poet's sublime "perceptions and ardors," is form-breaking discontinuity, a flux of symbols resistant to logic, paraphrase, or abstract definition. This is the rhetorical convention I have been calling a Longinian (or neo-Longinian, to be more precise) technique of variation. Williams embraces it virtually throughout his career. Consider, for example, his rather Emersonian pronounce-

15. Williams, "Revelation," in *Selected Essays,* 268.

ment that "there are no 'truths' that can be fixed in language. It is by the breakup of the language that the truth can be seen to exist and that it becomes operative again."[16] In *Paterson,* he appeals to this convention at several points, but it arises most explicitly in the notions of "the nul / [which] defeats it all" (77) and "the radiant gist that / resists the final crystallization" (109). These provide the ground of Williams' oft-cited celebration of "dissonance" (Book IV: 2):

> Dissonance
> (if you are interested)
> leads to discovery   (176)

Through dissonance, or through the breakup of conventionally expected pattern, the ineffable, extralinguistic truths beyond the common mind's hodiernal circle may be revealed or discovered. With this claim, Williams presents no startling breakthrough in aesthetics or poetics, as it is sometimes claimed. Rather, he is aligning himself with a commonplace of his literary generation. More distinctive, perhaps, is his use of this commonplace. As the passage proceeds Williams shifts the concept of dissonance to "antagonistic cooperation" and dialectical invention:

> Love, the sledge that smashes the atom? No, No! antagonistic
>   cooperation is the key, says Levy
>
> Sir Thopas (The Canterbury Pilgrims) says (to Chaucer)
>   Namoor—
>   Thy drasty rymyng is not
>   worth a toord
> —and Chaucer seemed to think so too for he stopped and went
> on in prose   (177)

The reader is asked to see that an antagonistic cooperation, or a conflict of voices, leads to original invention in Chaucer. The figure of Sir Thopas is the "back kick" to the self-image Chaucer has written into the text of *The Canterbury Tales,* and provides Chaucer with a dissociated counterego by which he criticizes himself and to which he responds—"and Chaucer seemed to think so too." The immediate result is formal invention: a switch from the "drasty rymyng" and fixed meters of traditional verse to what is probably, in this context, the more natural or flexible phrase-rhythms of speechlike prose.

16. Williams, *The Embodiment of Knowledge,* 20.

The larger result of Chaucer's self-dispersal in multiple, antagonistically cooperating voices is only implied, but it is visible in Williams' Burkean concept of dialectical invention—as well as in the notion, in *Paterson V,* that a poem presents "a complete little universe" constituting "a view of what the poet is" (224). In Chaucer, Williams suggests, a poetic deep self ramifies itself as an internal dialogue (or polylogue) between competing or antagonistic voices, and that self adumbrates, through its dance of differences, a complex, irreducible perception of the fullness of medieval English society *as it exists in the soul of Chaucer.* Chaucer "lives, himself in his world" through the processes of this internal dialectic. To achieve this adumbration, moreover, Chaucer has appropriated his society's language—English rather than Latin—and he has used, with the breakthrough occasioned by Sir Thopas, prose rhythms rather than the borrowed metrics of Scholastic verse. Chaucer, then, has crystallized an ethos for and of his world by means of a many-faceted voice out of the abysms of his consciousness. Also, like Whitman, Chaucer contains multitudes and can contradict himself. Williams' evocation of *The Canterbury Tales* neatly absorbs Chaucer into the picture of a Whitmanesque bardhood, and at the same time he establishes a key exhibit for the basic convention on which *Paterson* itself is built.

Self-dialectic—a neo-Longinian figure of "question and answer" or "conversation as design"—becomes the means of structuring a bardic *agon* over an entire text. This convention permits Williams to construct a dispersed or dissociated voice that appeals persuasively to ideas of "radical utterance out of the abysms of psyche" and that presents the reader with the voice of a multitude, such as that enacted in the *Cantos.* It also permits him to avoid the appearance of a lyrical hysteria, or *parenthyrson,* that the isolated voice of Crane's floating singer creates. Williams successfully identifies—like Pound, and unlike Crane—the means of constructing a bardic voice endowed with strong credentials in the eyes of a modernist audience. However, Williams' preferred figure accords him somewhat different possibilities than Pound's accorded him. Most significantly, he can more directly exploit the oppositional qualities of an antagonistic cooperation, in order to play out the terms of a controversy, and thereby advance a sort of dramatized argument through the unfolding of his text. By means of self-dialectic, then, Williams can put forth his own conception of the bardic enterprise against Pound's, and at the same time he can engage the same audience or sacerdotal tribe to which the *Cantos* potently speaks. The available means that Williams finds permit him to refute and supplant Pound—and Eliot, for that matter— as an exemplary figure for the American literatus, or the would-be sacerdotal bard. This is what the dance of differences in *Paterson* is largely meant to do.

After its somewhat hermetic epigraph—promising, among other things, "a reply to Greek and Latin with the bare hands" and "a plan for action to supplant a plan for action"—*Paterson I* begins with a question: "'Rigor of beauty is the quest. But how will you find beauty / when it is locked in the mind past all remonstrance?'" (3). Everything that follows is movement toward an answer. But the question itself has two distinguishing features. First, it is a quotation, of strangely unspecified provenance, which asks to be taken as some sort of representative voice: the initiating question seems put to Williams by his world—society, "that supplying female"—or by someone or something in it. This use of quotation allows Williams to suggest that the contractual issue for his text is not merely a private obsession, but instead is a task assigned to him, much as the *nekiya* that begins the *Cantos* is a task assigned to Pound-Odysseus by Venere-Circe. The implied source of Williams' question is a Muse. If the reader accepts the implicit claims to authority and the question the Muse proposes, the issue takes on a measure of seriousness, and even urgency. "Rigor of beauty" is the quest, and the problem is finding a way to "unlock" the mind.

Perhaps most important, Williams' contractual question raises an essentially aesthetic issue, one that contrasts markedly with the implied quest for kingdom-restoring knowledge that begins the *Cantos*. To some extent, Williams' contract parallels the Whitmanesque promise to give to the reader "the origin of all poems." The difference is that Whitman's confident generosity—the calm assumption that he does indeed possess that "origin"—is replaced by a problem, and one that Williams himself does not yet know how to solve. What he has at his disposal, as the immediate response to the question says, are "defective means" (3). This revision of the contractual issue, substituting a problem for a claim, indicates a shift, and indeed a narrowing, in the intended audience of the bardic poem. By opening with an aesthetic issue, Williams explicitly directs himself to an audience of fellow artists or (if we include critics, exegetes, and so forth) fellow members of the "creative class." And Williams presents himself, at the outset, as one who shares their problem, the problem, of discovering how to release the presumed beauty in the mind. Williams, then, postpones the Whitmanesque or Poundian urge to reach the citizen or city-making factive man. He addresses himself instead to the creative tribe on a question of artistic and poetic method.

The response to Williams' contractual question, in the Preface, serves a multiple purpose. It announces a methodological contract for the poem that is to follow:

> To make a start,
> out of particulars
> and make them general, rolling
> up the sum, by defective means.   (3)

Williams promises a catalogic accumulation, or a "phalanx of particulars," adumbrating some ultimate unity. He invokes, that is, a standard convention for American bardic discourse, a convention that holds for readers of Pound as well as of Whitman. The same idea reappears in the closing lines of the Preface:

> from mathematics to particulars—
>
>   divided as the dew,
> floating mists, to be rained down and
> regathered into a river that flows
> and encircles:
>
>   shells and animalcules
> generally and so to man,
>
>   to Paterson.   (5)

The unity that the poem's accumulation of particulars will adumbrate, Williams suggests, is "man"—a consciousness, a sensibility, a generalized ethos commensurate with the public identity of a city. Behind this announcement, and providing (for the proper audience) a certain amount of resonance, lies the Emersonian dictum (in "The American Scholar") that "the main enterprise of the world for splendor, for extent, is the upbuilding of a man." Also behind it is the notion of a Joycean "recorso," the celebrated cyclical structure of *Finnegans Wake*. Thematic recurrences are "regathered into a river that flows and encircles." Williams' methodological contract, then, not only invokes the prevailing conventions for bardic discourse. It also suggests—even if it falsely promises—a text embodying the formal properties admired by the then-dominant new-critical wing of modernist literary thought. Williams appears to engage a critical audience (or a critical stance) with which he has failed throughout most of his career, an audience (and stance) generally more receptive to Eliot, Joyce, and Pound.

This gesture toward a dominant critical attitude is apparent also in Williams' obvious and non-ironic echo of Eliot's *Four Quartets,* and the subsequent appeal to complexity, rather than ideas or knowledge (other than "poetic knowledge" of the textures of human experience), as the ground of literary value:

> For the beginning is assuredly
> the end—since we know nothing, pure
> and simple, beyond
> our own complexities.   (3)

The Preface turns, a few lines later, to an antithesis between literary "craft" and "thought." The latter, Williams asserts, betrays the poet to the closed-minded dogmatism of "minds like beds always made up" and results in "the writing of stale poems" (4). Williams appears, in these passages, to promote the sort of poem, or epic poem, that one version of high modernist taste could admire. In such a poem, "ostensible subjects" and "thought" serve as no more than foils for the virtuoso display of poetic sensibility, or of elaborate craft embodying the complex texture of an act of apprehension (as opposed, typically, to the communication of specific ideas, values, or moralizing "oughts"). A poem of subtle recurrences and intriguing formal complexities is precisely what Randall Jarrell saw in *Paterson I,* according to his highly enthusiastic and influential review in 1946. What Williams' general appeal to formalist aesthetics suggests, I think, is not so much a knuckling-under to prevailing tastes—though it may be partly that—but rather a will to address and succeed with a critical audience whose tastes and expectations Pound and Eliot have largely formed. For the Whitmanesque Williams, who was engaged in a lifelong polemic with the Pound-Eliot axis in modern poetry, this high modernist audience holds assumptions he would change. And to do that, he must first engage them: he must, and he does, meet his readers on their own ground.[17]

However, as Williams says, his text is also to be "divided as the dew," and will include the "obverse" as well as the "reverse." This suggestion quietly introduces the possibilities of a dance of differences, or a dialectical interplay that will render the poem's accumulative processes a cycle of "addition *and subtraction*" (4; emphasis added). The process is not immediately apparent in the Preface, though we see the beginnings of a multiple voice in the general "answer" to the contractual question. Williams' text enacts a self-interruptive progression, playing out each topic until the next one cuts into it, virtually as a non sequitur. Each cutting-in, moreover, can be regarded as the emergence (and intrusion) of a new voice. In the Preface, however, the general effect is probably closer to a composite "choral" voice such as Pound achieves, rather than a dialectical voice dissociated into "back kicks." In other words, Williams' opening voice enacts a discontinuous accumulation, iteratively building up the terms of his methodological contract. And since that contract is for a "rolling up" of unity through particulars and "interpenetrations" (3), the voice meets the terms of the very conventions it appeals to, and thereby its credentials are genuine in the eyes of its intended audience.

As Williams moves with his reader into *Paterson I,* the dissociative processes begin. First, a voice invokes the personification of Paterson as an autochthonous, unrecognized place-spirit:

> Paterson lies in the valley under the Passaic Falls
> its spent waters forming the outline of his back. He
> lies on his right side, head near the thunder
> of the waters filling his dreams! Eternally asleep,
> his dreams walk about the city where he persists
> incognito.   (6)

17. Randall Jarrell, review of *Paterson I,* in "The Poet and His Public," *Partisan Review,* XIII (1946), 493–98. Jarrell was a second-generation new-critical poet. Jarrell's (and Lowell's) interest in Williams, and Tate's continuing lack of interest, suggest that Williams' most persuadable audience consisted of younger high modernists, who were already beginning to react against the literary establishment. The older high modernists (and particularly the southern school), however, remained more fixed in their ways and tastes—constituting, for Williams perhaps, a version of the Eliotic ethos that his own rhetoric polemically opposed. The second-generation poets were the group that Williams could (and did, to some extent) pry away from Eliot, Pound, and Tate.

This reverie, as critics have pointed out, is carried on in rather commonplace romantic terms. It resembles a naïve appropriation of the premise of *Finnegans Wake*—which has been grounds for praise from some of Williams' more enthusiastic readers. At the same time, the reverie is carried on in language with little prosodic interest. The lines are loose, prosaic, and flat—qualities distinct from the laconic spareness of Williams' usual style. If we return to the terms of the Preface, Williams' opening gesture toward the Passaic Falls looks like the beginning of a "stale poem."

But as soon as Williams completes his panoramic gesture toward a city of "automatons" animated by the dreams of a sleeping giant, another and typographically distinct voice cuts in. This one is more terse, more rhythmically punctuated, and less given to easy symbolisms:

> —Say it, no ideas but in things—
> nothing but the blank faces of the houses
> and cylindrical trees
> bent, forked by preconception and accident—
> split, furrowed, creased, mottled, stained—
> secret—into the body of the light!   (6)

This sounds more like a description of an Edward Hopper painting than a romantically animated landscape. The retrospective and oblique criticism shows the previous voice as apparently forcing a standard figure onto things rather than deriving ideas from them. That voice, we are now asked to see, has been "subverted by thought," or by attraction to prepackaged ideas and easy comparisons. That explains, perhaps, its loose prosody, that is, the lack of formal invention.

The second voice, then, is the "back kick" to the first; Williams enacts for the reader the dissociation of a conventional epic voice, or the splitting-off into subsidiary aspects that form oppositions. It is important to note what this enactment does to the reader's perception of the overall voice in which these aspects are contained. The discourse, in effect, is mentalized. The reader is close to the supposed psychic process through which the text exfoliates, and, being thus situated within the consciousness of the poet (*i.e.,* "Williams"), the reader witnesses the emergence of a self-divided voice from the depths of the author's psyche. The voice, at this early stage, is only dual, but eventually becomes multiple. What the reader does not see, in this voice, is an authorial figure talking back to the textual voices in his memory, as in Canto I. Neither of Williams' voices is a locatable, "quoted" text. Instead, the authorial consciousness, or an ego, is in the process of breaking apart into antagonistically cooperative aspects. The discourse of *Paterson* is perhaps sufficiently and persuasively abysmic for a believable bardic voice—to Williams' audience. But the sense of a dissociating ego also suggests a voice that is more frankly and radically enclosed within the mind than is the voice of the *Cantos*. Williams' voice is thus more difficult to imagine as actually "performed" (*i.e.,* spoken or chanted)—despite his preoccupations with the spoken voice, and his efforts to represent it in his shorter poems. The self-interfering voice of *Paterson* suggests a language happening somewhere down in the brain.

But whether or not the reader perceives Williams' version of the mentalized abysmic voice, he or she is carried forward by the opening "dance" of the first two subvoices. As they continue to alternate (or interpenetrate), a sort of counterpoint evolves. Eventually, both aspects of the authorial psyche are meditating on a local place-spirit at the primitive root of all individual minds in Paterson. They meditate, however, in competing terms. The romantic voice develops trite similes ("a man like a city and a woman like a flower" [7]) and elaborates on a nonexistent pristine nature: "The Park's her head . . . Pearls at her ankles, her monstrous hair / spangled with apple-blossoms" (8). The countervoice, meanwhile, tends toward an urbanized ironic humor:

> Twice a month Paterson receives
> communications from the Pope and Jacques
> > Barzun
> (Isocrates). His works
> have been done into French
> and Portuguese. And clerks in the post-
> office ungum rare stamps from
> his packages and steal them for their
> children's albums   (9)

This is not the giant with a "stone ear" who sleeps under the Passaic Falls; this is the citified "Mr. Paterson" whose thoughts can be seen "sitting and standing" in the bus, and whose thought "is listed in the Telephone / Directory." Indeed, he is not so much an object of reverence as he is a sort of patrician figure—the gentleman who goes away "to rest and write" (9)—inviting jokes and petty vandalisms.

What develops from this play of romantic and urban voices is a contest of dictions, which may devalue or undercut specific terms while still affirming the basic percept. There is *something there,* and the text denies validity only to specific verbal formulations. Intruding upon this counterpointed reverie, scraps of prose assert the pressure of an actual, outer world upon the mind: a letter from a would-be poetess (presumably Cress in Book II) who is at odds with society and who is not flowerlike; and an account of the commercial rape of Notch Brook (for pearls) in 1857. These intrusions generate a dialogue between inner and outer experience, complicating relations between the two inner voices. First, Cress demonstrates that the romantic voice is not adequate to the facts; and second, the conventional notion of mercenary exploitation is the cause of nature's lost purity and therefore of Cress's womanly distress. But if the society oppressing her is the product of corrupting mercantile motives, then the urban voice, which is more adequate to actual conditions, must be understood as most probably corrupt also. Williams thus succeeds in sketching out the basic scheme of his historical mythos— namely, the suppression of a vital American "primary culture" by the spirit of a mercantile, puritanically oppressive "effigy culture"—while destabilizing the terms in which this mythos is presented. There is, as the opening sections of *Paterson I* continually suggest, no adequate language. Indeed, within a sublime poetic, there *cannot* be an adequate language for true poetic vision. The reader, then, is engaged with truth but denied a codified dogma, and this denial is largely intended as a demonstration of the poet's veracity. He virtuously refuses to fix upon any particular formulation, so as not to fall victim to the mental cramps of static belief.

But certain dogmas, after all, are in the poem. Williams' celebrated relativized perspective serves to relativize, more than anything else, the force of specific symbologies or dictions while Williams' underlying mythos abides as a "radiant gist that / resists the final crystallization" (109).[18] Thus, in essence, his mythic history hovers in the background of the poem, as an implied presence, or as an assumed ground to which the text sporadically alludes. The reader in this situation is engaged on terms quite similar to the requirements in the *Cantos.* The reader is to be a genial exegete, recognizing or reconstructing (if necessary) the vision of history that informs the poem and underlies its main rhetorical action.

18. See Bernstein, *The Tale of the Tribe,* Chap. 9.

Williams' preferred reader must accept and assume what the poet assumes, in order to be admitted to a communion of understanding with the "special" sensibility revealed through textual process. From one point of view, this built-in reconditeness of Williams' text might be a failure, or a deviation from his frequently stated wish to write a more accessible sort of poetry. It more truly reflects Williams' recognition of his actual audience. *Paterson* is addressed to a literary/sacerdotal tribe and indeed the exegetical cult the *Cantos* engages and creates. Of necessity, Williams speaks the language of this tribe—which is *his* tribe too.

Dispersed and allusive as its presentation is, however, Williams' assumed historical vision is by no means as recondite or inaccessible as is Pound's. Williams' version of the national history is close to a demo-liberal, even Parringtonesque myth of untransacted destiny grounded on the ubiquitous Jefferson-Hamilton antithesis—a standard mythology for Williams' generation (and subsequent generations as well). In consequence, Williams can establish the basic outlines of his history with little more than glancing references, such as the passing mention of Alexander Hamilton (10), whom conventional Jeffersonian typology has made the serpent in the garden of a now-lost Green Republic. The mention of Hamilton, significantly, sets off the topics of "gathering violence" and launches Williams into gestures toward a demented culture, a culture of "Elsies" and decayed families "taken to the hills," whose own minds are foreign to them or "divorced" from their blunted powers of articulation (11–12). This disturbing vision of an inarticulate, deranged society is immediately put into historical perspective. Williams refers to "Jackson's Whites," a "tribe" of half-breed runaways and exiled criminals running wild, during the colonial period and after, in the woods around the Ramapos (the place of origin of the inarticulate Phyllis in the opening segment of Book IV). With the advent of Hamilton, it seems, the national mind begins to go to seed. And there are throughout the text an assortment of inadequate, distorted, suffering people, among whom the outstanding figures are, in Book I, Mrs. Cumming and Sam Patch. They both succumb to pointless tragedy because they lack an adequate language and misinterpret the promptings of their own minds.[19]

Lack of an adequate language, then, yields distortion—the disasters

19. See James Breslin's discussion of Mrs. Cumming and Sam Patch, in *William Carlos Williams*, 177–78.

of history, brutalized consciousness, and the perversions and uglinesses of modernity. The text invites us to assume that this lack is caused by the repressive, puritanical agencies whose presiding figures in *Paterson* are Hamilton and Carrie Nation, the "American Artemis" (Book IV, p. 180). This vision of effigy culture's harmful agencies comes to focus, in Book I, with references to sequestered, private wealth "in time of general privation": a house with a private dairy, an empty swimming pool, uncut and unexhibited hothouse orchids, and a "special French maid" whose only duty is to groom the sleeping Pomeranians (33). The point is that the wealth is applied to no social benefit; it is torpid and self-concerned, and represents nothing more than the general loss or the witholding of what is needed elsewhere. Against this, Williams sets Cornelius Doremus, an old-time agrarian yeoman, who left to his heirs (in 1809) a working farm and a collection of personal goods, the catalog of which reads like the penny-wise accounting-lists in *Walden*. The point of the contrast is clear. Old Cornelius Doremus represents the virtues of wealth applied in proper measure—there is no private luxury hoarded "in time of general privation." As a virtuous yeoman, he represents also the thwarted, true America of standard Jeffersonian mythology. This example of vanished sensibility leads Williams to a declaration of the focal "stasis" of his historical argument:

> Who restricts knowledge? Some say
> it is the decay of the middle class
> making an impossible moat between the high
> and the low where
> the life once flourished   .   .   knowledge
> of the avenues of information—
> So that we do not know (in time)
> where the stasis lodges. And if it is not
> the knowledgeable idiots, the university,
> they at least are the non-purveyors
> should be devising means
> to leap the gap. Inlets? The outward
> masks of the special interests
> that perpetuate the stasis and make it
> profitable.
>
>   They block the release
> that should cleanse and assume
> prerogatives as private recompense.   (34)

This is the germ of an outright Poundian conspiracy theory. "Special interests," identified with "the university" and "sequestered wealth," block the release of knowledge and thereby suppress the flowering of a vital culture, in the pursuit of "private recompense." The "general privation," then, is the intentional creation of the "special interests." And the historical "stasis" is capitalistic pursuit of wealth versus a flourishing culture based on vital sensibility—the sort of sensibility that seems latent in Cornelius Doremus (and George Washington, who also appears in Book I), but that has been suppressed, deflected, or perverted.

Williams' historical argument is further expanded in the subsequent books of *Paterson*—additional elements arise, as it were, from the ongoing dialectic. In Book II, for example, prose intrusions on Hamilton's creation of the national debt, and his plan to stimulate industry as a means of creating a tax base to pay the debt, lead directly to a Poundian definition of the Federal Reserve as a "Legalized National Usury System" (67–74). Williams includes a gesture toward the end of the republic, though, he suggests, the republic is not *quite* ended:

> The bird, the eagle, made himself
> small—to creep into the hinged egg
> until therein he disappeared, all
> but one leg   (73)

And this leg, as Williams says, "would not . . . remain inside" (73). So the nearly born republic has gone back, unwillingly, into its egg—where it persists—because of a Hamiltonian usury system under which the people (the tax base) pay the interest charges, thereby enriching the banks. The consequence, we are clearly meant to see, is sequestered wealth and general impoverishment. We must, I think, take this argument as one that Williams seriously intended. It accords with what we know to be his actual private opinions; and in *Paterson,* this somewhat paranoid-seeming vision prepares the ground for Williams' lengthy and unequivocal celebration, in Book IV : 2, of Social Credit as " 'the radiant gist' against all that / scants our lives" (186). Williams says, in a sort of summing-up,

> Money sequestered enriches avarice, makes
> poverty: the direct cause of
> disaster   .
>   .   .   .   .   .

```
         .    the cancer, usury. Let credit
out       .         out from between the bars
before the bank windows
              .    credit, stalled
in money, conceals the generative
that thwarts art or buys it (without
understanding), out of poverty of wit        (182–83)
```

The validity, or probable invalidity, of Williams' economic thesis need not concern us. The point is that Williams appropriates the demo-liberal mythology of his intended audience, and joins with Pound's extension of that mythology into an economic thesis that implies a prescription for the ills of modernity. On these topics, Williams shares agreement with his tribe and with his bardic rival: he is establishing the middle ground on which persuasion can occur.

A significant feature of Williams' historical and economic argument is that as a system of sporadically invoked assumptions, it provides a direct link to the aesthetic or rhetorical issues that become the major ground of controversy. In the passage just quoted, stalled credit, Williams says, "conceals the generative" and "thwarts art." The result is a nonvital effigy culture that buys the art its impoverished wit cannot produce or even understand. Art is thus a sort of "vicarious" merit badge or "blue ribbon" (183) representing economic status. And the live arts, in turn, are thwarted by a general lack of interest and support. References to this situation, and examples of it, occur throughout the text. In the beginning of Book III:2, for example, Williams offers the observation that, for the poet, "the being / in a position to write (that's / / where they get you) is nine tenths / of the difficulty" (113). Amply illustrating this claim are the letters by the desperate Cress, which disturb the poet's progress in Book II, and the case of an impoverished woman writer in Denmark, reported (apparently) by Edward Dahlberg in Book V. In Book III:2, moreover, Williams' self-divided poet-hero himself faces isolation and incomprehension. The "fury" of his writing finds no audience, or meets an audience unable or unwilling to understand:

```
—the cyclonic fury, the fire,
the leaden flood and finally
the cost—

Your father was *such* a nice man.
I remember him well        .
```

> Or, Geeze, Doc, I guess it's all right
> but what the hell does it mean?   (114)

"[B]eing in a position to write" is "where they get you." And being in that position, the text of *Paterson* suggests, means in large part having an adequate audience, or a society in which the now-stalled "generative" or creative will is active and available for poetic articulation. Only in such a case, apparently, can the poet-sacerdote, or the artist, lead society forward to the attainment of a high civilization, of a vital and aristocratic culture. In principle, then, socioeconomic reformation—in this text, Social Credit as an antidote to usurious industrial capitalism—is a necessary precondition for a truly sacerdotal art, or a truly great art of any kind.

Williams' dispersed argument deals with the existence in the national mind (or the mind of Paterson) of an abiding but repressed primary culture, a native American sensibility grounded in vital apprehension of experience. In Book I, Williams calls this furtive, inexpressible vision of desire the "first beauty" or the "first wife." And what opposes or represses this "generative" urge toward "marriage" with vital reality is effigy culture: the culture of Hamilton, usurious banks, imported art, aesthetic insensitivity, sexual taboo, and corrupt scholastics blocking knowledge for the sake of the "special interests." Socioeconomic reform would "release the generative" and allow articulation of the Venerean urge toward "marriage" with the "first beauty"—"the temple upon / the rock" (23). The temple is the aesthetic, sacramental gesture that necessarily falls short of adequacy (because experience forever escapes our attempts to trap it in names), and that needs continual renewal. That, too, is standard modernist (and Emersonian) dogma. But the general outcome of a society turned toward its vision of beauty, a society that will raise a temple upon the rock, is what Williams calls "the Parthenon" (184), the "splendor of renaissance cities" (186). Williams is not suggesting ersatz Greek temples and campaniles as an image of the desirable. He is gesturing toward the notion of a revitalized American culture led forward to expression by its artists, and thereby crowned with the sort of aristocratic grace that previous high civilizations have attained. He is gesturing, in short, toward an untransacted destiny in which the artist/literatus has a crucial role.

All this is, we must remember, commonplace modernist dogma—a code of belief established in the mind of Williams' contemporary audience and, indeed, in the disciples the *Cantos* generates and *Paterson* inherits. The essential gist of this mythology is available from sources at least as early as Van Wyck Brooks's *America's Coming-of-Age* (1915): "In the back of [America's] mind lies heaven knows what world of poetry, hidden away, too inaccessible . . . to serve, as the poetry of life should serve, in harnessing thought and action together, turning life into a disinterested adventure." Between 1915 and 1921, Brooks argues for a (somewhat vague) socialism as the means of releasing the buried "poetry in the mind," and of arriving at a national culture of aristocratic distinction and radiant, even world-redeeming beauty.[20] Williams, then, is appropriating a well-established mythology—by 1946, a well-aged mythology—that forms the non-controversial ground of his text. And the key point, for Williams as for Brooks, is that the poetry or "rigor of beauty" hidden in the national mind is, after all, too inaccessible. The vital essence of the true national ethos is suppressed and smothered, and the artist (or literatus) thus loses his essential function. He is cut off from the sort of live society that would be both the source and the audience of highly developed art. And because the distorted culture around him is so inarticulate, he has no available language adequate to his own vital urge, "a sort of springtime" that is, the poet feels, "ice bound" within himself (36). All that remains for him is his frequently iterated defeat or despair, made poignant or distressing by his sense of unrealized but latent possibilities, as in Book III:

> What end but love, that stares death in the eye?
> A city, a marriage—that stares death
> in the eye
>
> [but]
>
> .   .   .   a world of corrupt cities,
> nothing else, that death stares in the eye,
> lacking love: no palaces, no secluded gardens,
> no water among the stones; the stone rails
> of the balustrades, scooped out, running with
> clear water, no peace.   (106, 107)

The reference here is to the Alhambra (or, more specifically, to its gardens). The Alhambra is one more version of the temple upon the

20. Van Wyck Brooks, *America's Coming-of-Age*, in *Three Essays on America*, 30, 109–11.

rock, an articulate embodiment of noble consciousness, which serves to define and distinguish an entire culture. But in the Alhambra's place, Williams sees nonlove or "divorce"—the "sign of knowledge in our time" (18)—and corrupted cities, in which finding an adequate language, "releasing the generative," often seems quite unlikely.

Williams' assumed argument brings us back to the stasis of his contractual question: *how* to release the "rigor of beauty" that seems to be "locked in the mind past all remonstrance." The aesthetic issue has arisen from the poet's vision of untransacted destiny. In consequence, that issue is also to be addressed in the context of the vision, or the problematic stasis it implies. Because of his supposed situation in history, the poet of *Paterson* necessarily has only "defective means" at his disposal. He is, his Preface suggests, a lame, three-legged dog; there are a lot of four-legged dogs who have "run out." These, implicitly, are Pound and Eliot (or their like), who have found an available poetic language, or a workable cultural tradition, but at the cost of becoming Europeanized and abandoning the American problem. This felt situation provides the basis of the poet's self-dissociations and antagonistic cooperations. He enacts the movement of a "special intelligence" toward a resolution of the aesthetic problem and through the deep-psychic world image that constitutes the origin of his abysmic, dialectical voice.

As *Paterson* exfoliates, its dissonant interplay of voices begins to adumbrate the fundamental antagonisms that determine the poem's rhetorical force. Probably the first clear development in this direction occurs at the close of Book I : 2 and the beginning of Book I : 3, when the poet receives and responds to the accusatory letter from E. D. (Edward Dahlberg). The thrust of E. D.'s letter is that Williams (or "Mr. Paterson") fails to measure up as an American poet because he makes a distinction between art and life, and therefore cannot respond to "the head and the heart that ached in the land, that you are not" (29). E. D.'s letter, however, is also crammed with "classic" allusions—to the Bible, to Unamuno and Goethe, for example—and with stereotyped, arch-sounding language: "It matters not so much how a man lies or fornicates or even loves money, provided that he has not a Pontius Pilate but an hungered Lazarus in his intestines" (28). E. D., in short, is attacking Williams from the position of a cosmopolitan, Euro-American (and essentially Christian) tradition, to which he evidently gives unquestionable authority. Williams' response is both an answer to E. D. and a restatement of the accusation:

> How strange you are, you idiot!
> So you think because the rose
> is red that you shall have the mastery?
> The rose is green and will bloom,
> overtopping you, green, livid
> green when you shall no more speak, or
> taste, or even be. My whole life
> has hung too long upon a partial victory.   (30)

At issue is a matter not so much of "mastery" but of American poethood.
E. D. speaks from a developed tradition, the "red rose"; Williams speaks
from a "green" and undeveloped one. Which can claim to speak for "the
head and the heart that ached in the land"? But at the same time,
Williams seems to admit the fault of dividing art from life—in the
pursuit of mastery, the finished aesthetic object, the red rose cut and
displayed. The red rose is a partial victory, because the vital essence of the
rose is in the "green, livid green" plant from which it has emerged (or
will emerge).

Then a narrative voice intrudes:

> He picked a hairpin from the floor
> and stuck it in his ear, probing
> around inside   (30)

The reader's perspective shifts to the poet's self-image. He stares at the
linoleum and lets his imagination "soar"

> to the magnificence of imagined delights
> where he would probe
>
> as into the pupil of an eye
> as through a hoople of fire, and emerge
> sheathed in a robe
>
> streaming with light   (31)

It is doubtful that this soaring is to be taken seriously; it looks more like
a withdrawal into self-indulgent (and self-aggrandizing) romantic fantasies. Soaring, after all, is the opposite of descent. E. D.'s accusation is
largely true, though garbed in a suspect language. The poet's fantasies,
moreover, fail to reach the sublime heights toward which he aspires. The
narrative voice asks, "What heroic / dawn of desire / is denied to his
thoughts?" (31) and then moves the reader toward an image of trees
"from whose leaves streaming with rain / his mind drinks of desire" (31).

But the trees, acquiring voice, become another "back kick" and deny the poet's aspired-to heroic dawn:

> Who is younger than I?
>   The contemptible twig?
> that I was? stale in mind
>   whom the dirt
>
> recently gave up? Weak
>   to the wind.
>   .   .   .   .   .
>
> A mere stick that has
>   twenty leaves
> against my convolutions.
>   What shall it become,
> Snot nose, that I have
>   not been?   (31–32)

This tree-voice speaks as E. D. does—from an established, convoluted, and in fact still-living tradition—and denies the value of the Paterson-poet's "green" beginnings. The poet's detached imagination, this voice suggests, is culturally groundless,

> too narrow to be engraved
>   with the maps
> of a world it never knew,
>   the green and
> dovegrey countries of
>   the mind   (30)

The question that emerges here is about "roots"—since "Everybody has roots" (31)—and whose are better. An important feature of this tree-voice is that, unlike the letter from E. D., it arises from the mind of the poet-hero and, by implication, the mind of the author as well. He is divided against himself, enthralled by the mystique of traditional (*i.e.,* European) high culture and its claims to authority, even as he steadily resists it. His choice is between a realized, complete, yet *external* cultural source, and one that is truer and more native, but that may be irretrievably lost within the mind, and poetic suicide to pursue:

> Moveless
> he envies the men that ran
> and could run off

> toward the peripheries—
> to other centers, direct—
> for clarity (if
> they found it)
>   loveliness and
> authority in the world—
>
> a sort of springtime
> toward which their minds aspired
> but which he saw,
> within himself—ice bound
>
> and leaped, "the body, not until
> the following spring, frozen in
> an ice cake"   (36)

The body is that of Sam Patch, whose stunt-leaping from the falls ended fatally because "speech had failed him . . . The word had been drained of its meaning" (17). A similar fate awaits the poet who would leap into the roar of his own mind without an adequate language. Yet the alternative, for the represented poet of *Paterson,* is unacceptable.

The grounds of this unacceptability are suggested in Book I: 3. Williams meditates on the traditional sources of "loveliness and authority in the world" and intersperses references to the chief redoubts of effigy culture—the university and (behind it) the world of sequestered wealth, imported art, and aesthetic insensitivity. In consequence, the voice or voices in the poet's mind that counsel traditionalism begin to represent a sort of Tory culture in the soul, a culture that looks to a collection of European heirlooms ("the maps of a world it never knew") as its source of beauty and authority. Williams takes this to be the culture of Pound and Eliot (and the other four-legged dogs). It has admittedly strong claims to superiority, but the literary patriot is obliged to resist it, in the interest of releasing the "springtime" frozen or trapped in his soul by the absence of an adequate language and culture. And since Tory culture is, in the poet-hero's mind, the presence that discourages the raw beginnings of a native, autochthonous language/culture—the convoluted tree that denies the contemptible twig—it constitutes the very ice in which his springtime is bound. The Tory voice of traditionalism is revealed, in consequence, as the voice of effigy culture, corrupt and corrupting.

Williams thus uses the dissociations of his voice to represent himself as a cultural patriot, faced with a powerfully antagonistic "back kick" in his own mind. The struggle between himself and the expatriate axis of Pound and Eliot for the status of American poethood is aligned with (or grounded on) the basic antagonisms of his mythic history—primary versus secondary or effigy culture, Patriot versus Tory, Jeffersonian republicanism versus Hamiltonian usury, Venerean vitalism versus Puritan restriction. For the reader who accepts Williams' underlying mythos—the reader most directly addressed by *Paterson*—the implicit appeal of these alignments is necessarily powerful. The patriot in Williams' self-divided sensibility becomes the hero in the dialectic, and the intended reader has some interest in seeing him prevail. Yet the Tory voice within this dialectic *is* authoritative, and the poet of Book I remains unable to completely overcome it:

> P: Your interest is in the bloody loam but what
> I'm after is the finished product.

> I: Leadership passes into empire; empire begets in-
> solence; insolence brings ruin.
>   Such is the mystery of his one two, one two.   (38–39)

"P," the genial exegete will recognize, is Pound. In 1946, both Williams and his tribal audience had ample evidence of the disastrous consequences of Pound's "empery" and "insolence," as the retort of "I" (Isocrates?) suggests.[21] Pursuit of authority and finished products may, and apparently sometimes does, betray the poet to ruin. Yet the attempt to do without the authority of an established tradition, Williams has suggested, may also lead to the disasters inherent in the lack of adequate language, namely, fatal immersion in the stream of the present, to which the death by drowning of Sam Patch and Mrs. Cumming figurally

21. Isocrates does, in his celebrated *Panegyricus,* advance a similar argument against the Persian Empire. At the height of their "insolence and power," the Persians saw fit to invade Europe, and they suffered ruin and humiliation at the hands of the "autochthonous" Athenians. The Persians' fate is not unlike that of the fallen Pound of Pisa and St. Elizabeths: "They were glad, by the most mortifying concessions, to purchase a dishonorable peace . . . [and they] waited in anxious and uncertain hopes of ever repairing their misfortunes" (Robert W. Connor [ed.], *Greek Orations* [Ann Arbor, 1979], 33). If Williams is using Isocrates here—and Isocrates is, as *Paterson* tells us, one of the correspondents of "Mr. Paterson" (9)—then Williams' refutation of Pound's borrowed authority is clearly compromised, since Isocrates is himself a borrowed authority (and his argument, in some sense, a prefabrication).

correspond. A refutation is begun, but it cannot be completed yet. Williams' "one two, one two" between the American poet-hero and competing Tory versions of himself emerges as the focal *agon* of the text. It appears to generate itself by an internal necessity arising from the latent tensions in the mind of the author. The represented bard of *Paterson* is caught, in Book I at least, in an unresolvable self-dialectic that comprises the contradictions and antagonisms of his world.

In Williams' rhetoric, a mythic history is the assumed ground of agreement between himself and his tribal audience, and a dissonant self-dialectic is the means of creating a persuasively abysmic, multiple voice that opens up a controversy between competing notions of American poethood. The advantages of this rhetoric are clear. In the first place, the controversy does not sacrifice Williams' claims to genuine poeticity in the eyes of his modernist reader. He is no browbeating case maker devoted to what the modernist aesthetic typically damns as "rhetorical self-assertion." He appears as one committed to disinterested revelation of the truth of experience, or what Emerson would have called "a man in alliance with truth and god," even as he rhetorically asserts his particular (if problematic) version of the American literatus. The rhetoric of *Paterson* permits Williams, quite ingeniously, to have it both ways.

In addition, the dramatistic possibilities of Williams' internal dialectic permit the importation of an intentionally constructed plot, namely, the sentimental education represented in the poet-hero's *agon* of sensibility, into what is, according to standard American epic decorum, an open-ended process. Moreover, with the mentalizing of his self-divided voice, Williams is able to introduce a narrative voice by which he comments on his own self-image, or even on the internal dialectic itself. He thereby creates overt narrative structures that do not appear as conventional narration. Such an appearance would almost certainly reduce the claims of his voice (in the mind of Williams' intended reader) to orphic status. In effect, the reader is presented with a deep psychic "movement of the intelligence," in which a narrative can arise, as if spontaneously, from the processes of dialectical invention. We are asked to see a narrative passing through the represented poet's mind, in the moment of invention/discovery.

This process is perhaps most visible in *Paterson II* as Williams meditates on a day in the park. More specifically, he represents himself thinking of himself (or of "Paterson" the poet, a transparent self-image) as he passes in imagination among the Sunday park-goers, listens to an evangelist's harangue, and goes home, finally, to write. What emerges from this abysmic narrative—in which the perspectives are those of the imagining author and of the imagined alter-ego—is affirmation of the positive side of Williams' controversy with the voices of tradition. There is, at the same time, reiteration of the poet's problem. In Book II:1, and particularly in the climactic hilltop vision of an archaic Mary dancing and spilling wine (56–57), Williams' poet-hero discovers an abiding but blunted Venerean energy in the "vulgar" pleasures of the "great beast" of the people, and is thus assured that a vital source remains available within the depths of the common mind. In Book II:2, however, he finds himself still "blocked." The causes are represented in the evangelist's harangue on the evils of money and in the account of the Federal Reserve as a "Legalized National Usury System." In Book II:3, he seeks to escape his blockage through "descent" into the vital core that his hilltop vision has assured him he will find (and he does find it). The narrative development is fairly straightforward as is the illustration of Williams' argument with Pound and Eliot. At the same time, however, that development is dispersed into the competing voices of Williams' inner dialectic and is therefore not so obviously straightforward.

In Book II:3, Williams' poet-hero emerges from his descent, and goes in to write, with what is declared "a war won"; but the unfolding of his story shows that he still is less than victorious. There are, as counter-evidence, the intrusive and accusatory letters from Cress, which suggest that he still holds the aesthetizing art/life distinction, as E. D. previously accused. There is also the evident disparity between the poem he is shown to write (or revise) and the inner voice that he has heard:

> On this most voluptuous night of the year
> the term of the moon is yellow with no light
> the air's soft, the night bird has
> only one note, the cherry tree in bloom
> makes a blur on the woods   (86)

There are three stanzas of such dreamy and detached imagery. As was true of the romantic voice that began Book I, the prosody is flaccid and dull. The inner voice, however, has a more spontaneous rhythmic energy, more of what Williams would call "measure" or "formal design":

"Her belly   .   her belly is like a white cloud / white cloud at
evening   .   before the shuddering night!" (86). The flatness
of the written poem and the vitality of the inner voice suggest that
the poet-hero is not yet writing what he hears, or does not yet have
a language commensurate with his inner will-to-speak. His poem
is of a piece with the dulled pursuit of desire that he witnessed in the
park: it is poetry with the right motive, but "stale poetry" all the same.
The represented poet-hero is trapped within the stasis of Williams'
history.

The problematics of the poet's situation, as defined by *Paterson,* do
not affect only the poet-hero represented in the text; to a large degree,
they affect the rhetoric of the text itself. Since Williams' historical
argument denies the availability of an adequate language or an established tradition, the dialectic of the poem tends to work against the
emergence of a voice accorded the strong declarative authority available
to Pound. In *Paterson,* most of Williams' subvoices are subject to an in-
cessantly ironic relativization. So he frequently cannot rise persuasively
to the lyric grandeur that the *Cantos* sometimes reaches. This is true even
in passages where Williams might want to endow a stance with strong
emotional force. We see this in the passage on "invention":

> Without invention nothing is well spaced,
> unless the mind change, unless
> the stars are new measured, according
> to their relative positions, the
> line will not change, the necessity
> will not matriculate: unless there is
> a new mind there cannot be a new
> line, the old will go on
> repeating itself with recurring
> deadliness   (50)

And Williams goes on, reiterating the phrase "without invention." This
is a curious passage. In the first place, it reflects what we know (from
external evidence) to be his actual position. Indeed, this is crucial for his
refutation of traditionalism and eventually for his advocacy of "measure"
(Book V). And in the second place, the passage attempts to achieve the
litanylike insistence of Pound's usura canto. However, this voice cannot
assume, as did Pound's, the resonant authority of a composite voice of

tradition, because the rhetoric of *Paterson* already denies the availability of such a tradition. Further, the intended point of this passage is made ironic (intentionally or not) by a diction and a scheme that are so obviously, imitatively, reminiscent of Pound's. Perhaps the thesis of the passage is meant to render ironic the *style* in which it appears, thereby implicitly and satirically criticizing the *Cantos*. In any case, the passage cannot claim the status of an unequivocal declaration, and it cannot (or will not) rise to the sort of soaring, apostrophic intensity that Pound sometimes attains, because it is caught within the ironies and the resulting tensions of the text. Indeed, any particular voice has extreme difficulty in rising above the dialectical antagonisms of the Patersonian rhetoric. In consequence, anything resembling high eloquence tends not to be available.

Williams' self-divided, multiple voice, then, takes on a somewhat paradoxical status. The voice as a whole has authority, when judged in terms of the conventions it appeals to. Yet particular voices within the dialectical process tend to be subverted by the tensions and oppositions of the "dance of differences." Indeed, the ironic deflation of particular voices and the short-circuiting of gestures toward high eloquence are in large measure the means by which the general voice acquires its credentials as a locus of poetic truth. The voice breaks down verbal codes or dictions in the interest of embodying or suggesting the ineffable vision of desire, the Emersonian "flying Perfect," toward which the poet appears to continually move. But while Williams thus has the ambiguous advantage of meeting conventional notions of poeticity in his modernist readers, he has no power to declare for particular values or "perceptions and ardors" with strong pathos. And in consequence, as every rhetorician knows, he lacks the ability to generate in readers the strong conviction that will cause them to act on ideas. Williams' self-dialectic risks impotence as an instrument for changing or affecting the sensibilities and real preferences of its intended audience.

A central problem in the Patersonian rhetoric is thus to discover a less equivocal voice that can escape the self-ironic pulling and hauling of Williams' "antagonistic cooperations." And such a voice does eventually emerge. Its root is the narrative voice that Williams periodically introduces, one that generally offers reliable and neutral commentary. Most of this commentary, in *Paterson,* reports the narrative situation—for example, when the poet-hero is shown (in Book I) to envy the poets who "ran off," or when his physical position and movements in the park are given (in Book II). In the "descent" passage in Book II, however, Williams introduces a commentary that provides a code of value by which the represented poet's subsequent action can be understood. The action stands as illustration or application of the thesis that the commentary proposes. Nothing undercuts this reliable voice: its diction and prosody (and typography) identify it as "original" to the mind of the author, and its emergence from a detached, narratival perspective removes it from the dialectic's process toward ironic leveling. This passage marks the first really distinctive emergence in *Paterson* of an "authorized" voice. The voice rises from the pulling and hauling, yet largely transcends and overlooks it, while absorbing much of its authority. The voice speaks for the well-credentialed poetic intelligence from which the overall dissociated voice emerges. Indeed, the "descent" passage lacks this persuasive authority in its appearance in *Selected Poems* as an individual lyric. Its real power derives from the way it resonates with, and speaks for, the dialectical consciousness that forms its ground.

But since the dialectic of the text provides the ground of Williams' authority—and hence the authority of the narrative and commentative voice—that process must work itself out before the authorized voice can come to center stage and freely operate, as it noticeably does in Book V. In Books III and IV, Williams confronts and eliminates the claims of his inward voice of tradition. In Book III, the imagined poet-hero is ensconced in the library, where he seeks to drown the roar of his own thought in a "roar of books," which, paradoxically, induces "Beautiful Thing" to assert itself through the interstices of his distracted attention. The story that develops shows him alternating between the desire to yield and let his voice be absorbed into the voices of the books, and the opposed desire to directly possess his "Persephone gone to Hell" and maintain a resistant separateness amid the cacophony. This results in at least four major voices: the narrative voice ("And as his mind fades, / joining the others, he / seeks to bring it back" [101]); the "ghostly" voice addressing "Beautiful Thing" (issuing from a "vague outline" that the poet-hero glimpses over his right shoulder [98]); the book voice invading the poet-hero's mind ("O Thalassa, Thalassa! / the lash and hiss of water // The sea! // How near it was to them! // Soon! // Too soon" [101]); and the voice of the poet-hero himself, reflecting on his own ambivalent condition:

> Say I am the locus
>> where two women meet
> One from the backwoods
>> a touch of the savage
>> and of T.B.
>> (a scar on the thigh)
> The other—wanting,
>> from an old culture   .   (110)

Clearly, the backwoods woman—in what the context implies is a lesbian encounter—is a version of "Beautiful Thing," who is always in her actualizations somewhat damaged:

> I must believe that all
> desired women have had each
>> in the end
>> a busted nose
> and live afterward marked up
>> Beautiful Thing
>> for memory's sake
> to be credible in their deeds   (127)

At the same time, the other woman "from an old culture" is identifiable with the voices of the books:

> (They do not yield but shriek
>> as furies,
> shriek and execrate the imagination, the impotent,
> a woman against a woman, seeking to destroy
> it but cannot, the life will not out of it)   .   (102)

The play of voices in Book III thus further amplifies the poet's ambivalent attraction to the aesthetics of effigy culture, which appears to possess his "Beautiful Thing" in an unnatural and corrupting embrace. Indeed, through this aesthetic, he could also possess a corrupted "Beautiful Thing," if he would buy into it. But he is also attracted to "Beautiful Thing" her/itself. In consequence, a sort of love triangle develops between the major dissociated aspects of the poet's mind.

Book III also includes a refutation of the library aesthetic and provides the basis for the poet-hero's repudiation of the book-voices. The so-called counterpoetics in Book III have been discussed at some length, and recently by Joseph Riddel.[22] So I need make but few comments. First, the counterpoetics are not really "counter" at all; rather, they amount to an evocation of Emersonian as well as modernist common-places. This is clear in what Riddel apparently regards as a crucial passage:

> We read: not the flames
> but the ruin left
> by the conflagration
>
> . . . .
>
> Dig in—and you have
> a nothing, surrounded by
> a surface, an inverted
> bell resounding, a
>
> white-hot man become
> a book   (123)

The book, then, is only an "ash," a trace left behind by the original "fire" of poetic inspiration—what Williams once called "the track of some-thing which has passed." Behind this idea stands Emerson's dictum (in "The Poet") that "Art is the path of the creator to his work," or that which reveals the movement of an inspired intelligence toward its un-graspable vision of the "flying Perfect." The book can only suggest the inspiration that caused it, of which it is the mere shadow, or hollow remnant. As Emerson says, books serve us primarily when they "in-spire," or give us a glimpse of the original inspiration (the "white-hot man") behind them, but tyrannize over us when we fix upon their language or formal configuration. These things, Pound once said, be-come "arrests of the truth."[23]

So we are back, evidently, to familiar modernist dogma regarding dogmas and mental cramps, a dogma that Pound appealed to conspicu-ously. Yet it is Williams' adroit and consistent portrayal of texts as ashy remnants of a vital process that enables *Paterson* to treat the book-voices, in Book III : 3, as detritus choking the mind, a poisonous "mud" left by textual "inundation." In effect, Williams manages to refute the Pound-

22. See Riddel, *The Inverted Bell.*
23. Williams, *The Embodiment of Knowledge,* 93; Emerson, "The Poet," "The Ameri-can Scholar," in *Essays and Lectures,* 466, 57.

ian rhetoric on its own ground: a voice of tradition whose basis is the language of prior texts, according to Pound's own assumptions, is a symptom of "mental arrest"—soul-stifling "mud"—and hence can have no authority as the voice of a truly vital ethos. Since Williams has demonstrated, in Book II, the availability of a vital spirit in the immediate social context, Book III's refutation of Pound's and Eliot's library aesthetic clears the way for persuasive declaration of a rhetoric more suitable for the bardic poet and his sacerdotal tribe. Indeed, Williams suggests at the end of Book III that his poet-hero has now arrived at such a rhetoric: "Let / me out! (Well, go!) this rhetoric / is real!" (145).

But the poet-hero has not, in fact, arrived; in a sense, neither has the rhetoric of *Paterson*. The elimination of library rhetoric still leaves open the question of where the poet will get a language adequate to his purposes, when what surrounds him (*i.e.,* the available source for a poetic language) is distorted or corrupt. As the poet-hero remarks, on his way out of the library, "And yet, unless I find a place / / apart from it [*i.e.,* the world and history], I am its slave, its sleeper, bewildered" (145). The problem, in essence, is finding a "place to speak" that is outside the hodiernal circle of the common mind, and without resorting to the sort of "permanent tradition" that Pound and Eliot invoke. Indeed, that tradition is part of what the liberty-seeking mind of Williams' struggling American poet needs to escape from. The past enslaves, the present is corrupt. Where to go?

In Book IV, Williams finds no way out, at least not for the modern poet. Instead, he once again plays out the fundamental antagonisms of the text and brings them to a final crisis. In the "Idyl" of Corydon and Phyllis (Book IV: 1), we see the love triangle from Book III expanded into a complete little drama. The authorial consciousness breaks up into the fully separate and named characters of the two women, plus "Paterson" and "The Poet." The drama reveals the final inability of the sophisticated Corydon, the wealthy, lesbian poetess, and of the desperately ineloquent Paterson to win the love of the crude and inarticulate but somehow virtuous (or invincibly dumb) Phyllis, though Phyllis does remain primarily under the influence of Corydon's money. As always, the autochthonous native psyche and the poet who would speak to/for it are kept from union by the unnatural seductions and the economics of a false but impressive culture.

But Corydon is important also as a parodic representative of modern poetry: her poetry sounds, by turns, like bad Pound, bad Eliot, bad Crane, and even bad Williams. We can also hear, if less distinctly, snatches of bad Yeats, bad Zukofsky, and bad Whitman—deciding just who is being parodied where can become a minor pastime. Corydon's Crane-aspect, though, is worthy of special note. A long segment of the poem she reads for Phyllis is clearly a parody of *The Bridge,* and particularly of "The Tunnel." She emotes rather archly about "the tunnel under the river," the claustrophobic and frenetic atmosphere of "the tall / buildings" where "the money's made," and the depressing tawdriness of city lunch-hour crowds, which resemble Crane's exhausted, shabby subway travelers. Corydon concludes this segment by gesturing toward a salmon, "our crest and guerdon," but interrupts herself to ask "(what's a guerdon?)" (164–67). The emotion is false and sentimental, and the language is likewise false, even unimpressively pretentious. The basic vision expressed, however, is one with which Williams can at least partially sympathize. *The Bridge,* then, is a failed effort in the right direction; and so, implicitly, is the poetry of all the other poets Williams parodies. Modern poetry is failed poetry, and the cause of its failure is the falseness and perversion of the culture in which it is situated.

After Williams' celebrations, in Book IV:2, of Marie Curie (who is a counter-Corydon), dissonance/invention, antagonistic cooperation, and Social Credit as "'the radiant gist' against all that / scants our lives," his *agon* of divided sensibility reaches its final crisis. In Book IV:3, as old Paterson's nostalgic thoughts drift down the Passaic and into the ocean, the voice resolves into a dialectic between the library-voice from Book III, which wants the poet to yield to the "time sea" of dream and history, and a firmer voice that wants to resist:

> The sea *is* our home whither all rivers
> (wither) run   .
>
>   the nostalgic sea
> sopped with our cries
>   Thalassa! Thalassa!
> calling us home   .
> I say to you, Put wax rather in your
> ears against the hungry sea
>   it is not our home!
>   .   draws us in to drown, of losses
> and regrets   .

> Oh that the rocks of the Areopagus had
> kept their sounds, the voices of the law!
> Or that the great theatre of Dionysius
> could be aroused by some modern magic
>   to release
> what is bound in it, stones!
> that music might be wakened from them to
> melt our ears   .
>
> The sea is not our home   .   (201)

The argument here, as throughout *Paterson* and throughout Williams'
career, is that the forms of the past cannot be resuscitated, and that to
dwell within them is to drown. The poet holds out virtuously, if laconi-
cally, for immediacy and primary sensibility. Yet the Thalassa voice
expresses one of the poet's central concerns in *Paterson*, namely, the
recovery of a lost first beauty—which is, at one point, invoked through
the image of Venus (202). The conflict is thus, as ever, between two
approaches to the same problem: one seeks renewal in the memory of
history and the languages the past affords; the other looks toward "descent" into a primary self that bottoms out in vital apprehension of the
actual world it occupies. This final *agon* of the poet-hero's (and the
author's) self-divisions, which is probably the most extended counterpoint of directly antagonistic voices in *Paterson*, is abruptly cut off by a
narrative voice drawn apparently straight from the old *Superman* series:
"What's that? / —a duck, a hell-diver? A swimming dog?" (202). The
voice is American, and it narrates the hero's emergence from the sea,
having survived the shipwreck or the drowning of his other half (as
Williams survived the shipwreck of much of the Pound generation), and
his striking in again toward Paterson, ready now (probably) to write the
poem in which he has just appeared.[24]

24. That the swimmer is heading inland toward Camden, New Jersey, is a frequently accepted interpretation of this passage; yet there is no evidence whatsoever for it
in the text. If we take into account matters of literal fact, moreover, we must recognize
that the Passaic (down which the thoughts of "Mr. Paterson" are supposedly running to
the sea) debouches in Newark Bay, and that Camden sits on the opposite side of the state,
facing Philadelphia across the Delaware River. Saying that the swimmer is headed for
Camden is thus no more accurate than saying he is headed for New Jersey or North
America. The idea that the swimmer *is* headed for Camden derives not from *Paterson* but
from Williams' *Autobiography* (Chap. 58), where the statement is made. But Williams
also says that the swimmer's dog is "obviously" a "Chesapeake Bay retriever," a "fact"

The reader is to feel the triumph of the swimmer's rather Odyssean emergence. The poem and the poet-hero together have managed a refutation and an ultimate repudiation of the Pound and Eliot aesthetic, the traditionalism that the text has linked with effigy culture and the perversion of sensibility it brings about. *Paterson,* in sum, enacts a casting-off of what oppresses the American poetic psyche as well as the civic psyche. The audience, insofar as it accepts the poem's argument and the authenticity of Williams' abysmic dialectic, is strongly encouraged to join this act of liberation. Yet the triumph is only partial, for the poet still confronts the problem of defining the "place apart" from the dream/nightmare of history, an ongoing debacle that reasserts itself, at the close of Book IV, with the reported hanging of one John Johnson (in 1850) for murder. History, as in the *Cantos,* comes to be seen as a chaos of violence, disasters, and despoliations interspersed with occasional, even rare, moments of beatitude. Williams' rhetoric has denied tradition as a valid perspective on history and immediate experience, and has advocated grounding vital intelligence in direct apprehension of the world. So the poet-hero, or the would-be bard, has no plausible way—at the end of Book IV—to escape an ultimate immersion of the poetic psyche in the ongoing dream/nightmare, or the "time sea" as it washes over and includes the present moment. As Charles Olson said, Williams' rhetoric tends to let history "roll him under."[25]

Williams, however, seems to recognize and accept this—he appeals in Book IV:3 to the notion that "Virtue is wholly / in the effort to be virtuous" (189). He thus concedes the impossibility of escaping from the dream of history, but accords virtue to the constantly renewed, if futile, effort to find a higher ground for the poet's apprehension of his world. In doing so, Williams lays claim, as did Pound, to the virtues of a tragic hero—the man who pursues the beautiful impossibility, the "flying Perfect," the constantly receding and perhaps chimerical horizon of the mind. This conclusion establishes Williams as a "virtuous poet" and, indeed, as a poet who is more virtuous than is Pound (or Eliot). He has

---

that also gets no mention in the actual poem. Williams is kidding his genial exegete; the wonder is that he has so frequently been taken straight. As for the American voice from the *Superman* series, consider: "What's that? Up in the sky? Is it a bird, a plane? . . . It's SUPERMAN!"

25. Charles Olson, *Mayan Letters,* in *Selected Writings,* ed. Robert Creeley (New York, 1966), 82–83.

resisted the temptation to yield his voice to the "time sea," even though he must limp along, a "three-legged dog," with defective means and more limited access to the wellsprings of "beauty and authority" in the world and in art. For the reader responsive to Williams' rhetoric, Williams emerges (like his swimmer walking up the beach) as an exemplary figure for the modern American poet.

Yet for the would-be sacerdotal bard, or the reader inspired toward Williams' definition of the noble literatus, this conclusion is less than satisfactory. It leaves the problem of discovering a rhetoric, or a poetic language, commensurate with the poet's world—a language capable of "meeting and winning" the public mind and guiding it toward a truer vision of desire. Indeed, as Williams' historical and economic argument and the celebration of Social Credit in Book IV:2 suggest, such a rhetoric or language must wait upon the redistribution of wealth and the elimination of a social structure based upon "sequestered wealth" and an exploited, ignorant, mass-cultural mob. The answer of Books I through IV of *Paterson* to Williams' original contractual question—how to find the "rigor of beauty" lost in the mind—is, *you can't,* not yet. The poet can only limp along and hold out against the temptations of effigy culture, the seductions of Corydon. He must wait, that is, until his society provides him the materials for a beautiful art, or for a "Parthenon." [26]

This "answer" is hardly adequate, at least not for the aims of the bardic project. It fails to address the need for an intermediate kind of poetry—namely, a poetry equipped to inspire the national and civic ethos to a redeemed society that would eventually make a "Parthenon" possible. The role of the bard, after all, and even as Williams conceives it in his own prose, is to *lead* his society, by declaring for its latent, truer sensibility. He emphatically is not simply the mouthpiece for a cultural status quo, another "slave" of the dream in which his world, the scene of history, is immersed.

The problem then remains: how to formulate a means of declaring to the inarticulate, dream-bound world in which the poet swims? The solution, Book III suggests, involves the need to find a "place apart," a perspective on experience that escapes the compromised, conventional perspectives of the quotidian mind or the fixed perspectives of a "permanent tradition." Williams once wrote, "The way out is for the mind to

26. Williams wrote in 1941, "The entire apparatus of an era is little more than a sconce to its poetry" ("Let Us Order Our World," *William Carlos Williams Review,* III:2 [Fall, 1982], 18).

conceive itself as standing beyond its processes"; Emerson said, "The field cannot be well seen from within the field." [27] The poet, then, must find a "higher ground" above the "field," a horizon outside the mind's horizon: he must launch himself into the sublime. And Williams, as the virtuous poet of *Paterson,* is obliged to move toward that ever-receding perspective—or to show himself doing so—and, at the same time, to search for a bardic rhetoric commensurate with the world, yet one sublimely free of "the past" that tyrannizes over the conventional mind.

In consequence, Williams returns, in Book V of *Paterson,* and announces to his sacerdotal tribe an *ars poetica.* He returns, moreover, as one *authorized* to speak. The antagonisms of his self-dialectic are now played out; and what polyphony remains is now more choral than dissonant. The reliable, narrative/commentative aspect of the author's voice comes to the fore and muses at length upon the life of art. Prose incursions, meanwhile, serve mainly to chime in with the poet's musing, rather than to complicate it or render it ironic (as in Books I through IV). Williams now speaks as the virtuous bard of Paterson—a bard, as the letters from Allen Ginsberg and Gilbert Sorrentino suggest, with a following—and a bard now at peace with himself and his imagination. Assuming the status of such a figure ("I, Paterson, the King-self" [234]), he can now presume to speak with some persuasiveness on matters artistic and rhetorical before the tribal audience his text has met and won. So Williams moves toward resolution of his original contract with the reader, and he propounds.

Williams' propounding arrives at, most distinctly and most distressingly for some readers, a celebration of "A WORLD OF ART / THAT THROUGH THE YEARS HAS / / SURVIVED!" (209). The "world of art" is now the "place apart," the perspective outside history, the vantage from which experience may be seen, understood, and articulated. This discovery resembles, suspiciously, an Eliotic embrace of tradition, or a world of artistic and literary monuments, as the ground of the poet's imagination. As Bernstein has said, Williams appears suddenly to choose one term of his original problem as its solution, and the term, moreover, he has spent Books I through IV repudiating. [28] And indeed, we do see Williams poring over a medieval tapestry and a

27. Williams, *The Embodiment of Knowledge,* 49; Emerson, "Circles," in *Essays and Lectures,* 409.
28. Bernstein, *The Tale of the Tribe,* 214–15.

Brueghel Nativity, and those seem to worsen the case. But Williams' "world of art" can be seen from another perspective.

Art, in Book V, is generally associated with notions of imagination and craft: imagination as the pursuit of a vision of desire in "the thing itself" (or pursuit of the virgin in the whorish world, as the Unicorn Tapestry and Book V's dedication to Toulouse-Lautrec suggest), leading to enlightened, passionate, even visionary observation (as the Brueghel Nativity suggests); and craft as *measure* employed in the articulation, or the "dancing," of that vision. These notions have their plainest statement in the Mike Wallace interview, at the close of Book V:2, wherein Williams tries to define "what poetry is." A poem, Williams says, is "words, rhythmically organized"—a "complete little universe" that "gives a view of what the poet is" (224). A poem communicates a sensibility, or a way of seeing through which a version of reality (imagined or perceived) may be constituted, and it does so by means of "words, rhythmically organized" or what Williams goes on to call (referring to American verse) "a jagged pattern." The poet's high ground is vital apprehension of the world, and his voice may occupy that ground by means of "measure," craft, or formal invention. Williams' "world of art," then, is the world that each true artwork evokes anew—and not a Poundian (or Eliotic) world of masterpieces, fragments, and ruins constituting the poet's "literary source."

At this point, *Paterson* returns us to the question of bardic rhetoric. Williams' "world of art," insofar as it applies to poetic technique, moves his reader toward a surprisingly non-modernistic conception of poetic language as versified language, with versification defined essentially as prosodic arrangement. If the reader accepts this notion, the essential poetic quality does not exist in symbolic flux, in the adumbration of sublime words beyond formulated language (through elaborate systems of "meaning"), or even in the orphic "ejaculation of logos in solitude." *Any* mode of discourse, when versified, may now be recognized as "poetry"—as Williams clearly suggests in his interview, when he states that "rhythmic treatment" of even "a fashionable grocery list" yields what he would call a poem. And if any discourse may be "poetry," then the ordinary discourses of the world—implicitly including the profane, prosaic structures of rational discursus and narration—can enter the realm of versification, the realm (for Williams) of jagged rhythmic patterns. According to this line of thought, then, the source of the poet's language is the world around him, and the source of his authority in speaking as a poet for and to that world is his prosody, or the "dance" of his phrasing. These conceptions move Williams and his audience toward a rhetoric by which "the world" (*i.e.,* the world beyond the poet's inner circle of fellow literati, exegetes, and disciples) may be "brought to the wonders of the poem." And such a rhetoric would essentially speak to the world in its own language, or a version of that language, uttered from the high ground of the world of art.

This line of thought implies a rhetoric for pursuing the ultimate goal of the bardic project, that is, cultivation of a civic or public ethos commensurate with the creation of a worthwhile civilization. A rhetoric that appropriates the public language can speak to the public mind. Yet the rhetoric implied here amounts, we must recognize, to a virtual cancellation of the general conventions of bardic rhetoric prevailing from *Leaves of Grass* to *Paterson.* Indeed, the Williams of Book V : 1 appears to repudiate the entire appeal to orphic revelation as a source of authority, as he declares, "Not prophecy! NOT prophecy! / but the thing itself!" (208). The kind of rhetoric that Williams is moving toward is visible in the poems surrounding and following *Paterson*—the sustained, discursive address of poems such as "Asphodel, That Greeny Flower" (which Williams once thought to use, interestingly enough, as Book V of *Paterson*), or the forthright narrative construction of "The Desert Music." But the same rhetorical tendency exists in the earlier "Danse Russe," "Tract," "To Elsie," and "At the Ball Game"—a tendency toward direct statement, often "prosaic" or explicitly argumentational, set to verse in jagged, halting, prosodic patterns. These patterns create the distinctive Williams voice and, indeed, the ethos behind the poem (the careful observer, slowly winning through to an intense perception of the facts). And this tendency toward versified, direct statement, I suggest, is the main rhetorical urge of the Whitmanesque or "American" Williams who wants to "speak to people." At the same time, he sees his literary world, the world of his primary audience, conquered and colonized by the rhetoric of Pound and Eliot.

Of course, we also see intimations of Williams' preferred rhetoric in *Paterson*—the adversarial, argumentational cast of his self-dialectic; the generation of narrative structures out of that dialectic; and ultimately the generation of an authorized voice equipped for direct, discursive statement. He smuggles these strategies into a rhetorical system that generally militates against them; as we have seen, Williams tends to have it both ways. But not quite. *Paterson,* in the end, cannot break the conventions that form the ultimate ground of its poetic authenticity in the eyes of its tribal audience. The orphic polyphony remains committed to the historical "stasis" reiterated in Book V and to an aesthetic that defines the artwork as a sacred locus for the communion of a sacerdotal elect. This leads him, in his meditation on the Brueghel Nativity, to evoke a community of redeemed understanding, a community apart from the "vulgar," corrupted world that Williams' history requires him to repudiate:

> —they [*i.e.,* the magi] had eyes for visions
> in those days—and saw,
> saw with their proper eyes,
> these things
> to the envy of the vulgar soldiery   (227)

The magi stand as figures for regenerate, aristocratic understanding. Such persons are the peers of Brueghel, the man "who painted what he saw" (226) and who understands the scene as the magi do, or perhaps better than they do. Brueghel and the magi together form a peerage, for the speaking poet who understands the painting, and also for the reader who understands the poet. As Emerson said, prophet and apostle may be understood by prophet and apostle, while the "vulgar soldiery," or what Williams damns as "this featureless tribe that has the money now" (228), look on with envy and incomprehension. Williams here appeals to the notion of a sacerdotal tribe engaged in exegetical self-communion, in the sanctum of a "world of art."

Paterson evokes not only a "world of art" that speaks to the world from its privileged vantage but also another "world of art" that speaks primarily and essentially to itself, withdrawn into the temple upon the rock, or, in Book V, a museum appropriately named The Cloisters. These two notions overlap and coincide: The Cloisters could be either a church for the world or a monastery. But Williams' rejection of the "age of shoddy" in which he lives, and the picture of redeemed understanding in the Brueghel Nativity, strongly suggest the monastery. And to this suggestion, a perhaps more damaging suggestion is added, in Williams' closing appeal to the notion that

> We know nothing and can know nothing
> but

                    the dance, to dance to a measure
                    contrapuntally,
                              Satyrically, the tragic foot.   (239)

For an audience inclined to the "monasterial" view of art, this appeal
evokes the notion, originally raised in the Preface, of a poetry in which
nothing matters but formal complexity, or some sort of aesthetic quality
detached from whatever ideas the poem may be thought to communicate. This notion resurfaces in the Mike Wallace interview, wherein
Williams makes—despite the implications of a poetics of versification—a distinction between poetic and ordinary language, and denies
that "sense" is a feature of poetic language (225). Williams' closing
evocation of the "tragic foot," then, represents—from a point of view his
intended audience is likely to hold—the congealing of his apparent
abandonment of history as a scene of unredeemable disaster with an urge
to withdraw to a formalist aesthetic, or a cult of art "divorced" from (or
"transcending") the world and history. The poet speaks for an elect of
understanders, amid a world that neither hears nor responds to him, and
that proceeds to its inevitable disasters; as Pound said in Canto CXVI,
litterae nihil sanantes. There is nothing to do but "dance," dance the
perceptions and ardors of a tragic perspective, in The Cloisters.

    This view of things may not be what Williams intends, but the text
of *Paterson* invites it. This is especially true for the modernist reader who
wants to regard the "ostensible subjects" of a poem as nothing more than
a foil for the display of artistic genius, or to regard a bardic poem (as Tate
regarded the *Cantos*) as brilliant conversation about nothing, yet full of
paradox, irony, and inconclusion, a purposeless instance of formally
intriguing beauty. Perhaps such a reader will automatically interpret a
poetic text in this way. It is also part of Williams' intention to engage
and alter the sensibilities of this reader. The conventional patterns of
expectancy that *Paterson* does evoke, the ground upon which Williams'
voice can persuasively appear as genuinely bardic to his modernist audience, tend to pull the poem toward an aestheticized, formalistic perspective in which Williams' specific ideas (historical, aesthetic, rhetorical)
become incidental decor. And for the reader's mind that already manifests this tendency, Williams' intimated notion of a poetry that "speaks
to the world" begins simply to disappear, like an appealing mirage.

    What, then, do we finally see in *Paterson*? It is a field of mixed, even
contradictory motives. What we see, in general, is the appropriation of a
bardic rhetoric in service of an intent to move the poet's tribal audience

toward a changed conception of its rhetorical means: Williams speaks *through* one set of conventions to recommend or, rather, suggest another. Thus Williams attempts to succeed with his audience on its own terms—to speak its own language—even as he tries to alter the terms themselves. And for this reason, Williams' success is also, in part, his failure. For the audience convinced of Williams' bardic stature or his stature as "major American poet," the conventional decorums of bardic discourse are substantially revalidated, as a direct result of Williams' successful reification of them in his poem. They therefore create a pattern of expectancy and response that works against the poet's intentions, as he cannot negate the very conventions in terms of which he succeeds, and still succeed. In consequence, the poet and the audience of *Paterson* pull up short of the poet's destination; he succeeds in the very role that the urge toward a public or worldly voice would abandon, even as he gestures beyond himself. To put it briefly, Williams uses *Paterson* to validate the kind of poet he cannot be in *Paterson,* but that he elsewhere can be and sometimes is. The "radiant gist" of *Paterson,* then, is a sacerdotal rhetoric beyond the rhetoric of *Paterson*—a distinctly un-bardly rhetoric toward which the bardic poet moves, with defective means, through the *agon* of his text.

Williams' prime audience is the inner circle of the sacerdotal tribe— the would-be bards, disciples, and extenders of the Whitmanesque project for a "great psalm of the republic." And this is the audience for which the suggestion of a worldly poetry of versified direct statement, or even of oratorical address to a public beyond the tribe, should not (and probably will not) wholly dissolve in hyperaesthesia. And out of this audience emerges the subject of the next chapter: Charles Olson and *The Maximus Poems.* The basic question is one that has hovered over this chapter, just as it hovers over the text of *Paterson* itself: Where can you get, with a Whitmanesque, or bardic, inspiration, and what rhetoric should be used? But more specifically, we will consider how the bard of *Maximus* appropriates the tradition worked by Williams, Crane, and Pound; how he exploits (or fails to exploit) the possibilities created by his predecessors; and how he moves (or fails to move) the sacerdotal tribe toward a rhetoric more commensurate with its public goals. Olson and *Maximus* bring the bardic poem to something like a consummation.

VIII.   The Maximus Poems

Nor judge, nor give what is holy to dogs.
　　　—"In the Hills / South of Capernaum, Port"

Celebrations of the union of poetry and rhetoric, or of a breakthrough to
a poetry of direct statement and public address, have appeared in critical
discussions of *The Maximus Poems,* and indeed of the work of Charles
Olson generally.[1] The chronic modern gap between author and audience,
it seems, is closed. These assertions carry an undeniable appeal, on first
hearing at least, but we must question whether they are really war-
ranted, and approach them with the skepticism appropriate to the
rhetor. First of all, if we define *rhetoric* as the use of available means to
create some desired effect in the mind of an intended audience, we must
doubt whether poetry and rhetoric could ever be really separated, or
subsequently unified, unless we suppose that poets have earnestly been
practicing an art with no audience, no intention, and no effect whatsoever.[2] And we must also doubt whether the pursuit of a public poetry,
or a poetry of frankly suasory intent, can really be considered Olson's
special contribution to modern literature. The urge to engage and ethically transform an audience of public selves—citizens, "factive" men of
affairs, "artifexes," or latent aristocrats—is endemic to the bardic enterprise in America, from Whitman onward. The issue is not *whether*
Olson's version of the bardic is rhetorical, or whether it seeks a public
audience. The issue, rather, is *what kind* of rhetoric Olson invents, and
how adequate that rhetoric is to the ultimate, and perhaps quixotic,
goals of the sacerdotal tribe.

　　Olson set himself the characteristic task of the American epic bard—

　　1. See Bernstein, *The Tale of the Tribe,* 246; and Robert von Hallberg, *Charles Olson:
The Scholar's Art* (Cambridge, Mass., 1978), 29–34, 209.

　　2. But even "effectlessness," or absolute boredom, would still be an effect—and
the intention to have no effect, if such a thing were possible, would still be an intention.

most strikingly evident in his self-conception, during his Black Mountain College rectorship, as a sort of literary, pedagogical Mao at Yenan.[3] In taking on this role as cultural revolutionary, Olson enters into the rhetorical situation faced by Whitman, Pound, Williams, and Crane. He must speak from outside the dominant conventions of belief in the public mind, and, in seeking to change those conventions, he must find a source of authority for his own position. He must, that is, discover a voice equipped for a polemical meeting with the prevailing ethos of his polis. Olson's solution is a reappropriation of the rhetoric he inherits from his predecessors. He presents his reader with a version of the myth of untransacted destiny, and presents himself as the voice of a long-suppressed, redemptive identity. And the voice of his poem is grounded on the conventions of abysmic utterance, thereby invoking the orphic authority those conventions support. Insofar as Olson's rhetoric is a recapitulation of the work of Whitman, Pound, Williams, and (to a lesser extent) Crane, there seems to be considerable cause for skepticism toward the celebratory claims sometimes made on behalf of *The Maximus Poems*. Yet we must also recognize the sometimes striking ingenuity with which Olson appropriates his inherited conventions, just as we must recognize the effect of Olson's bardic text on subsequent poets, and the implications of that effect for the sacerdotal project itself. For the moment, then, we might keep skepticism in reserve as we turn to Olson's reinvention of the myth of untransacted destiny.

In its earliest form, Olson's myth appears to derive from his time as a Harvard graduate student of F. O. Matthiessen, for whose *American Renaissance* Olson did research (mainly on Melville and Hawthorne). In Matthiessen's view, the major American writers in the mid-nineteenth century were striving to "give fulfillment to the potentialities freed by the revolution, to provide a culture commensurate with America's political opportunity." Further, those potentialities originated from the English seventeenth-century sensibility, whose spiritual aspirations, Matthiessen maintains, found manifestation in its literature *and* "the settlement and early life of New England." Elizabethan mind, in short, lies at the root of the New England mind and, therefore, the national mind. Behind this line of argument lies the work of Vernon L. Parrington, who maintains in his *Main Currents in American Thought* that the "liberal equalitarian" spirit of the Renaissance, which produced the

3. Von Hallberg, *Charles Olson*, 14–21.

Reformation and its "doctrine" of natural rights, crossed the Atlantic and persisted in the conscience of the common American—eventually breaking free of Calvinist domination in the Revolution, flourishing briefly in the Jeffersonian political philosophy, and suffering betrayal by Federalists (and, of course, Hamilton). The implication that clearly emerges from the juxtaposition of Matthiessen and Parrington is that the American renaissance was a transplanted reflorescence of *the* Renaissance and, as such, was an affirmation of the potentials of natural, secular man. Or to put it another way: the spirit of the English Renaissance died out under Cromwell and the drift of Europe into modern industrial capitalism, but persisted in America and resurfaced in the "golden" period from 1776 to the Civil War.[4]

Olson seems to take this implication. In a letter to Robert Creeley, dated June 24, 1950, about one month after the composition of the first *Maximus* poem, for example, he capsulizes the myth it leads to: "date, 1607, America was drawn off fr. England. My argument wd be, that 250 years thereafter . . . we got the 2nd flowering, heave of, the Elizabethan in MELVILLE? WHITMAN."[5] Whether or not this judgment is correct, it forms the essential germ of Olson's early mythology—a mythology that ramifies, in his different presentations of it, to a vision of elemental struggle between the vital, secular humanism of the Renaissance mind and the repressive, exploitive mercantilism of the post-Cartesian mind (especially as manifest in Puritanism). In the opening volume of *The Maximus Poems*, this vision emerges in typical fashion for bardic rhetoric, namely, as an implicit schema revealed through scattered, elliptical references. An important and early reference occurs in "Letter 10" as Olson brings the reader through his first major engagement with Gloucester history:

> Elizabeth dead,
> and Tudor went to James
> (as quick as Conant's house
> was snatched to Salem

4. Charles Boer, *Charles Olson in Connecticut* (Chicago, 1975), 17ff. See also Matthiessen, *American Renaissance*, xviii, xv, 104; and Parrington, *Main Currents in American Thought*, I. Matthiessen cites Parrington as one of two primary influences on his work; the other is Van Wyck Brooks.

5. *Charles Olson & Robert Creeley: The Complete Correspondence*, ed. George F. Butterick (Santa Barbara, 1980), II, 11.

> As you did not go,
> Gloucester: you tipped, you were our
> scales[6]

The reference is elliptical indeed: the genial reader, with the help of Butterick's *Guide,* is obliged to amplify. What the passage implies is that Elizabethanism gave way to James, or to the encroachment of a mercantile spirit, but survived (briefly) in Gloucester—or in the independent Gloucester fishermen—until the triumph of Puritanism under Endecott in 1626 and the removal of Roger Conant to Beverly, Massachusetts. Endecott's "snatching" of Conant's house thus represents the conquest of one sensibility by another, even as it illustrates the predatory, acquisitive mentality (according to Olson) of the culture the Puritans inaugurated. Gloucester, then, is a scales upon which the opponents in an elemental moral struggle may be weighed.

Olson's basic historical stasis receives a more succinct presentation in "Stiffening, in the Master Founders' Wills":

> Canaan
> was Cane's, and
> all was faulting,
> stiffening in the master
> founders wills—
>
> the things
> of this world (new
> world, Renaissance
> mind named
> what Moses men tried
>
> to twist back to Covenantal
> truth)   (134)

This passage leads eventually to notions that the European mind "dried out" inside of "continental loci" and underwent a transformation in America. The nature of the transformation, Olson implies, was a shift to the Cartesian perception of a gap between matter and spirit—which Olson illustrates with Anne Hutchinson's antithesis between works and grace. "[T]he things / of this world" became mere objects for mercantile exploitation: "Descartes / 's holding up / another hand . . . The

6. Charles Olson, *The Maximus Poems* (Berkeley, 1983), 50. All further references to *The Maximus Poems* are to this edition.

apple . . . was now / / already merchandise" (134). "The apple" had ceased to be the focal happening in a devoted and communal engagement with nature. In consequence, according to Olson, John Winthrop's dream of a commonwealth as "a greate family" had already become, without his knowing it, impossible.[7] The New World venture, then, had gone off track almost from the beginning, Olson here suggests and directly affirms in "Capt Christopher Levett (of York)": "About seven years / and you can carry cinders / in your hand for what / / America was worth" (139).

Behind this general notion of a transformation or "faulting" in the will of early New England, as Olson's references to "Renaissance / mind" and "Moses men" suggest, is a Parringtonesque antithesis between the Renaissance and Reformation sensibility of the early colonists and the "Hebraic" or Calvinist sensibility that succeeded and oppressed it. At the same time, "naming," "continental loci," and "drying out" suggest that the general theses of *In the American Grain* also underlie (and resonate with) Olson's interpretation of early American history. In effect, Olson conflates his available modern sources, using them to extend, complicate, and qualify each other. He produces what looks like an exemplary rendition of the general myth of thwarted or unrealized promise. That promise, according to the general myth and *Maximus* as well, remains immanent and redeemable as long as the true native spirit, or Renaissance mind, or the mind of (a de-Europeanized) seventeenth-century humanism, survives in a saving remnant such as Olson's "root person in root place" (16), or what he calls the "Divine Inert" (126), borrowing a phrase from Melville. To this point, then, Olson's mythic history seems to be fairly well grounded in the available authorities— authorities, that is, in the eyes of his tribal audience, as well as a larger, demo-liberal audience—and this groundedness gives his vision of early New England a persuasive validity. Or it does so, at least, for the tribal

7. John Winthrop, for reasons that are not fully clear, generally escapes Olson's condemnation of the Puritan mentality. Olson apparently regards Winthrop as a "pre-Cartesian" man and therefore not responsible for the "feral," mercantile ethos that came to possess the Plymouth colony, Boston, and the nation. In *Maximus,* II and III, Winthrop appears as a "Vedic" magistrate (305) and as a "wanax" (Mycenaean king) "who imagined / / that men / cared / for what kind of world / they chose to / live in / and came here seeking / the possibility" (408–409). But Winthrop was mistaken, in Olson's opinion, because Cartesian man no longer cared about what kind of world he occupied, seeing it only as an external object for exploitation and consumption.

and demo-liberal audiences whose conventions of belief are directly engaged.

However, Olson goes considerably beyond the mainstream topoi from which his mythology derives. His major departure is an extension of the term *humanism* to global application, which probably would have surprised Matthiessen. Yet the Olsonian humanism does derive, by an Olsonian twist, from germinal elements in *American Renaissance*. Emerson's age discovered a mythic American identity, Matthiessen argues, by reading the present in terms of a virtually timeless, heroic antiquity, and by attending to the abiding, ancient aboriginal mind in the ongoing present. This argument seems to imply that Matthiessen faithfully takes the transcendentalists at their word. His best example of American mythic vision is Thoreau, who engages with the primal meaning of America by "fronting facts" and by striking an "autochthonous vein" where "he could penetrate almost immediately to a savage past." In consequence, Matthiessen's Thoreau discovers that "the perennial mind did not die with Cato, and will not die with Hosmer" and that "the New Englander is a pagan suckled in a creed outworn." Matthiessen, in what seems to be a gesture of keeping the faith, applies these notions to Thoreau and reads him as "most nearly an antique Roman" at large in New England. Melville, similarly, makes contact with "the primitive" and, intuitively grasping Whiteheadian process, understands and re-enacts in his fiction the major "heroic myths" that give meaning to American life. Matthiessen's American renaissance figures discover a prototype of the modernists' "mythical method" and, by doing so, revive not only the spirit of the English Renaissance but also the animus of a mostly Greco-Roman heroic antiquity as well. As Thoreau once said, and as Matthiessen apparently believes, "*this was the heroic age itself, though we know it not.*" These appeals to the notion of an archaic, heroic ethos as the root of a mythic and true American self give the notion of "humanism," that spirit inherited directly from the Renaissance, a deeper resonance—or so Matthiessen seems to suggest, though he stops short of openly declaring it.[8]

Olson has taken the suggestion, with what at times seems to be heroic literal-mindedness. If we start with genial consent to Matthiessen's reading of the American renaissance in terms of Rome, Greece,

8. Matthiessen, "Man in the Open Air," in *American Renaissance*, 628, 632–33, 648, 654–55.

and the "perennial mind" of natural man (which joins the New Englander, the Indian, and the pagan of European antiquity), we are
prepared for an equally genial consent to such period rhetoric as
Melville's nostalgic evocation of the second century A.D. in his poem
"The Age of the Antonines," not to mention the representation of
aboriginal self in Emerson, Whitman, and Thoreau. From a willingness
to believe in these representations, then, we quickly arrive at nearly all
the material required to reconstruct Olson's mature historical myth. We
need only add the minute if miscellaneous particulars from his voracious,
eclectic, and sometimes eccentric readings in archaeology, anthropologi-
cal linguistics, theosophy, metaphysics, and ancient intellectual history
(starting with Ezra Pound's sources and including Eric Havelock's *Preface
to Plato*), to obtain Olson's notion and history of humanism.[9]

The essential outline can be reconstructed from Olson's elliptical but
explicit presentation in "Proprioception" (1961) and other more fragmentary references. Olson's history begins with the "true humanism,"
which stands in opposition to the "big false" one supposedly perpetrated
by Socrates and his tradition. The *true* humanism is centered in Whiteheadian agentive sensibility and first appears in Olson's history with the
"original town-man" of the Aurignacian-Magdalenian period in Eurasia
(7000–5000 B.C.). This is the same sensibility that Olson finds, but in a
degraded form, among the Indians of Yucatán and writes of in *Mayan
Letters,* where his main historical thesis makes one of its earliest appearances. In that text, he defines humanism as "(homer) coming in [to
Western history] and (melville) going out." He also presents fragments
of his "imaginative thesis of the sea," which makes America the "Ultima
Thule" of ancient mythology, and the Maya civilization the product of
"Armenoid-Caucasoid" prehistoric seafarers. "Humanism" comes from
somewhere near the Tigris and Euphrates.[10]

We should note, however, that Olson's rejection of the Socratic tradition does not entail wholesale rejection of the Greco-Roman ethos or of
the *heroic* ethos of the Mycenaeans and the Etruscans. Olson's true humanism, as "Proprioception" makes clear, is the dominant will-to-

9. Von Hallberg discusses Olson's reading of Whitehead as an example of reading
texts for confirmation of ideas he already holds, rather than coming to grips with the
details of an author's argument (*Charles Olson,* 82–125).

10. Olson, "the hinges of civilization to be put back on the door," in "Proprioception," *Additional Prose* (Bolinas, 1974), 25–26; Olson, *Mayan Letters,* in *Selected Writings,* 93, 98, 112–13.

civilize, which he perceives as progressing from the proto-cities of the Near East to the Greece of the pre-Socratics. This humanism finds its last full expression for Western culture, according to Olson (after Havelock), in the poetry of Homer and Hesiod. From then on, humanism intermittently disrupts the Western estrangement from the real, at moments of renaissance—such as the first to second centuries A.D. (the Age of the Antonines, the Second Sophistic, Longinus, and Maximus of Tyre), the period of Aquinas (1200–1250), the Renaissance to the seventeenth century, and the American twentieth century.

Humanism, in other words, moves northwest, through its various manifestations, and arrives on the shores of North America. In consequence, the task of the present is to reclaim this westward-moving, long-suppressed mode of sensibility. Otherwise, Olson says, "the present will lose what America is the inheritor of: a secularization which not only loses nothing of the divine but by seeing process in reality redeems all idealism fr[om] theocracy or mobocracy, whether it is rational or superstitious, whether it is democratic or socialism." [11] The referent of the final doubled "it" is theocracy/mobocracy—perhaps simply mobocracy. Olson's history of humanist civilization excludes all the major periods of democratic or republican government, with only the possible exception of the present, which is itself in doubt. In this respect, and despite his occasional claims to reject "hierarchy," Olson appears to follow Pound and most of his modernist predecessors in the sacerdotal enterprise, by favoring the leadership of an enlightened elite, or an unofficial aristocracy of "artifexes" and charismatic men of affairs. The more egalitarian political ideals expressed by Whitman, or by such demo-liberal voices as Matthiessen, are at least partly rejected or quietly abandoned. "Root person in root place" is the factive, the vital and superior individual who determines the actual unfolding of historical process: he (or she) is the "Divine Inert."

The sociopolitical preference implicit in Olson's humanism reveals itself in *The Special View of History*. There he adopts an essentially negative and curiously Platonic stance toward democratic process. The object of creative will in a "man of achievement" is not "to get elected or something—which is the vulgar way in which the factor of majority operates. . . . What I am striking at here is . . . the incredible notion

---

11. Olson, "Proprioception," in *Additional Prose*, 26.

that value is relative . . . and that the Four Qualities are any more
dependent on the vote of many than the Four Objects." It does not
matter, for our purposes, what the Four Qualities and the Four Objects
are, though we should note that they sound suspiciously like the sort of
abstract, ideal, and timeless categories that the post-Socratic discourse of
the big false humanism supposedly prefers, and that Olson supposedly
rejects. The point is that value, for Olson, is *absolute,* and beyond the
domain of "vulgar" public discussion and decision. What Olson is after,
he explicitly says, is a return to faith in place of "politics, government,
athletics and metaphysics" (all consequences of the big false humanism).
Communal will in Olson's polity of faith, which will somehow not be
theocracy, is to be grounded instead in men of achievement—whose own
wills, in turn, are grounded in direct, intuitive perception of the absolute through, Olson says, Keatsian negative capability. The bases of the
directio voluntatis in the "Divine Inert" are non-negotiable. Men of genius
will set the pattern, by announcement or example, and the common folk
will obediently, faithfully follow along.[12]

The result of this preference, in Olson's own discourse, is a tendency
toward the authoritarian. Heraclitus, Olson says, *"laid down the law"*
that the humanist now must follow, and that the many presumably must
not subject to rational debate or the play of mere opinion—and Olson,
aligning himself with Heraclitus, asks his students to "put yourselves in
my hand." The general drift of *The Special View of History* is rather
strange, considering Olson's attitude toward Socrates, since Olson apparently holds the Socratic/Platonic position that truth is above and
beyond the "vulgar way in which the factor of majority operates," and is
available only to the philosopher or, for Olson, the Keatsian man of
achievement. This apparent self-contradiction cannot be resolved or
avoided as long as Olson sees truth as absolute and non-negotiable within
a secularized "idealism" that "loses nothing of the divine." As a result,
Olson's claims to a non-hierarchic stance must eventually succumb to the
suspicion of majority opinion that the absoluteness of truth, or the
divine inertness of truth, entails. Truth belongs to him who knows, and
knows from his own direct perception, since Olson has canceled rational

12. Olson, *The Special View of History* (Berkeley, 1970). A course of lectures delivered
in a "seminar" at Black Mountain College in 1956. See Ann Charters' Introduction, and
pp. 21, 28–29, 34–35, 41–46.

inquiry as a path to knowledge. The only hierarchy that this stance can validly reject is abstract public institutions that deny the primacy of the truth-beholding individual—the institutions of government, mass politics ("mobocracy"), and the law. Olson's lack of interest in the "vulgar majority," and indeed his eventual hostility to it, is a point we shall return to. For the moment, we may note that his attitude bodes ill for the possibilities of a public rhetoric in bardic poetry, or at least limits such a rhetoric to an *ars praedicandi,* the rhetoric of the sermon and the fiat.

But we have not quite finished looking at Olson's humanist history. In making America the inheritor of a cultural event that begins perhaps at El-Amarna and that includes the entire sweep of Western history *and* prehistory, Olson achieves a grand enlargement of the major nineteenth-century topos in the rhetoric of American destiny—namely, the westward course of empire. In Olson's discourse, "empire" becomes "humanism" or "civilization," but an overview of his favored eras (including, most conspicuously, the Roman imperium in the second century A.D.) makes ambiguous the usual distinctions between these terms. And as Robert von Hallberg has pointed out, Olson treats the period after World War II as the opening of an American imperium, and finds encouragement in that perception. His time, apparently, is a decisive moment, or *the* decisive moment, in which virtually all will be decided. America's role in history is to culminate the westward course and to redeem a lost or deflected possibility by bestowing (if not imposing) upon the world a humanist civilization. In Olson's historical thought, then, the American event is the final and decisive showdown between the true and false humanisms, or the completion of a vast historical *agon*: we are, in Olson's recurrent phrase, the "last first people" or "the apocalypse people." In general, the historical myth that provides the rhetorical ground of Olson's bardic enterprise is a repossession, transformation, and application of Whitman's myth of national destiny—or, more broadly, the core myth of the American renaissance as it came to Olson through Matthiessen.[13]

In *The Maximus Poems,* Olson appeals to this mythos at various points. The notion of a live humanism of active, independent, enterprising individuals ("yeomen" and their leaders) struggling with a deathly scientific-abstract corporate entity is present in the Elizabethan-Puritan

13. Von Hallberg, *Charles Olson,* 21–28; Boer, *Charles Olson in Connecticut,* 12.

(or Conant-Endecott) conflict and in the opposition between fishermen and Puritans (then) or fishermen and Gorton-Pew (now). Further, the "westward course" topos is obliquely present at many points in the text and directly invoked at others. For example, Olson announces that "the motion / (the Westward motion) / comes here, / to land" (125). Or again, more fully, in the second volume, as he tells the wanderings of Maximus:

> He sent flowers on the waves from the mole
> of Tyre. He went to Malta. From Malta
> to Marseilles. From Marseilles to Iceland.
> From Iceland to Promontorium Vinlandiae.
> Flowers go out on the sea. On the left
> of the Promontorium. On the left of the
> Promontorium, Settlement Cove [*i.e.,* Gloucester]
>
> I am making a mappemunde. It is to include my being.   (257)

This version of Olson's historical thesis, and there are several, apparently derives from his reading of Victor Bérard, who believed that Homer's *Odyssey* translated a Phoenician original (a metrically encoded oral sea chart, directions for a *periplum*). Bérard, supplemented by other archaeological sources, allowed Olson to describe the ancient Near Eastern spirit of civilization as passing westward (or to the left, on the map) from the mouth of the Orontes at Tyre, via Phoenician mariners, through the Mediterranean world and beyond—to the Norse and Anglo-Saxon world (via Pytheus of Marseilles). The movement then continues its vaguely northwest-tending line, toward its terminus (via the Vikings, and later the English) at Newfoundland/Vinland and Cape Ann. In sum, the sea migration of humanist culture is effected mainly by Phoenicians and Nordics, and it passes through the partially resisting and eventually distorting medium of the Greco-Roman, or false humanist, mind. The "man of the Midi," Olson suggests *contra* Pound, is neither the origin nor the major agent of the true civilizing spirit. We should perhaps add that Maximus of Tyre, in this perspective, becomes a Levantine Semite, a Phoenician, practicing a pre-Socratic (sophistical) mode of discourse in the midst of a Hellenized, Romanized society.

But Olson's thesis has deeper sources than Bérard and "recent" archaeology. A version of it appears in Emerson's rendition of mythic history, in *English Traits*. The ancient Druids, Emerson claims, were Phoenicians, and their central mystery, "a compass-box" permitting navigation, "was lost with the Tyrian commerce" as the Roman Empire cut off Druidical England from its sources. The Briton, then, derives his virtues, which are the virtues of the American yeoman as well, from a mixture of Druidical/Celtic and Saxon/Nordic influences. Underlying this view, and integral to it, is the Real Whig "secret history" of Saxon virtue, and particularly Noah Webster's version of it, which sought to locate in the Teutonic "tribe" the prelapsarian root of all European languages and cultures. That is to say, in effect, Teutonic or Nordic man is the essential European or Indo-European man.[14] This may not be the correct reading of Webster or the Real Whig mythology (or of Emerson either), but it is, apparently, Olson's reading. In a book review (*circa* 1964), for example, he describes Noah Webster as "the creator of the only dictionary which has now permitted the English-American language to become the re-issue of the original Indo-European experience."[15] In a passage (1964–1965) from the third volume of *The Maximus Poems,* he celebrates "Norse" as the essential European ethos:

> Norse are
>   Anglo-
> Saxons. Norse are
> early Greeks. Norse are
> Kelts. Norse are
> Gauls. Norse are
>   Rus (Russia)
>
>   Norse are
>   all but
>   Constantinople   (444)

"Norse" is the wellspring of virtually all of Western civilization. "Constantinople" means (apparently, if wrongly) the Byzantine opposition of "Roman" to "Asiatic," or the distinction of "Mesopotamian / and European," a product of compartmentalizing "Mediterranean / mindedness" that Olson (on the authority of Josef Strzegowski, an art historian) rejects in a subsequent passage (445). There is a single cultural stream, then, arising with "Mesopotamian" or Near Eastern peoples and flowing

14. Emerson, "Stonehenge," *English Traits,* 282. See also Bynack, "Noah Webster and the Idea of a National Culture."

15. George F. Butterick, *A Guide to The Maximus Poems of Charles Olson* (Berkeley, 1978), 724.

through to the "Norse" and ultimately to England and America (with stopoffs in Greece and Rome). As Butterick's note to this passage makes clear, Olson's "Mesopotamian" conflates Indo-European (Iranian) and Semitic (Phoenician) cultures in a single general entity.[16]

In sum, then, Olson's "history of humanism" eventually reveals itself as a resurrection of the Real Whig mythology. That resurrection, at least in part, takes the form of an Aryan/Nordic mythology (with "Aryan" including, by conflation, the Phoenician/Semitic), grounded in an up-to-date-sounding appeal mostly to archaeological and antiquarian authorities, such as Bérard and Strzegowski. As a result, the Olsonian humanist civilization/imperium, which abides in the text of *The Maximus Poems* as America's untransacted, apocalpytic destiny, comes periodically into view as a grand, indeed sublime object—the ultimate issue and culmination of the true and westward-tending Indo-European ethos.

Undoubtedly more could be said about Olson's history, and about his "humanism" as well, but greater detail would do little to change the basic scheme. The crucial point is that Olson's myth allows him to present "Maximus," or the bardic figure through which he speaks, as the voice of humanism, and to invoke the authority of a tradition encompassing all Western and Near Eastern history and prehistory. But in order to acquire that authority, to speak persuasively as the voice of his tradition, Maximus must display the qualities appropriate to his humanist ethos. This necessity brings Olson to a mixture of the oratorical, the rhapsodic, the primitivistic, and the abysmic, in his self-representation as an American sacerdotal literatus.

The place to begin, again, is F. O. Matthiessen. In *American Renaissance,* Matthiessen convincingly argues that the republican aspirations and neo-Roman pretensions of Americans in the nineteenth century led to the preeminence of oratory as the *only* developed native literary tradition. It evolved from Puritan and Unitarian pulpits to the post-Revolutionary political forum and the public lecture hall, in the years preceding (and including) Emerson. Emerson and most of his peers believed, as had Cicero and other ancients, that the appearance of the orator, with his ability to persuade, organize, and lead his peers in

16. *Ibid.,* 582–83.

cooperative groups, marked the birth of civilization. At the same time they—following Strabo, Sidney, and late neoclassical bellettrists, such as Hugh Blair and E. T. Channing—found this primitive, civilizing orator identified as the bard of heroic prehistory. Oratory suited America's nineteenth-century vision of itself as the successor to Rome and Greece, and thus became (according to Matthiessen) the governing paradigm for other literary genres, including Whitman's poetry and Emerson's essays. Further, and perhaps because of the mixed Ciceronian and Strabonian concepts of the orator/bard, oratorical and poetic genres tended to conflate, so that (in Matthiessen's opinion) Whitman's poetry often indulged in declamatory assertion "instead of building up the exact plastic shape of what he felt," and Emerson's addresses became a "rhapsodic" (*i.e.*, accumulative or catalogic) stitching-together of lines from his journals. Matthiessen finds a great many puzzling difficulties in the transcendentalists' tendency to collapse the sermon, the political address, the lecture, and the poem all together in a single notion of sublime eloquence, but Olson sees no problem. Maximus is an orator, a poet, and a rhapsode all at once, and he is engaged with subjects that are political, historical, and pastoral by turns. To the extent that he successfully does all this, he fulfills the expectations for a sacerdotal literatus that his historical-mythic premises create.[17]

But Olson's Maximus must display one essential quality to believably represent the humanism predicated by his mythology. According to "Human Universe," *The Special View of History*, and other pieces, the cultural revolution wrought by the followers of Socrates involved the substitution of an abstracted rational discourse, or what Olson considers speculation enclosed in an unreal "universe of discourse," for the more concrete and experiential discourse of the pre-Socratics. The conspicuous Western examples of the earlier and truer discourse, for Olson, are Hesiod and Homer. This line of thought appears to be directly taken from Havelock's *Preface to Plato,* a text that Olson enthusiastically recommends in most of his bibliographies. In any case, Olson and Havelock reach identical conclusions: after 500 B.C., the philosopher replaced the epic poet, or the primitive orator/bard, as the educator of the polis. The inference for the humanist poet is clear. Olson, in choosing to speak as Maximus and as an epic bard, consequently must operate in a restored

17. Matthiessen, *American Renaissance,* 14–24 ("Eloquence").

Homeric/Hesiodic (or primitive pre-Socratic) mode, to display properly his own credentials. This necessity has a double consequence.[18]

First of all, if we assume with Olson the validity of his and Havelock's understanding of the Homeric ethos, Olson's bardic job (in Havelock's terms) is to constitute himself as a cultural "encyclopedia." He must construct a "narrative" that will allow him to present as many of his culture's essential items of knowledge as possible, and most conveniently through presentation or dramatization of the education of his exemplary hero. However, as Havelock points out, the narrative is only a device for making the encyclopedia *memorizable* in a preliterate culture—as are the techniques of metrical composition. For the epic poet in a literary culture, then, narrative structure (like metrical prosody) is dispensable for the encyclopedic work. The Hesiod of *Works and Days,* rather than Homer, may be Olson's best model.[19]

But Olson sees his tradition in slightly different terms, probably because of the conventional assumptions within which he and his American predecessors are situated. The suppression of narrative structure leaves not the rational discursus of Hesiod but the Poundian "grab-bag" or Whitmanesque addition as the essential means of encyclopedic accumulation. Indeed, what Olson especially praises in Pound is the suppression of narrative linkage in order to render time as a "space-field," so that all points in history become contemporaneous. In "Projective Verse," he insists that "the conventions which logic has forced on syntax must be broken open" and that poetic energy must not be "sapped" by the structures of "argument in prose." At the same time, Olson defines art and poetry as reenactment of the "kinetics" of psychic experience, praising the "*dramatic sense*" of Pound's "method" in the *Cantos* and suggesting the potentials of "projective verse" for "some sort of drama, say, or of epic." What all this suggests is a fairly clear recognition of the nature of the rhetoric Olson has inherited. As Olson wrote to Robert Creeley on June 22, 1950, his true rhetorical tradition is

18. Olson, "Human Universe," in *Selected Writings,* 53–56; Olson, *The Special View of History,* 21–25. See also Eric A. Havelock, *Preface to Plato* (Cambridge, Mass., 1963), 91.

19. Havelock, "Epic as Record Versus Epic as Narrative" and "The Oral Sources of the Hellenic Intelligence," *Preface to Plato,* Chaps. 5, 7. See also Olson, "Letter 23," *The Maximus Poems,* 104.

> Ezra/
>
> out of Whitman by/
>
> Homeros/

We must understand "Homeros" in Havelockian terms.[20]

The second consequence of Olson's necessity to speak according to conventional ideas of primitive pre-Socratic discourse is largely evident in the first. Insofar as Olson follows modernist (and transcendentalist) convention in dispensing with the supposed falsities of the "universe of discourse," logic and "prose argument," and insofar as he wants to speak as a true humanist, he must devise a language that can persuasively claim to reflect the operations of the essential human mind. This language is defined for Olson by his chief linguistic authority, Edward Sapir. According to Sapir's *Language*, "Language is primarily a pre-rational function," a psychic faculty that lies at the threshold of conscious thought and, to a large extent, determines its form. Sapir speaks, for example, of "thought riding lightly on the submerged crests of speech." When he speculates on the origins of language, Sapir conceives of undifferentiated mental energy and intuitive experience giving rise to the prerational categories of language, categories that in turn make defined, abstract "concepts" (and thus names) possible. To this point, "the latent content of all languages is the same—the intuitive *science* of experience." These concepts, however, when turned back upon the language faculty so as to organize it, make possible the more purely rational activities of conscious reasoning and formal logic. The "intuitive *science* of experience" ends in abstraction, categorization, and systems of entailment and relation that follow a dance of their own.[21]

This final stage in Sapir's language evolution can be interpreted— from an Olsonian (and romantic) point of view—as the invention of a "universe of discourse," which substitutes fossilized and false convention for experiential truth. Olson's task as a poet, then, is to return the voice of Maximus to this hypothetical prerational stage of language, and to appear to allow "the submerged crests of speech" to be vocalized before the categories of logic and syntax can apply. Olson's poet thereby refastens his utterance, like Emerson's Poet, to the supposed facts of direct

20. Olson, *Mayan Letters,* "Projective Verse," "Human Universe," in *Selected Writings,* 82, 16, 20, 21, 26, 61; *Charles Olson & Robert Creeley,* I, 141.

21. Edward Sapir, *Language* (New York, 1927), esp. Chaps. 1, 10, 11.

deep-psychic experience, what Sapir called the "generalized linguistic layer." But he does so on the strength of a more modern-sounding appeal to the speculations of linguistic scholarship (just as he grounds his neo-Whig mythology in contemporary archaeology). For Olson, as for his predecessors, a language that struggles toward expression of the "generalized linguistic layer," "deep structure," or the mind's inherent, experiential language remains the sign of the poet's authority or authenticity as a member of the humanist "Divine Inert." Olson's poet, at least in his Maximus-aspect, is clearly obliged to speak such a language.

And yet he must struggle—or appear to be struggling—to break through convention and give true utterance to his latent, universally human speech force. Sapir's point, and Olson's point as well, is that a primitive, prerational language is not available to modern, Western man, if it ever was available at all. In consequence, the characteristic figures (*i.e.,* the required credentials) for Olson's humanist bard emerge as asyndeton (or variation, interpreted broadly as convention-breaking and fractured syntax) and *correctio* (adjusted iteration, as the speaker "tries again" and seems to grope toward the truest expression of his urge)—as well as the more global structuring figure of accumulation. He rhapsodically and oratorically moves upon waves of submerged linguistic energy (thought riding on the crests), and reenacts/dramatizes a psychic *agon* of discovery.

The voice that Olson's mythology requires him to manage in the figure of Maximus is an eclectic compound of the oratorical, the bardic, and the primitivistic. This compound is, to say the least, a problematic one. Rendering the encyclopedic and pedagogical bard through an orator may be advantageous in Olson's rhetorical situation. His essentially polemical stance toward the mores of mainstream culture and his cultural-revolutionary ambitions—the stance and the ambition, in essence, of the Whitmanesque tradition—both imply the need to meet and convert an audience that is, by definition, alien at first to the values Olson wants to promote. "Rhetorizing" the bardic voice may, in principle, give it a sufficiently public access. This is the signal contribution to modern poetry with which Olson is sometimes credited. However, a primitivistic prerational discourse, as defined through Sapir and Olson's other sources, implies an essentially psychologistic, privatized language, *especially* in a society whose operant public speech is primarily literate, grammatically formalized, and more or less rational. Olson is caught in the same contradiction as were his bardic predecessors. The urge toward a public audience seems to dissolve (and historically has dissolved) in the conventions of abysmic orphism. What also dissolves is any theoretic advantage gained by adopting the pose of "orator." The question that emerges from this contradiction is how or whether Olson's Maximus could actually "rhetorize" the bardic voice in any meaningful or purposeful way, if rhetorizing means engaging an audience beyond the poet's tribal circle. What remains to be seen is Olson's actual use of his available means—the persuasion effected, the audience engaged, and the education delivered—in the text of *The Maximus Poems*.

The voice with which Olson begins his bardic undertaking, in "I, Maximus of Gloucester, to You," is unmistakably a mentalistic one:

> Off-shore, by islands hidden in the blood
> jewels & miracles, I, Maximus
> a metal hot from boiling water, tell you
> what is a lance, who obeys the figures of
> the present dance   (5)

The fictive speaker here, if he is truly located "by islands hidden in the blood," cannot be imagined as corporeal. He rises, along with the "off-shore" scene, into the consciousness of the "you" he addresses—and since he *is* offshore, this "you" cannot be Gloucester. Presumably, the addressee at this point is Olson himself, though it may also be the reader, who may participate with Olson in this experience. If the reader at this point congenially takes "you" to mean himself, he is effectively engaged on a contract that requires accepting the terms of Olson's psychic experience, including the voice of Maximus, as his own. Or, if the reader is more resistant—the more likely case, particularly for a reader who wants to maintain his intellectual independence, and the almost certain case for Olson's as-yet-unconverted reader—he has available the alternative contractual position of privileged witness of this imaginary auditory event. Olson, for his part, contracts with his audience to act the part of exemplary recipient of a moral education. He (and thus his reader) will hear from the spectral voice in the mind "what is a lance, who obeys the figures of / the present dance." He will hear what constitutes a proper leader or "metal hot from boiling water" like Maximus (and in the distant background, oddly, Melville's Ahab) and what constitutes correct behavior (obedience to the dance).[22] Olson thus becomes, in one sense, the simultaneous channel and locus of the works and deeds of Maximus; in another sense, he implicitly takes upon himself the role of Havelock's Homeric hero.

The next two sections of this opening "letter" continue the fiction of a mentalistic discourse, by developing an apparent counterpoint between the imagined address of Maximus and the associated or responsive thought of the figure we can call "Olson himself":

> the thing you're after
> may lie around the bend
> of the nest (second, time slain, the bird! the bird!
>
> And there! (strong) thrust, the mast! flight
>   (of the bird
>   o kylix, o
>   Antony of Padua
>   sweep low, o bless
> the roofs, the old ones, the gentle steep ones
> on whose ridge-poles the gulls sit, from which they depart,
>
>   And the flake-racks
> of my city!   (5)

Maximus speaks first, opening the topic of desire ("the thing you're after"); and everything that follows, in the never-closed parenthesis, happens in the mind of "Olson." This ideation fluctuates between 1) asyntactic or sublinguistic responses to the mental imagery of a bird commencing flight (and probably, the conventional romantic association of that flight with "soaring" poetic imagination), and the superimposed imagery of a mast (presumably Maximus' sailship, since there is at this point nothing else to attach it to); and 2) the emergence of articulated verbal sequences that accomplish, through asyntactic accumulation and *correctio* ("the roofs, the old ones, the gentle steep ones"), a somewhat oblique epic invocation. The reader is invited to regard this ideation as rising on the submerged crests of an autonomous speech faculty, moving in waves from the initiatory speech impulse of Maximus/Olson through

22. In *The Special View of History*, 45–46, Olson defines the ethical will of the truly great man as a "will of achievement," or the "*obeying function*" of the true self, which he grounds in a vaguely Whiteheadian notion of psychic experience. One obeys the process-in-reality, the "dance."

an endless, digressive parenthesis, which allows inclusion of more material than any overtly propositional language would formally permit, and which simply plays itself out until the next wave enters consciousness.

As the reader thus engages with the terms of Olson's voice, Maximus advances his second main proposition—"love is form, and cannot be without / important substance." This extends the topic of desire and generates in the subsequent parenthesis an exegetical discursus by the poet, including an announcement of his epic method as well as a second invocation to "my lady of good voyage," who will prove in subsequent "letters" to be Olson's favorite Muse. The announcement of method, an evident paraphrase of the proem-ode in *Paterson,* invokes what by Olson's time is standard procedure in modern verse epic:

> feather to feather added
> (and what is mineral, what
> is curling hair, the string
> you carry in your nervous beak, these
>
> make bulk, these, in the end, are
> the sum   (5)

Feathers, minerals, hairs, and animalcules generally—rolling up the sum—and so to man, to Maximus. The "important substance" of the "form" that "love" (or desire) creates is, like the nest of the bird addressed by Olson here, an accumulation of particulars that are, in Pound's "grab-bag" fashion, to be incorporated as they come to hand (or beak). In this way Olson engages his reader, in the first two segments of the opening "letter," with his characteristic mode of voice and establishes his methodological contract—through the dramatized apparition of the Maximus-aspect of himself, and his consequent reception of the bardic inspiration. If the reader accepts the terms of this voice, and thereby the premises that justify it, Olson establishes from the outset his credentials as an Olsonian "humanist" and modern bard. The reader most likely to accept these terms, it seems most probable, is going to come from the existing tribal audience for whom the conventions invoked are reasonably familiar and valid. Olson's prime audience emerges fairly quickly as the audience left him by Whitman, Williams, and Pound.

The subsequent three sections of Olson's first "letter" expand Maximus' initial phrases to a complete oration. This largely exhortational piece begins by announcing and amplifying the basic problem that the promised moral education must resolve: "But that which matters, that which insists, that which will last, / that! o my people, where shall you find it . . . / when all is become billboards, when, all, even silence, is spray-gunned?" (6). Without really answering this question—in effect, the contracted-for education is the answer, so the audience must wait— Maximus/Olson makes a direct and extreme appeal for action: "(o Gloucester-man . . . o kill kill kill kill kill / those / who advertise you out)" (7–8). The rhetoric of this speech is truly surprising, since it offers no intelligible motivation for the violent action, and it does not offer persuasive proof that the real impediment to finding out "that which matters" is the commercialized culture that encloses Gloucester. Obviously, the warrant for Olson's exhortation is the conventional vision of a conflict between "billboard culture" and live culture, between usurocracy/pejorocracy and civilization, which Olson inherits from his modernist masters. This convention (by the mid-1950s, if not sooner) had degenerated to such a cliché that no argument need be made, at least not for Olson's tribal audience. The argument is assumed as self-evidently true. In opening from the stasis of an assumed truth, and then moving from it to amplification and exhortation, Maximus/Olson adopts the rhetoric of a sermon. The speaker's persuasiveness depends entirely on the already granted authority of both the proposition and his ethos. In short, one directs this rhetoric to an inside audience whose values are to be intensified rather than changed. In Olson's case, this means an audience that has to some extent already undergone the proposed moral education. The skeptical witness-audience of *Maximus* is not here directly addressed, nor is the average Gloucester-man, despite Olson's diction.

This hortatory and violent sermon may indirectly engage the reader, either as witness or believer, but fictively it is not addressed to anyone at all, as we soon discover. Maximus is still offshore. In section 6, he and the bird head in toward Gloucester:

> in! in ! the bow-sprit, bird, the break
> in the bend is, in, goes in, the form
> that which you make
>
> . . . .
>
>   The nest, I say, to you, I Maximus, say
>   under the hand, as I see it, over the waters
>   from this place where I am   (8)

Maximus thus appears, if we imagine him as anything more than an abstract urge in Olson's psyche, as standing at the gunwale of a boat (or floating in the air or water), saying what he *would say* to the city across the water, a city that cannot yet hear or understand him. The actual audience of the text—tribal readers, believer-participants, and skeptical witnesses—is thus engaged with Maximus/Olson's central problem: how shall he gain the understanding and obedience of the city? How will he get the Gloucester-man to carry out the dire command of humanist conscience? This unsolved problem is the object of the poet-hero's education, and to the extent that the audience identifies with Maximus/Olson's problem, it will be theirs also. For the would-be poet-pedagogues among the tribe engaged by Olson, this implies a fundamentally rhetorical education.

The text of the first "letter" of *Maximus* thus attracts to itself an audience amenable to the terms of Olson's psychologized voice—and an audience, moreover, that can initially grant the value of the proposed undertaking. In the second and third "letters," which complete the overture to *Maximus,* the initial contract is both amplified and refined, and the role of the audience is confirmed. "Letter 2" contrasts a culture subverted by "pejorocracy" and the acts of a series of heroic fishermen, and then closes with the hope that "the demand / will arouse / some of these men and women" (12). "Letter 3" essentially expands the negative side of this antithesis, elaborating on the perverting effects of absentee ownership—"they whine to my people, these entertainers, sellers / they play upon their bigotries" (14). It concludes with an "oratorical" address to the fictive audience, defined now as a saving remnant:

> o tansy city, root city
> let them not not make you
> as the nation is
>
> I speak to any of you, not to you all, to no group, not to you as citizens
> as my Tyrian might have. Polis now
> is a few, is a coherence not even yet new (the island of this city
> is a mainland now of who? who can say who are
> citizens?   (15)

Maximus of Gloucester thus appears to depart, very early on, from the ways of Maximus of Tyre. Instead of addressing the anonymous inhabitant, or the vulgar mass, he speaks to the true citizen who must claim his rightful inheritance. The audience of the text, if it holds "true citizenship" as valuable as it must to be engaged with Olson's undertaking, is invited to think of itself as an elect minority whose duty is to become the humanist conscience of the polis. Finally, Maximus/Olson announces the authoritative action of the educator of true citizens:

> Root person in root place, hear one tansy-covered boy tell you
> what any knowing man of your city might
>
> .   .   .   .
>
> they'd tell you
> the condition of the under-water, the cut-water of anyone   (16)

The true poet-pedagogue will reveal the substratum of consciousness in which all his rightful and privileged understanders must participate. That is what Olson's psychologized voice, in dramatizing the mental apparition of Maximus and his fictive address to the city of Gloucester, has been doing all along. Olson thus demonstrates his ethical authority for an audience that accepts the initial terms of his voice, and contractually affirms the future action of his epic as dramatized psychic experience—an education through accumulative, encyclopedic examination of the materials of an American humanist ethos.

From this point on, the figure of Maximus as a fictive orator exhorting the saving remnant of Gloucester tends to disappear, as Butterick and others have noted. The exhorter does, however, have moments of resurgence—which is to say that the whole idea of an oratorical poetry figures in the text more and more as an idea, or a conceit toward which Olson may sometimes gesture, and less and less as a reality. And, if it need be said (though Olson's explicators seldom say so), a comparison of the Olsonian discourse that follows "Letter 3" with any oration of consequence—Isocrates' *Panegyricus,* for example, a major speech in the sophistical (and pre-Socratic) tradition, and a speech that means to inspire a sense of citizenship in its audience—makes the non-oratorical quality of Olson's voice abundantly obvious. In general, as the text of *Maximus* piles up, the name "Maximus" becomes a transparent cover for Olson himself in the role of poetic culture-pedagogue, who speaks in his privacy for an enlightened few. And along with this withdrawal from the stance of civic orator, there is a necessary shift of emphasis from consideration of civic virtue to an insistent and abiding concern with the ethical qualities of the poet himself.

In "letters" 5 through 7, for example, following a short lyric interlude ("The Songs of Maximus") in which the poet celebrates the virtues of poverty in a consumer civilization, Vincent Ferrini is dealt his famous drubbing for publishing Olson in poor company (in the pages of *Four Winds*). Foregrounded, in consequence, is literary and artistic virtue, or, more specifically, the proper function of a little magazine. Olson's criticisms are various: *Four Winds* is vaguely spiritual and removed from the sharp facts of life; it evokes a nostalgic past instead of engaging the present; and (worst of all) it simply publishes Ferrini's friends, a poetic clique, instead of seeking first-rate material. It contributes nothing to the cultural growth of Olson's citizens and so has no place in the polis. This moves Olson to consider examples of "the old measure of care" (which Ferrini lacks) in the lives of fishermen and of Ezra Pound (whose status is ambiguous). His point is that a literatus *ought* to have the same judicious attentiveness to the actual details of his life and work that a fisherman does. Olson humbly includes a pair of anecdotes from his youth to show that he has lacked this carefulness and has been hurt thereby (bad eyes from looking into the sun-blaze on the water, and a weakened heart from pridefully racing an Englishman up a mountain trail), thus demonstrating his own need for the education that the *Maximus* poems enact. These considerations provide the motive for the conclusion of "Letter 6":

> So few need to,
> to make the many
> share (to have it,
> too)
>
> but those few . . .
>
>> What kills me is, how do these others think
>> the eyes are
>> sharp? by gift? bah [. . .]
>
> There are no hierarchies, no infinite, no such many as mass, there are only
> eyes in all heads,
> to be looked out of   (33)

The literatus, or any other citizen, can acquire the desirable sensibility through the effort of attention: becoming one of the "few" who can "make the many share" is a consequence of applied virtue rather than natural gifts. Olson thus disclaims any natural superiority and appeals to the virtues of "caring" as the measure by which both he and Ferrini must be judged. However, at the same time, he creates the basis of a severely negative judgment against "these others" who fail to join the "few." Their fault becomes disinclination to apply or exercise their latent virtue, and thus a sort of willful, lazy, uncaring stupidity. At this point, though, the judgment is not made. Olson moves on, in "Letter 7," to amplify his notions of the "measure of care." He culls the necessary traits of Maximus-figures from consideration of the life of an early Gloucester shipwright ("the first Maximus"), the arrogance of Ezra Pound, an assortment of Gloucester characters who display "exactness," and the sharp eyes and skilled hands of the artist Marsden Hartley. The "Ferrini letters" thus initiate the body of *The Maximus Poems* by raising the issue of the poet/artist's proper role in the polis; and, at the same time, the "letters" develop the criteria that form the basis for a definitive resolution of the issue, through reference to ethical exempla. This foregrounding of a question of literary ethics, at the outset of the work, implies an intended audience for whom the issue can matter—an audience composed essentially of fellow poets or would-be poets, rather than citizens (unless *poet* and *citizen* have become synonymous terms, which seems probable). The "Ferrini letters" decisively change the audience image projected by the text of *Maximus,* and they likewise shift the emphasis of the education which that audience will undergo as witness and/or participant in Olson's self-enactment.

The subsequent section, "Tyrian Businesses," forms another interlude comparable in function to "The Songs of Maximus." Instead of exhortation, invective, or moral exempla, the reader is presented with the inner life of Olson/Maximus as he sets himself a "morning exercise"—"how to dance / sitting down" (39). This exercise involves, mainly, some fanciful studies in semantics and etymology; a number of minute observations, some of which become the basis of metaphor; and a prose journal entry dealing with a seafaring episode, followed by thoughts on "lady luck" and her symbol, the fylfot/swastika. The basic exercise, learning the "dance" that Olson as a poet must "obey," is attention to the materials he must work with. Olson shows himself as living up to the ethical criteria developed through the "Ferrini letters": he is training his virtue. In so doing, he becomes an exemplum, the prime exemplum in his own text, for an audience of potential or would-be Maximuses. This explicit foregrounding of himself as preferred subject—and his psychic experience has, at least implicitly, been the preferred subject all along (though the object of that experience need not be himself)—sets the stage for "Letter 9" and the remainder of Volume I of *The Maximus Poems*.

In "Letter 9," the poet speaks in his own person, perhaps directly to the reader—but more likely to himself, if the role of the reader is still to be privileged witnessing or participating in his psychic experience. He celebrates the publication of his latest book, and muses on the vicissitudes of authorship: "in another spring, I learned / the world does not stop / for flowers" (46), meaning poems. He thinks of his poems as "those self-acts which have no end no more than their own" (48). He reconfirms an ethic based on what Olson has called (in relation to his fishermen) "the practice of the self" (35), a vitalistic ethic based on the pursuit of one's individual vision of desire, and a poetics of self-dramatization for the poem he now appears in. This notion of poems as "self-acts" comes dangerously close to, and perhaps is, a version of "art for art's sake," and as such may be a betrayal of the entire public or culture-reforming motive from which *The Maximus Poems* (and bardic poetry generally) springs. The way out for Olson, possibly, is a claim that "self-action" is the essential quality of directed will in a factive man, or a member of the "Divine Inert": action based on non-corrupted, non-ulterior motives from the deep self puts the polis on its true humanist path. And yet, at the same time, the skeptical reader cannot help but see in this ethic the beginnings of withdrawal toward a private world, and indeed a rejection of the "vulgar" processes of politics and other public action, such as we have seen already in *The Special View of History*.[23]

Olson's inward turn becomes emphatic at the close of "Letter 9." He forges what amounts to a new contract for the ensuing text:

> I measure my song,
> measure the sources of my song,
> measure me, measure
> my forces   (48)

The audience is now engaged to watch Olson/Maximus inspect himself and his sources (meaning his humanist tradition and its history, which is "his-story") as he moves in "Letter 10" to presentation of his myth of frustrated destiny. This presentation goes forward under the guise of an investigation—"on founding: was it puritanism, / or was it fish?" (49).

23. See Bernstein, *The Tale of the Tribe*, 262, for another view of this withdrawal.

In fact, however, the myth has already been accepted in its general shape by the audience that has granted the terms of Olson's voice and the ethical antitheses upon which textual movement to this point has largely depended. Olson knows this, and so closes the historical question only nine lines later: "It was fishing was first." This proposition, as Perry Miller has noted, is fairly commonplace, but hardly uncontroversial; Miller treats it as oversimplification and misconception.[24] But Olson, as he did in his early "oration" in "Letter 1," simply ignores the actual controversy (or potential controversy), assumes the position, and elaborates upon it. He reflects, for example, upon the "Elizabethan-Puritan" confrontation, the passage of "Tudor" to "James," and Endecott's seizure of Conant's house. In the entire historical consideration that develops from this point and runs through all three volumes of *The Maximus Poems,* Olson's interpretation of history is not really at issue. The audience is engaged with the poet-hero's self-educational process. He pores over his sources, "measures" them according to the ethical criteria that the text has established, and thereby accumulates a series of moral exempla that give concreteness and particularity to the notions of virtue to which he himself (and his audience) must measure up.

As the "encyclopedia" ramifies, Olson maintains his ethical authority through periodic foregroundings of himself, rather than the moral lessons of history, as the immediate object of attention. In "Maximus, to Himself"—a moment of rare and appealing humility—he reflects upon his own shortcomings, his estrangement from familiar things, and the "undone business" before him. In "Letter 15," he revises a minor historical thesis and elliptically defends his poetics of digressive "rhapsodia," combining this defense with reflections on "The American epos" in an age of advertising and an explicit address to an audience of literati: "(o Po-ets, you / should getta / job" (75).[25] Through such episodes as these, which demonstrate his humble attentiveness and his adherence to a "humanist" concept of poetry, Olson somewhat circularly fulfills the ethical criteria he has established *through his own authority.* He thereby

24. See Perry Miller, in his Prefatory Note (1956) to "The Marrow of Puritan Divinity" (1935) in *Errand Into the Wilderness,* 49.

25. Or as Hart Crane once said to Waldo Frank: "[I]s there any good evidence forthcoming from the world in general that the artist isn't completely out of a job?" (*Complete Poems and Selected Letters and Prose,* 230).

defines himself to his insider audience as an exemplary bardic poet within a closed system of values.[26]

To the extent that this is true, the rhetoric of *Maximus* is certainly a rhetoric of authority. The ultimate appeal, as with Olson's bardic predecessors, is to the ethical qualities of the poet-hero himself. This rhetoric is, further, primarily sermonistic or "pastoral" in nature: truths are announced and then amplified; to maintain the credibility of the teaching, they are (at least fictively) lived up to. This kind of rhetoric is perhaps in keeping with a sacerdotal role—and indeed, it is the general sort of rhetoric we have seen from Whitman onward as the bard requires and persuades the reader to assume what the text assumes. Such a rhetoric also implies (and consistently causes) deep difficulty for the entire culture-shaping project, because it simply excludes the audience that fails or declines to agree with its initial and very large assumptions. And this excluded audience is the very one that a cultural revolution must "meet and win." Olson's rendition of the bardic rhetoric, moreover, seems to suffer from this even more acutely than did the attempts of his major predecessors, since the inital assumptions of *Maximus* are so insistent and, beginning with the exhortation of "Letter 1," so extreme. Olson confines himself, nearly from the outset, to a fairly restricted audience of citizen-poets, or fellow humanists—and then he tells them what they need is "humanism."

This exclusion of the unredeemed from Olson's rhetorical field implies, at least potentially, a certain amount of collusion in the author-audience relation. The audience is invited, insofar as it accepts the proliferating terms of Olson's self-representation, to regard itself as a sacred band of fellow communicants in a virtually timeless truth, themselves surrounded by a lapsed, degenerate world. Author and audience can huddle together in self-congratulation and let the rest go by. Still, it may be arguable that since *Maximus* foregrounds the sacerdotal life as its preferred subject, the audience can be propaedeutically brought to the

26. Olson uses the authority of his *voice* to establish himself as a representative of his "humanist" tradition; this permits him to pass ethical judgments on the past and present; the judgments yield a set of *particular* ethical qualities as the constituents of virtue; and these constituents then compose the ethos that Olson, as "Maximus," displays—thereby renewing his ethical authority . . . and so on, in something of an endless spiral.

materials required for the rhetoric of some future cultural revolution. Certainly, by foregrounding "Maximus" as a figure for the sacerdotal will, Olson does at least suggest that his audience of citizen-poets enter into some sort of forum (however restricted its entry may be), rather than retreat into the sort of detached, sociopolitically irrelevant aestheticism that Ferrini's "clique" and *Four Winds* represent.

This line of thought, however, brings us back again to the rhetoric embodied in the text. Maximus himself is a sermonizer; and Olson is a pedagogue. Both depend on the rhetoric of authority. Further, what Olson ultimately proposes as a humanist response to the historical situation—in addition to the example set by himself—is problematic. We see this solution emerging as early as "Capt Christopher Levett (of York)":

> cheapness shit is
> upon the world. We'll turn
> to keep our house, turn to
> houses where our kind,
> and hungry after them,
>
> not willing to bear one short walk
> more out into even what they've done
> to earth itself, find
> company.   (138)

This is not the imaginary address of "Maximus" to a distant city of fishermen across the water; this is Olson, speaking with an inclusive "we," for himself and his humanist tribe, the "Divine Inert." The world is befouled, and they will henceforth have nothing more to do with it. They turn to "houses" where "our kind . . . find company." This sort of appeal recurs at intervals as Volume I of *The Maximus Poems* progresses toward its close. The most arresting instance is Olson's sudden breaking-off of the historical excursus, in "Letter, May 2, 1959," to deliver this exhortation:

> step off
> onto the nation   The sea
> will rush over   The ice
> will drag boulders   Commerce
> was changed the fathometer
> was invented here the present

> is worse give nothing now your credence
> start all over   (155)

Olson's audience of citizens is thus enjoined to simply reject present reality, and indeed to refuse to deal with it on its own terms. The sacerdotal elite is now apparently to withdraw to its private world, to shelter and preserve its own probably ever-hardening position. This is absolutely disastrous advice for a rhetorical project intending cultural change, since it entails refusal to speak to or even consider those still living in the rejected present. Yet Olson himself, in the subsequent *Maximus* poems, seems to act upon the sort of conclusions that his exhortation embodies.

In "Maximus, to Gloucester, Sunday, July 19," Olson presents what is ostensibly an "address to the city" once again. He speaks of the annual memorial service for the city's drowned fishermen: "and they stopped before that bad sculpture of a fisherman" (157). Yet the Gloucester-people are actually spoken about, in the third person, for all but a last brief segment of the poem, which itself is an uncompleted gesture. The utterance beginning "let you who paraded . . ." simply shades off in digressive thought-waves, and reaches no verb. The gesture, as dramatically represented by the text, is imaginary. Olson is musing in his privateness. The audience for this musing is, as always, Olson's humanist literati, for whom he presents the virtue of his own memorious, imaginary act: "The drowned men are undrowned . . . The disaster / is undone" (157). The implication is fairly clear. The literatus may reclaim the wreckage of the past by *remembering,* and he becomes thereby the keeper of a sacred trust. This appeal to a sort of holy stewardship, conjoined with the exhortation in the previous poem, prepares the way for Olson's retreat into oracular pronouncements, private (and rather fanciful) mythologies, "Jungian" archetypes, and an ever-narrowing audience through the subsequent two volumes. It also prepares the way, most probably, for the self-indulgent deterioration of Olson's style, which most of his critics (beyond, perhaps, an inner circle) have found cause to censure.

The rhetorical situation of the later *Maximus* poems has undergone a transformation. Olson can and does assume the devoted, world-repudiating audience that the exhortations in the first volume finally require. He can and does assume, in fact, an audience almost wholly predisposed to agree and ready to regard his least utterance—fragments and jottings on the back of an envelope, for example—as important and significant, simply because he was the source.[27] In consequence, Olson's oracular stance veers off into the rhetoric of the memo, the word game, and the doodle. There are, of course, some striking moments of recovery, especially in those occasional short lyrics where Olson returns to the stasis of "Maximus, to Himself," and the sort of honest self-examination it involves. Those moments, however, are few and far between.

In the end, Olson's polis becomes no more than a few close friends, as in "OCEANIA" (Volume III): "And no one / to tell it to / but you / / / for Robert Hogg, Dan Rice and / Jeremy Prynne" (540). The reading audience, certainly, is still invited to consider itself as part of this privileged company. However, the audience that does join with Olson in these later volumes commits itself to collusive regression into a private world—a regression at times resembling a boy's make-believe, and at times resembling something worse. On pages 467–69 in Volume III, for example, Olson develops two untitled poems in which he fancies that the "menhirs and cromlechs" lining the shores of Gloucester are the legendary Roman soldiers turned to stone by Saint Cornély as he fled from them into northwestern France. This is undoubtedly meant as "metamorphosis" of the beach rocks, or an instance of mythic perception, but as poetic invention it is embarrassingly puerile; Olson resembles Tom Sawyer more than he does Thoreau.

As Olson withdraws with his preferred audience into the "republic" which he pretends to write "in gloom on watch-house point" (III, 377), the relation between this republic and the outer world becomes increasingly untenable and hostile. In the first place, it seems to take shape as the result of a *repopulation,* or the restitution of a time in which "human beings came back," who "listened / / to the sententious" (384). This, in effect, defines "humanity" as Olson's limited audience. On the other hand, Olson's stance toward "nonhumanity" degenerates to a murderous if impotent hatred. In one of his untitled spiral-poems, for example, he declares that "human lives are so much trash," and tells his reader "how right / it is to hate" as he represents himself shooting "big scared rats" on

27. Such an assumption seems clearly to underlie the posthumous compilation of the third volume of *Maximus,* which George F. Butterick and Charles Boer carried out at Olson's request. But much the same could be said for the second volume. Olson presents his readers with an album of largely unfinished scraps and miscellaneous jottings, in which no principle of selection or arrangement (other than chronology) appears to operate.

a rubbish heap (498). Shooting the "rats," perhaps, is how Olson would have his citizens prepare the way for his repopulation of the republic with "human beings." This suggestion is not excessive. In one of the final segments of Volume III—"His health, his poetry, and his love all in one"—Olson brings his stance toward the vulgar world to its consummate expression:

> One does only wish
> that these poor stuffed people,
> & their hopelessly untreated children
> —except to anything they want—
> cld either be removed
> to the cemetery
> or to the moon   (620)

At this point, the "rats" become everyone outside Olson's narrow audience of fellow humanists, and Olson's fantasy revolution becomes a kind of righteous genocide. The outer world and the people in it, in the end, are nothing but an obstacle, or as Olson actually says at one point, a *distraction* to the clarity of "my attentions" (585). Meanwhile "an Earth like this one we / few American poets have / carved out of nature and of God" (556–57) becomes the only world in which the Maximus-figure willingly moves. In sum, then, Olson refuses to talk to, or even regard, the society of "poor stuffed people" or anyone who does not already agree with him. This is disaster for a countercultural project, unless Olson has the means to kill off everyone who denies or simply fails to notice his authority. Indeed, this is what he would like to do; moreover, it is the very action that he, as Maximus, recommended to his imaginary listeners in his opening *Maximus* poem ("I, Maximus of Gloucester, to You"). The refusal to talk is nothing new at this point, nor is the shrill and violent hatred that accompanies that refusal. Both are characteristic of Olson's rhetoric, and he consequently dooms himself and his followers to fail in his cultural-revolutionary ambitions. It is as if Saint Paul refused to address the Gentiles, and dreamed of their extermination instead.[28]

28. In Volume II, Olson asks the question, "[O]n what grounds shall we criticize the City Manager?" (258). At the end of his text, we are compelled to turn this question on Olson/Maximus himself, and wonder what sort of "City Manager" or republic maker he would be, if actually given the power.

At the end of *The Maximus Poems,* then, our skepticism remains, or is increased. In what sense can Olson be said to really advance the goals of the sacerdotal tribe? In *Paterson,* as we have seen, Williams manages to intimate a somewhat different rhetorical direction, namely, movement toward a poetry that substitutes "formal invention" as its sign of authority for the orphic voice of tradition. And it appropriates the language available from the "supplying female" of live society—including "the hurley-burley" of political encounters—in order to speak as the voice of existing public culture. Certainly, pursuit of such a poetry seems to be in the best Whitmanesque tradition. The Olson of *The Maximus Poems,* however, declines to pursue this alternative direction in bardic rhetoric; and in fact, his hostility to the "vulgar" people around him suggests an outright repudiation of the possibility Williams raises. It is true, of course, that *The Maximus Poems* may in some sense make a contribution to the American bardic tradition by proposing the rhetor as a model for the literatus. But in further proposing for this rhetor a sermonistic rhetoric of authority, conjoined with a retreat from the public forum to an audience of virtual acolytes, Olson destroys whatever potential use this proposal may have. His rejection of the public world, in the end, commits him to the rather paradoxical status—considering his original ambitions, and the ambitions of the bardic project generally—of a cult leader, a demagogue to the withdrawn few. And by rendering his devoted followers politically inert, Olson betrays his own humanist mythology, for the ideal of even his own humanism is the "original town-man"—civic man and, therefore, political man.

The bardic poet, if he is to fulfill his role as educator of the polis, or as proponent of the true national ethos, must address the many and not the few. If he speaks *for* the many, he may perhaps use a rhetoric of authority, or a sermonistic rhetoric intending a sublime beholding of an assumed mythology, since he and his audience then stand together, within a closed system of values—a shared and unquestioned system of conventional beliefs available for public celebration. But if he speaks for the few, and seeks a transformation of the many—which is the situation of an advocate for Olson's humanism, and of the Whitmanesque bard generally—he must adopt a different rhetoric, one that the pedagogical action of *The Maximus Poems* fails to either embody or provide.

IX. Phaeacia

To have great poets, there must be great audiences, too.
  —Whitman, "Ventures, on an Old Theme"

From Whitman onward, the poet succeeds in gaining an audience of sacerdotal literati, or a tribe responsive to the conventions with which he works, and succeeds (if he makes good use of his available, conventional means) in establishing himself as an authoritative, *poetic* spokesman for the tribal ethos he represents—but only in the eyes of the tribe itself. In *The Maximus Poems,* we see this rhetoric brought to a sort of ultimate extreme, as bard and tribe withdraw, in a mood of impotent hostility, from the field of public discourse. In summary, then, we may say that Olson's main achievement in bardic poetry is to enact for us an exaggerated paradigm of the rhetorical tradition created by his major predecessors. The rhetoric of countercultural authority is grounded in a mythic history and the figural credentials of a "sublime," abysmic voice, and it favors self-dramatization, tending to make the bard himself the foreground subject of his poem. History (or "his-story"), in this context, takes on the status of assumed belief, of background for the poet's *agon,* or even of incidental decor—what Allen Tate called Pound's "ostensible subjects." Where can you really go with such a rhetoric? Consistently, the poet succeeds in the first of the Whitmanesque goals—and sometimes quite impressively, as did Pound and Williams—as he speaks to his tribe, and renews the sacerdotal call. At the same time, he fails in the second and ultimate goal, which is to find a way for either bard or tribe to engage and cultivate the ethical will of the nation. From Whitman to Olson, the bardic poet's untransacted (literary) destiny remains what it always was: a splendid, quixotic, unattainable ambition.

It will not do, in the end, to praise the poets for what has been called their "epistemological honesty." As we have seen, the "honesty" of a superficial incoherence consists of a conventional stylistic appeal, a decorum in which the poet fictively pretends that his vision outpaces total comprehension, and defies conventional articulation. Epistemological honesty, in other words, is little more than a euphemism for the device that calls the tribal reader to the role of genial exegete, and implicitly requires assent in advance (or, at least, an initial assumption of "poetic truth"). It will not do, either, to excuse the poets for their failure, for their willingness to do no more than advance themselves as heroes for a literary cult, by declaring them somehow an "image of ourselves," or by gesturing toward what one critic calls "the peculiar dynamics of American culture, which can absorb eccentric individuals with tolerance and even admiration, but has difficulty answering challenges to common belief."[1] We cannot doubt that American culture is possessed of "peculiar dynamics," and that it is (for all that) resistant to "challenges"— such resistance is, most probably, a consequence of the flexible, absorbent, and tolerant dynamic itself. Neither can we doubt that American culture has its share of disturbing and disillusioning shortcomings (though, perhaps, resistance is not one of them). But mainstream public culture, with all its faults, cannot be cited as the cause of its failure to be engaged or affected by the American epic poem. That failure, as we have seen, is in fact a direct consequence of the conventions with which the poet works.

Consider, for example, another if nonpoetic version of the sacerdotal literatus, Martin Luther King, Jr. King's rhetorical situation was in many ways the same as that of the countercultural bard, for his rhetoric intended a change in the public ethos of the nation, and he spoke from a minority position, a position largely outside the cultural dynamics of American life. The point is that King succeeded. He entered the public conscience, and did alter the direction of the national will. We can argue that King's success was not complete, and that the American mind remained (and remains) slow to respond, or indeed resistant, to the

1. See Pearce, *The Continuity of American Poetry*, 133–36; and von Hallberg, *Charles Olson*, 42–43. The notion of "peculiar dynamics" is from von Hallberg. "Epistemological honesty," of course, is Bernstein's phrase, in *The Tale of the Tribe*, 276. Bernstein's euphemism seems, more than anything else, an effort to end what is, in fact, a highly critical study on an upbeat note. What we see at work is a major convention in the rhetoric of modern literary criticism—the imperative to celebrate, to strike an essentially encomiastic stance. The critics who characteristically break with this convention are few, and they stand out—as in the case of Yvor Winters.

challenge he presented. But we can hardly maintain that King was simply "absorbed," by a sort of amorphous, amoebalike dynamic, and thereby became nothing more than an oracle or demagogue to an alienated cult. In no sense, then, is it true that a sacerdotal polemic with the mainstream American ethos will necessarily be neutralized by the hurley-burley of opinion into which that polemic must go; the polemic will only be neutralized if it fails to find the necessary and available rhetorical means. King found the means, and thereby succeeded as a sacerdotal literatus in the truest sense, if not in Whitman's sense. It is no wonder that Williams looks upon the evangelist (Klaus, in *Paterson II*) and sees the poet as "rivaled" and "in disgrace." With King, certainly, the rhetorical skill and public effectiveness of the bardic poet are brilliantly surpassed.

The differences between the rhetorics of King and of the bardic poet are, perhaps, sufficiently obvious; but let us briefly note what they are. In the first place, King's ethical authority is typically grounded in sublime appeals to the constituent elements of American conscience—such as, for example, the Western (Judaeo-Christian) tradition in moral philosophy, democratic ideals, and the American identification with the rights of man—and he gives his reader the choice of joining with him or disavowing these fundamental ideals. Once the ideals are accepted, the reader (or listener) cannot avoid the logic of King's argument, since it is grounded in those same ideals. King's audience is compelled to admit the justice and the reasonability of his argument, or suffer the pain of a bad conscience. The bardic poet, in contrast, really has precious little ground from which to derive a source of ethical authority in the eyes of a public, non-tribal audience. His mythic history typically favors non-egalitarian, non-democratic, and non-Christian (*i.e.,* supposed archaic or pagan) values, and sets the poet in implicit opposition to the codes of value that King evokes, and with which most Americans identify themselves. The poets are more concerned with the rights of an elite of energetic geniuses or "artifexes" to order the world according to their heart's desire. What they tend toward, in essence, is a polity of faith in which all argument (or politics) will disappear, a polity of trusting selves who "listen to the sententious" simply because they *are* sententious. Should we be surprised if the national mind resists the challenge embodied in such values? Should we complain of this resistance?

But let us suppose, for a moment, that the poets are right. Their argument is not, after all, wholly without sources of appeal. The mythic history with which they work, not to mention the elemental antithesis of Jefferson and Hamilton (or a sort of populist republicanism versus Federalism, big government, and the banks) is a version of a mainstream political mythology that is still viable today. The poets also have available to them a potent, commonplace notion of personal liberty, as well as a belief in the moral responsibilities of legislators and men of affairs. It is conceivable, then, that the literatus could use his mythic history to convince us that the rights of man—conceived in terms of personal liberty within a stable and beautiful social order—could be best served by an enlightened authoritarianism, or by a privileged, aristocratic intelligentsia that looks to the artist for its ethical guidance and promotes the enterprise of factive, inventive individuals. It may be possible to demonstrate that the demo-liberal, egalitarian ideals of "anonymous government" or "mobocracy" really are absurdities (as William James suggested) and inconsistent with the lessons of history. It may be true, in short, that the poets' preferred authoritarian polity is really most consistent with the high national ambition to create a splendid, world-redeeming civilization equal to, or better than, the greatest civilizations of the past. If the poets could really convince us of the justice and reasonability of their preferences, we would unquestionably be driven to a hard choice, one involving a profound redefinition of the national ethos.

As rhetors, then, we must recognize the *sic et non* of things, and admit that the sacerdotal bard does have an available argument, however unpalatable its conclusions may be, and however (justifiably) resistant the "peculiar dynamics" of the national mind may be. His ultimate problem is presenting this argument. Within the conventions of bardic poetry, a direct discursive or narrative presentation—the means by which the poet might argue from a history to ethical and/or political conclusions, in something like a language accessible to the common mind—is virtually impossible. Poetry, within the tribal context, is generally defined as a language of prerational, affective, sublime (*i.e., unparaphrasable*) apprehension, and is so defined in opposition to the language(s) of reason and the conventions of public, "prosaic" discourse. This fundamentally romantic compartmentalization of language and of the mind divides the vital, intuitive beholding of experiential truth from the supposed falsities of common thought and discourse. And this inherited, conventional compartmentalization is the implicit, validating topos in the poets' preferences for a vital (or "humanist") elite, those who can apprehend reality directly, by intuition, those who are above the "vulgar ways" of political argument and democratic process. Within the tribal context, as a result, the so-called language of poetry reveals itself as the aboriginal language of the vital elite, and as the language of nonnegotiable truth. These tribal conventions of belief place the bardic poet in an irresolvable dilemma: insofar as he wants to write what will be acceptable *as poetry* to his inner audience of fellow tribesmen, and insofar as he wants to be regarded, by this audience, as an appropriate representative for the higher sensibility he wants to promote, he is obliged to speak what is self-consciously *not* the language of common understanding. The bard, in short, is obliged to reject the available means for effectively communicating his historical, political, and ethical vision to the public mind *insofar as he wants to succeed with his tribal audience*.

The sacerdotal literatus with ambitions for an ethical and cultural transformation of the nation, then, has two essential choices: he can proceed as a sacerdotal literatus in the nonpoetic manner, perhaps, of Martin Luther King; or he can proceed as a poet, as a bard, in the eyes of his tribal cult. But he cannot really be both bard and sacerdote (in the sense that King is a sacerdote) at the same time. Nor, we should add, can he play the role of bardic poet according to an arbitrarily constructed set of conceits, or a decorum unintelligible or unacceptable to the available tribal audience for bardic verse. To fail (or decline) to engage the primary and literary audience for poetry in terms of its prevailing codes of expectation and response is, in the present scheme of things, to have virtually no audience at all—a fate that Crane approaches in *The Bridge* (but does not quite reach, since parts of his text are salvageable as symbolist lyrics). To a certain extent, the necessary inability to reconcile the public with the poetic ambitions of the bardic project is acknowledged in the poets' generally voluminous explanations of themselves in prose. In texts such as *Patria Mia, The Spirit of Romance,* and *Jefferson and/or Mussolini,* Ezra Pound is a sacerdote who argues (after a fashion) for a vision of history and politics, and argues in something like an accessible public language. Even in prose, however, Pound regularly refuses to "fool" his reader with the "old trick" of "syllogistic arrangement" as he waxes inspirational with disconnected, aphoristic, peremptory assertion. In the *Cantos,* on the other hand, Pound is the bardic poet, presenting an extended picture of himself beholding a vision he cannot coherently articulate, thereby giving us, regardless of his actual intention, *himself* as the focal (and only coherent) object of our own response. As long as the conventions of bardic poetry remain as they have been, the poet will have no exit from this recurring and untenable situation. His literary tribe encircles him, a *cordon sanitaire* between himself and the world his high ambition wants to change.

Or the poet can try to persuade his tribe to change the conventions, to redefine the meaning of the term *poetic discourse.* This is a main intention in the rhetoric of *Paterson,* though it seems doubtful whether Williams' rhetoric goes far enough, or whether it can go far enough, in the necessary direction. But what Williams suggests, if fleetingly, is interesting: a definition of poetic discourse purely in terms of versification—in terms, that is, of prosodic pattern and "formal invention." This conception is not the same as formalistic concern with the poem as an autonomous, autotelic aesthetic object. This conception opens into concern for the poem as a rhetorical act, an act that appropriates any and all of the available conventional discourse-systems operant in public life—including the rational structures of narration and discursive argument—and raises them to the status of poetic eloquence. The poem could actually be, for example, a versified oration, such as we find in the odes of Pindar. Such a poetry, a poetry of versified (but otherwise "normal" or conventional) public language, may indeed be a vehicle for "meeting and winning" an audience of public selves in an act of ethical, historical, or political and economic persuasion; but it will only be available to the poet, as a vehicle, if his literary tribe decides that a poetry of versified "normal discourse" is poetry in the truest sense, and is the thing they want to hear.

This definition of poetic discourse effectively collapses the antitheses that underlie the major conventions of bardic rhetoric: the sublime and the rational are reintegrated, and the argumentative (discursive or narrational) replaces simple oracular declamation. Likewise, the romantic valorizing of the intuitive or vital truth-beholder above the codes of public common-sense is deprived of its ground, and there is little place left for a politics or a rhetoric of sublime authority. With its fundamental assumptions and antitheses collapsed, the bardic rhetoric dissolves. In sum, then, a sacerdotal poetry really adequate to the ultimate public goals of the Whitmanesque literatus would not be bardic, and perhaps not even Whitmanesque, at all.

Will the tribe of sacerdotal literati rewrite its conventions? One can only speculate, but the answer seems to be probably not. For one thing, the antirational stance within which the literatus is situated—and particularly in his modernist incarnation—militates against a skeptical confrontation with assumptions, and likewise discourages a rational examination of the logical consequences of those assumptions. One beholds truths; one knows them to be truths by the intensity, or the sublimity, with which they strike the perceiving mind; and these truths do not fall out in relations of logical entailment, but simply constellate in "simultaneous orders," or obsessional clusters. The skepticism of the rhetor, within this frame of mind, is something of a moral failure. As Olson once said, "[T]he trouble with professors today . . . is that they don't *believe* what they know."[2] The failure to believe, for Olson at least, is evidence of the failure to perceive. His skeptical professors are degenerate cases. This perception transfers to the vulgar world as a whole, where general failure to recognize the truth of the poet's obsessional system stands as an indictment of corrupt contemporary mores. The bardic literatus, as long as he sincerely holds to the characteristic antirational stance of his tradition, is unlikely to be persuaded out of his intense convictions; a criticism is only proof of the critic's depravity. The bardic mind is "resistant" indeed. And insofar as the bardic literatus does decline to confront his own assumptions or their probable consequences, he is compelled—as he has been compelled—to live out the logic of his own position.

What, then, shall we say to the bardic literatus, or to the tribe with whom his authority is greatest? Shall we try to propose a rewriting of the tacit rules for sacerdotal poetry? All we can do, perhaps, is say that the bard's available means, as presently constituted, defeat his greatest ambitions. Before he can engage the public mind, he must speak the public language; and before he can speak the public language, his immediate audience, the *cordon sanitaire* of literary peers, disciples, exegetes, and critics, must shift its ground. The inner tribe may prefer a dance of exegetical communion in the cloisters of an orphic discourse. Within that situation the bardic poem itself becomes a rather pointless ritual, serving only to establish the poet's canonical status within the shrine. That state of affairs amounts to an abandonment and indeed a betrayal of

2. Boer, *Charles Olson in Connecticut*, 13.

the original motive of the bardic undertaking. The tradition of the bardic poem can continue in this false position, and it can probably continue for a very long time; or it can change. And the initiative, ultimately, rests not only with the poet but also with the tribe that constitutes his primary and encircling audience—the tribe with whom, like Odysseus among the Phaeacians, he is marooned.

Bibliography

By the Poets

Crane, Hart. *The Bridge: A Poem by Hart Crane.* 1933; rpr. New York, 1970.
———. *The Complete Poems and Selected Letters and Prose of Hart Crane.* Edited by Brom Weber. New York, 1966.
———. *The Letters of Hart Crane, 1916–1932.* Edited by Brom Weber. Berkeley, 1965.
Olson, Charles. *Additional Prose.* Bolinas, 1974.
———. *Call Me Ishmael.* San Francisco, 1947.
———. *The Maximus Poems.* Berkeley, 1983.
———. *Selected Writings.* Edited by Robert Creeley. New York, 1966.
———. *The Special View of History.* Berkeley, 1970.
Olson, Charles, and Robert Creeley. *Charles Olson & Robert Creeley: The Complete Correspondence.* Edited by George F. Butterick. 2 vols. Santa Barbara, 1980.
Pound, Ezra. *ABC of Reading.* New Haven, 1934.
———. *A Lume Spento and Other Early Poems.* New York, 1965.
———. *The Cantos of Ezra Pound.* New York, 1981.
———. *Collected Early Poems of Ezra Pound.* Edited by Michael John King. New York, 1976.
———. *Confucius: The Unwobbling Pivot, The Great Digest, The Analects.* New York, 1951.
———. *Confucius to Cummings.* New York, 1964.
———. *Gaudier-Brzeska: A Memoir.* 1916; rpr. New York, 1960.
———. *Guide to Kulchur.* 1938; rpr. New York, 1970.
———. *Jefferson and/or Mussolini.* 1935; rpr. New York, 1970.
———. *Literary Essays of Ezra Pound.* Edited by T. S. Eliot. New York, 1968.
———. *Personae.* New York, 1971.

————. *The Selected Letters of Ezra Pound*. New York, 1971.

————. *Selected Poems of Ezra Pound*. New York, 1957.

————. *Selected Prose 1909 – 1965*. Edited by William Cookson. New York, 1973.

————. *The Spirit of Romance*. New York, 1968.

————. "Vorticism." In *The Modern Tradition*, edited by Richard Ellmann and Charles Feidelson, Jr. New York, 1965.

Whitman, Walt. *Complete Poetry and Collected Prose*. New York, 1982.

Williams, William Carlos. "America, Whitman, and the Art of Poetry." *Poetry Journal* (November, 1917), 27 – 36.

————. "Appendix IV." *New Directions* 17 (1961), 307 – 10.

————. *The Autobiography of William Carlos Williams*. New York, 1967.

————. "Danse Pseudomacabre." In *The Farmers' Daughters*. New York, 1961.

————. *The Embodiment of Knowledge*. Edited, from an unpublished manuscript (1928 – 30), by Ron Loewinsohn. New York, 1974.

————. "An Essay on Leaves of Grass." In *Leaves of Grass One Hundred Years After*, edited by Milton Hindus. Stanford, 1955.

————. *Imaginations*. Includes *Kora in Hell* (1918, 1920, 1957), *Spring and All* (1923), *The Great American Novel* (1923), *The Descent of Winter* (1928), and *A Novelette and Other Prose* (1932). Edited by Webster Schott. New York, 1970.

————. *Interviews with William Carlos Williams*. Edited by Linda Wagner. New York, 1976.

————. *In the American Grain*. 1925; rpr. New York, 1956.

————. "The Later Pound." *Massachusetts Review*, XIV : 1 (Winter, 1973), 129.

————. "Letter to an Australian Editor." *Briarcliff Quarterly*, III : 2 (October, 1946), 207 – 208.

————. "Let Us Order Our World." *William Carlos Williams Review*, III : 2 (Fall, 1982), 18.

————. *Many Loves*. New York, 1961.

————. *Paterson*. New York, 1963.

————. *Pictures from Brueghel*. New York, 1962.

————. *Selected Essays*. New York, 1969.

————. *Selected Letters*. Edited by J. C. Thirlwall. New York, 1957.

————. *Selected Poems*. New York, 1969.

————. "The Situation in American Writing." *Partisan Review*, IV : 4 (Summer, 1939), 41 – 44.

————. "A Study of Ezra Pound's Present Position." *Massachusetts Review*, XIV : 1 (Winter, 1973), 118.

Classical/Neoclassical Rhetoric and Bellettristic Theory

Adams, John Quincy. *Lectures on Rhetoric and Oratory.* Cambridge, Mass.,
    1810.
Aristotle. *The Rhetoric and the Poetics of Aristotle.* Translated by W. Rhys
    Roberts and Ingram Bywater. New York, 1954.
Blair, Hugh. *Lectures on Rhetoric and Belles Lettres.* London, 1783.
Channing, E. T. *Lectures Read to the Seniors in Harvard College.* 1856; facsimile,
    Carbondale, 1968.
Charvat, William. *The Origins of American Critical Thought, 1810–1835.* Phila-
    delphia, 1936.
Cicero. *De Inventione.* Translated by H. M. Hubbell. Cambridge, Mass., 1949.
————. *De Oratore.* Translated by E. W. Sutton and H. Rackham. Cam-
    bridge, Mass., 1942.
Horace. *Odes and Epodes.* Translated by C. E. Bennett. Cambridge, Mass.,
    1978.
Kames, Henry Home, Lord. *Elements of Criticism.* Edinburgh, 1762.
Longinus. *On the Sublime [Peri Hypsous].* Translated by W. Hamilton Fyfe.
    Cambridge, Mass., 1932.
Monk, Samuel H. *The Sublime: A Study of Critical Theories in XVIII-Century
    England.* New York, 1935.

American Modern Epic Verse as a Genre

Bernstein, Michael. *The Tale of the Tribe: Ezra Pound and the Modern Verse Epic.*
    Princeton, 1980.
Dickie, Margaret. *On the Modernist Long Poem.* Iowa City, 1986.
Miller, James E. *The American Quest for a Supreme Fiction: Whitman's Legacy in
    the Personal Epic.* Chicago, 1979.
Pearce, Roy Harvey. "The Long View." In *The Continuity of American Poetry.*
    Princeton, 1977.

Studies Focused on Individual Poets

Allen, Gay Wilson. *The Solitary Singer: A Critical Biography of Walt Whitman.*
    New York, 1955.
Asselineau, Roger. *The Evolution of Walt Whitman: The Creation of a Personality.*
    Translated by Roger Asselineau and Richard P. Adams. 2 vols. Cam-
    bridge, Mass., 1960, 1962. Originally published in French in Paris, 1954.
Boer, Charles. *Charles Olson in Connecticut.* Chicago, 1975.

Bloom, Harold, ed. *Modern Critical Views: Walt Whitman.* New York, 1985.

Breslin, James E. B. *William Carlos Williams: An American Artist.* New York, 1970.

Brooke-Rose, Christine. *A Structural Analysis of Pound's Usura Canto.* The Hague, 1976.

————. *A ZBC of Ezra Pound.* Berkeley, 1971.

Brunner, Edward. *Splendid Failure: Hart Crane and the Making of The Bridge.* Urbana, 1985.

Bush, Ronald. *The Genesis of Ezra Pound's Cantos.* Princeton, 1976.

Butterick, George F. *A Guide to The Maximus Poems of Charles Olson.* Berkeley, 1978.

Chaffin, Tom. "Toward a Poetics of Technology: Hart Crane and the American Sublime." *Southern Review,* XX : 1 (January, 1984), 68–81.

Chase, Richard. *Walt Whitman Reconsidered.* New York, 1955.

Clark, David, ed. *The Merrill Studies in The Bridge.* Columbus, 1970.

Craig, Cairns. *Yeats, Eliot, Pound and the Politics of Poetry: Richest to Richest.* London, 1982.

Davie, Donald. *Ezra Pound.* New York, 1975.

Davis, Earle. *Vision Fugitive: Ezra Pound and Economics.* Lawrence, Kans., 1968.

Dembo, L. S. *Hart Crane's Sanskrit Charge: A Study of The Bridge.* Ithaca, 1960.

Doyle, Charles, ed. *William Carlos Williams: The Critical Heritage.* London, 1980.

Erkkila, Betsy. *Walt Whitman Among the French.* Princeton, 1980.

Flory, Wendy Stallard. *Ezra Pound and the Cantos: A Record of Struggle.* New Haven, 1980.

Giles, Paul. *Hart Crane: The Contexts of The Bridge.* Cambridge, England, 1986.

Hindus, Milton, ed. *Leaves of Grass One Hundred Years After.* Stanford, 1955.

Hollis, C. Carroll. *Language and Style in "Leaves of Grass."* Baton Rouge, 1983.

————. "Rhetoric, Elocution and Voice in *Leaves of Grass*: A Study in Affiliation." *Walt Whitman Quarterly Review,* II : 2 (Fall, 1984), 1–27.

Kaplan, Justin. *Walt Whitman: A Life.* New York, 1980.

Kearns, George. *Guide to Ezra Pound's Selected Cantos.* New Brunswick, 1980.

Kenner, Hugh. *The Pound Era.* Berkeley, 1971.

Lloyd, Margaret Glynne. *William Carlos Williams' Paterson: A Critical Reappraisal.* London, 1980.

Loving, Jerome. *Emerson, Whitman, and the American Muse.* Chapel Hill, 1982.

Malin, Stephen D. "'A Boston Ballad' and the Boston Riot." *Walt Whitman Review,* IX (September, 1963), 51–57.

Mazzaro, Jerome. *William Carlos Williams: The Later Poems.* Ithaca, 1973.

Nassar, Eugene Paul. *The Cantos of Ezra Pound: The Lyric Mode.* Baltimore, 1976.

Nilsen, Helga Normann. *Hart Crane's Divided Vision: An Analysis of The Bridge.* Oslo, 1980.

Norman, Charles. *The Case of Ezra Pound.* New York, 1960.

Paul, Sherman. *Olson's Push: Origin, Black Mountain, and Recent American Poetry.* Baton Rouge, 1978.

————. *Hart's Bridge.* Urbana, 1972.

Pearlman, Daniel D. *The Barb of Time: On the Unity of Ezra Pound's Cantos.* New York, 1969.

Read, Forrest. *'76: One World and The Cantos of Ezra Pound.* Chapel Hill, 1981.

Riddel, Joseph N. *The Inverted Bell: Modernism and the Counterpoetics of William Carlos Williams.* Baton Rouge, 1974.

Sankey, Benjamin. *A Companion to William Carlos Williams' Paterson.* Berkeley, 1971.

Stock, Noel. *The Life of Ezra Pound.* San Francisco. 1982.

Surette, Leon. *A Light From Eleusis: A Study of Ezra Pound's Cantos.* Oxford, 1979.

Tapscott, Stephen. *American Beauty: William Carlos Williams and the Modernist Whitman.* New York, 1984.

Terrell, Carroll F. *A Companion to the Cantos of Ezra Pound.* 2 vols. Berkeley, 1980.

Tomlinson, Charles, ed. *William Carlos Williams: A Critical Anthology.* New York, 1972.

Torrey, J. Fuller. *The Roots of Treason: Ezra Pound and the Secret of St. Elizabeths.* New York, 1984.

Trachtenberg, Alan. *Brooklyn Bridge: Fact and Symbol.* New York, 1965.

Traubel, Horace. *With Walt Whitman in Camden.* 5 vols. New York, 1906–64.

Von Hallberg, Robert. *Charles Olson: The Scholar's Art.* Cambridge, Mass., 1978.

Weaver, Mike. *William Carlos Williams: The American Background.* Cambridge, England, 1971.

Wilhelm, James J. *The Later Cantos of Ezra Pound.* New York, 1977.

Witemeyer, Hugh. *The Poetry of Ezra Pound: Forms and Renewal, 1908–1920.* Berkeley, 1969.

Zweig, Paul. *Walt Whitman: The Making of the Poet.* New York, 1984.

Related Studies and Sources

Abrams, M. H. *The Mirror and the Lamp: Romantic Theory and the Critical Tradition.* Oxford, 1953.

————. *Natural Supernaturalism: Tradition and Revolution in Romantic Literature.* New York, 1971.

Ahearn, Barry. *"A": An Introduction.* Berkeley, 1983.

Altieri, Charles. "Objective Image and Act of Mind in Modern Poetry."
Publications of the Modern Language Association of America, XCI : 1 (January,
1976), 101–14.

Barfield, Owen. *Poetic Diction: A Study in Meaning.* 1928; rpr. London, 1964.

Bercovitch, Sacvan. *The American Jeremiad.* Madison, 1978.

———. *The Puritan Origins of the American Self.* New Haven, 1975.

Bergson, Henri. *Creative Evolution.* Translated by Arthur Mitchell. 1907; rpr.
London, 1919.

———. *The Philosophy of Poetry: The Genius of Lucretius.* Translated by Wade
Baskin. 1884; rpr. New York, 1959.

———. *The Two Sources of Morality and Religion.* Translated by R. Ashley
Audra and Cloudesley Brereton, with the assistance of W. Horsfall Carter.
1935; rpr. Notre Dame, 1977.

Blackmur, R. P. *Language as Gesture.* New York, 1952.

Bloom, Harold. *Agon: Towards a Theory of Revisionism.* Oxford, 1982.

———. "The Breaking of Form." In *Deconstruction and Criticism.* New York,
1979.

Booth, Wayne. *The Rhetoric of Fiction.* Chicago, 1961.

Brooks, Cleanth. *The Well-Wrought Urn: Studies in the Structure of Poetry.* New
York, 1947.

Brooks, Van Wyck. *Fenollosa and His Circle.* New York, 1962.

———. "On Creating a Usable Past." *Dial,* LXIV (April 11, 1918), 339.

———. *Three Essays on America.* Includes *America's Coming-of-Age* (1915),
Letters and Leadership (1918), and *The Literary Life in America* (1921). New
York, 1934.

Browning, Robert. *Sordello.* In *Robert Browning: Poetical Works 1833–1864,*
edited by Ian Jack. Oxford, 1975.

Buell, Lawrence. *Literary Transcendentalism: Style and Vision in the American
Renaissance.* Ithaca, 1973.

Bundy, E. L. *Studia Pindarica, I–II.* In *University of California Publications in
Classical Philology,* No. 18. Berkeley, 1962.

Burke, Kenneth. *Counter-Statement.* 1931; rpr. Berkeley, 1968.

———. *A Grammar of Motives.* 1945; rpr. Berkeley, 1969.

———. *Language as Symbolic Action: Essays on Life, Literature and Method.*
Berkeley, 1966.

———. *A Rhetoric of Motives.* 1950; rpr. Berkeley, 1974.

Bynack, Vincent P. "Noah Webster and the Idea of a National Culture: The
Pathologies of Epistemology." *Journal of the History of Ideas,* XLV : 1 (January-March, 1984), 99–114.

Carey, Christopher. *A Commentary on Five Odes of Pindar.* New York, 1981.

Chadwick, Nora Kershaw. *Poetry and Prophecy.* Cambridge, England, 1942.

Chatman, Seymour. *Story and Discourse: Narrative Structure in Fiction and Film.* Ithaca, 1978.

Chomsky, Noam. *Language and Mind.* New York, 1972.

———. *Rules and Representations.* New York, 1980.

Connor, Robert W., ed. *Greek Orations.* Ann Arbor, 1979.

Culler, Jonathan. *Structuralist Poetics.* Ithaca, 1975.

Delasanta, Rodney. *The Epic Voice.* The Hague, 1967.

De Man, Paul. "Literary History and Literary Modernity." In *Blindness and Insight: Essays in the Rhetoric of Contemporary Criticism.* 2nd rev. ed. Minneapolis, 1983.

Eliade, Mircea. *Shamanism: Archaic Techniques of Ecstasy.* London, 1964.

Eliot, T. S. *The Three Voices of Poetry.* New York, 1954.

———. "Tradition and the Individual Talent." In *Selected Essays.* New York, 1964.

Elliott, Robert C. *The Literary Persona.* Chicago, 1982.

Emerson, Ralph Waldo. *English Traits.* 1856; rpr. New York, 1903.

———. *Essays and Lectures.* New York, 1983.

———. *Selections from Ralph Waldo Emerson.* Edited by Stephen Whicher. Boston, 1960.

Feidelson, Charles, Jr. *Symbolism and American Literature.* Chicago, 1953.

Fenollosa, Ernest. *The Chinese Written Character as a Medium for Poetry.* Edited by Ezra Pound. San Francisco, 1936.

Fish, Stanley. *Self-Consuming Artifacts.* Berkeley, 1972.

Frye, Northrop. *Anatomy of Criticism.* Princeton, 1957.

———. *Fearful Symmetry: A Study of William Blake.* Boston, 1947.

Gage, John T. *In the Arresting Eye: The Rhetoric of Imagism.* Baton Rouge, 1981.

Gilpin, William. *Mission of the North American People, Geological, Social, and Political.* Philadelphia, 1873.

Gould, Stephen Jay. *The Mismeasure of Man.* New York, 1981.

Graff, Gerald. *Literature Against Itself: Literary Ideas in Modern Society.* Chicago, 1979.

———. *Poetic Statement and Critical Dogma.* Chicago, 1970.

Havelock, Eric A. *Preface to Plato.* Cambridge, Mass., 1963.

Haviaris, Stratis, ed. *The Poet's Voice.* Recordings of Pound, Williams, Eliot, and others. Cambridge, Mass., 1978.

Hirsch, E. D. *Validity in Interpretation.* New Haven, 1967.

Hulme, T. E. *Speculations: Essays on Humanism and the Philosophy of Art.* London, 1924.

Hynes, Samuel. *The Edwardian Turn of Mind.* Princeton, 1968.

James, Henry. *The American Scene.* 1907; rpr. New York, 1947.

Jameson, Fredric. *Fables of Aggression: Wyndham Lewis, the Modernist as Fascist.*
    Berkeley, 1979.
Jarrell, Randall. "The Poet and His Public." *Partisan Review,* XIII (1946),
    493–98.
Jespersen, Otto. *Language, Its Nature, Development and Origin.* London, 1922.
Johnson, W. R. *The Idea of Lyric: Lyric Modes in Ancient and Modern Poetry.*
    Berkeley, 1982.
King, Martin Luther, Jr. "Letter from Birmingham Jail." In *Why We Can't
    Wait.* New York, 1963.
Lawrence, D. H. *Studies in Classic American Literature.* 1923; New York, 1981.
Lentricchia, Frank. *After the New Criticism.* Chicago, 1980.
Lord, Albert B. *The Singer of Tales.* Cambridge, Mass., 1960.
Lowell, Robert. "Thomas, Bishop and Williams." *Sewanee Review,* LV (1947),
    500–503.
Lukacs, Georg. "The Epic and the Novel." In *The Theory of the Novel.* 1920.
    Translated by Anna Bostock. Cambridge, Mass., 1971.
———. "The Ideology of Modernism." In *The Meaning of Contemporary Real-
    ism.* London, 1962.
Matthiessen, F. O. *American Renaissance.* Oxford, 1941.
May, Henry F. *The End of American Innocence.* Oxford, 1959.
Miller, Perry. *Errand Into the Wilderness.* Cambridge, Mass., 1956.
Milton, John. *Paradise Lost.* In *The Complete Poetry of John Milton,* edited by
    John T. Shawcross. Garden City, N.Y., 1971.
Mullen, William. *Choreia: Pindar and Dance.* Princeton, 1982.
Mumford, Lewis. *The Brown Decades: A Study of the Arts in America.* New York,
    1931.
———. *The Golden Day: A Study in American Experience and Culture.* New
    York, 1926.
Ong, Walter J., S.J. *Orality and Literacy.* London, 1982.
———. "The Poem as a Closed Field: The Once New Criticism and the
    Nature of Literature." In *Interfaces of the Word: Studies in the Evolution of
    Consciousness and Culture.* Ithaca, 1977.
Ouspensky, P. D. *Tertium Organum.* Translated by Nicholas Bessaraboff and
    Claude Bragdon. 1920; rev. ed. 1922; rpr. New York, 1970.
Parrington, Vernon L. *Main Currents in American Thought.* Vol. I of 2 vols.
    New York, 1927.
Perelman, Chaim. *The Realm of Rhetoric.* Translated by William Kluback.
    Notre Dame, 1982.
Perelman, Chaim, and Olbrechts-Tyteca, L. *The New Rhetoric: A Treatise on
    Argumentation.* Translated by John Wilkinson and Purcell Weaver. Notre
    Dame, 1969.

Peterson, Merrill D. *The Jefferson Image in the American Mind*. Oxford, 1960.

Richards, I. A. *The Philosophy of Rhetoric*. 1936; rpr. New York, 1979.

————. *Poetries and Sciences*. 1937; rpr. New York, 1970. Originally published as *Science and Poetry* in 1926 and revised in 1935.

Riffaterre, Michael. *Semiotics of Poetry*. Bloomington, 1978.

Rosenmeyer, Thomas. "Aristotelian Ethos and Character in Modern Drama." *Proceedings of the IXth Congress of the International Comparative Literature Association*. Vol. I, *Classical Models in Literature*. Innsbruck, 1979.

Ross, Andrew. *The Failure of Modernism: Symptoms of American Poetry*. New York, 1986.

Sapir, Edward. *Language*. New York, 1927.

Schwartz, Sanford. *The Matrix of Modernism: Pound, Eliot, and Early Twentieth-Century Thought*. Princeton, 1985.

Seven Arts, ed. James Oppenheim. All issues (November, 1916–October, 1917).

Smith, Barbara Herrnstein. *Poetic Closure: A Study of How Poems End*. Chicago, 1968.

Smith, Henry Nash. *Virgin Land*. Cambridge, Mass., 1950.

Stevens, Wallace. *The Necessary Angel: Essays on Reality and the Imagination*. London, 1942.

Tate, Allen. *Essays of Four Decades*. Chicago, 1968.

Thoreau, H. D. *Walden and Civil Disobedience*. 1854, 1849, respectively; rpr. New York, 1966.

Wellek, René. *Confrontations: Studies in the Intellectual and Literary Relations Between Germany, England, and the United States During the Nineteenth Century*. Princeton, 1965.

Wesling, Donald. "Difficulties of the Bardic: Literature and the Human Voice." *Critical Inquiry,* VIII (Autumn, 1981), 69–81.

Whitehead, Alfred North. *Science and the Modern World*. New York, 1925.

————. *Symbolism: Its Meaning and Effect*. New York, 1927.

Wilson, Edmund. *Axel's Castle*. New York, 1931.

Wilson, R. S., ed. *Darwinism and the American Intellectual*. Homewood, Ill., 1967.

Winters, Yvor. *In Defense of Reason*. Chicago, 1947.

————. *Uncollected Essays and Reviews*. Edited by Francis Murphy. Chicago, 1973.

Wright, George T. *The Poet in the Poem: The Personae of Eliot, Yeats and Pound*. Berkeley, 1960.

Ziff, Larzer. *Literary Democracy: The Declaration of Cultural Independence in America*. New York, 1981.

Index